Emotionally Intelligent Design

Rethinking How We Create Products

Pamela Pavliscak

Beijing · Boston · Farnham · Sebastopol · Tokyo

Emotionally Intelligent Design

by Pamela Pavliscak

Printed in the United States of America.

Published by O'Reilly Media, Inc., 1005 Gravenstein Highway North, Sebastopol, CA 95472.

O'Reilly books may be purchased for educational, business, or sales promotional use. Online editions are also available for most titles (*http://oreilly.com/safari*). For more information, contact our corporate/institutional sales department: (800) 998-9938 or *corporate@oreilly.com*.

Acquisitions Editor: Jessica Haberman
Developmental Editor: Angela Rufino
Production Editor: Melanie Yarbrough
Copyeditor: Octal Publishing, LLC
Proofreader: Rachel Monaghan

Indexer: Lucie Haskins
Cover Designer: Ellie Volckhausen
Interior Designers: Ron Bilodeau and Monica Kamsvaag
Illustrator: Rebecca Demarest
Compositor: Melanie Yarbrough

November 2018: First Edition.

Revision History for the First Edition:

2018-11-01   First release

See *http://oreilly.com/catalog/errata.csp?isbn=0636920049036* for release details.

978-1-491-95314-3

[GP]

[contents]

[*Preface*]

That Feeling When (TFW)...

TFW you've replayed that cute otter video more than 10 times.

TFW you see yourself reflected back to you in your Spotify Discover Weekly songs.

TFW you made your Kickstarter goal much faster than expected.

TFW you discover your child having a heartfelt conversation with Alexa.

TFW your tweet goes viral and you don't have a Soundcloud to promote.

TFW your WiFi goes down and takes your smart locks with it.

TFW Twitch subscribes you to yourself.

TFW you lose your teen's Snapchat streaks while they are away at phone-free summer camp.

TFW your love language is texting links to those near and dear, and then you realize that you've become the next generation of your aunt sharing links on email or your grandmother sending newspaper clippings.

Our so-called life with technology is complicated. It's becoming profoundly stranger at an exponential rate. And the most important parts of it are invisible.

At times, we're keenly aware of the highs and lows of digital life. We feel an overwhelming sense of camaraderie after a serendipitous conversation. Or we feel a rage hangover after a particularly difficult news cycle. Sometimes, the emotional undercurrent shifts just below the surface.

Technology is deeply embedded in every aspect of our daily lives. It collects our secrets, it bears witness to our everyday actions, and it circumscribes our relationships. Yet somehow, it's still radically insufficient for our messy, beautiful, emotional reality.

With all the focus on ease, efficiency, and convenience, we might miss what's truly essential. We worry about our attention, while technology toys with our affections. We idealize calm, when tech takes us on an emotional rollercoaster.

Now more than ever, we need technology that respects what it means to be human. That's what this book is about.

The True Story Behind This Book

It was the summer of 2014. Our team collected about 50 diverse characters—film crew, makeup artists, agency team, agency clients, agency clients' clients, other consultants—in a space not uncommon in New York City: an airy loft with a bright-blue sofa, a whimsical display of globes, a carefully arranged bookshelf of faux tomes, a rough-hewn table in front of a chalkboard decked in flowcharts. It was the sort of space that you might rent out for wedding photo shoots or cooking shows or bespoke events.

But this was a research project: the kind of research that happens every day in little rooms and not-so-little rooms, with little devices and not-so-little devices, all over the world, but usually without the makeup touch-ups and outfit changes and pauses for microphone adjustments and careful rephrasing of questions for the final cut. We were trying to figure out that special future something, couched in a high-quality persuasive film for a corporate audience.

Here I was in a room full of cameras, bright lights, and the bustle of strangers, and into our study walks Matthew. On paper, the usual suspect. Millennial, tech-savvy, does all the right things online—shops, rideshares, streams. Ultimately, that tells me almost nothing about Matthew.

After some small talk, we huddle around his phone, and I ask him to give me a tour—kind of an ice-breaker. When he got to photos, he hesitated. "You are going to think I'm weird." I assured him that "Weird is secret code for interesting." He went on to show me photo after photo after photo of butterflies.

And I thought, well, if that's weird then I'm truly odd. But I put on my best research face and asked him to tell me more. He told me about the last time he saw his father a butterfly had landed on his father's shoulder. Matthew felt like it was sort of this magical moment when time stood still:

> And I guess I was trying to bring that magic back. I don't have many photos of my dad. So, I started taking pictures of butterflies, and then learning about butterflies, and then other people—people I'd barely spoken to in years—started sending me pictures of butterflies. I guess I've become a kind of a modern-day butterfly collector.

The room was suddenly silent except for the low buzz of film gadgetry. Observers leaned in. We were all connected. Everything changed. That interview convinced me that we all need to collect those *butterfly moments*—the rare and beautiful and meaningful.

As a designer and researcher, I didn't start out studying emotion. But every time I looked at how people engaged with technology, there it was. Every experience was infused with sentiment, from intense emotions to fleeting feelings to lingering moods.

The past few years of my life have been devoted to the study of our emotional life with technology. Not always directly. After all, talking about feelings with strangers can invoke face-melting terror. So, I tried to get at it in all kinds of ways.

An "emotion exegesis" study had people annotate each tap and swipe with emotion. I encouraged people to sketch their experiences from memory. I asked people for their mantras, distilling their coping strategies into pithy advice. Just like the phone has "driving mode" to stop notifications or your laptop has "night mode" to soften the glow, I asked people to describe their personal modes for using technology. In another, I gifted people a magic wand that would instantly change the technology in their lives. I followed people charting new kinds of relationships with artificial intelligence (AI) companions. I hosted research playdates with kids to try out Cozmo and Aibo and Jibo. I orchestrated emotion tech hackathons.

I'd consider myself to be one of those highly sensitive people; you know the type—the one who winces at an unkind word, who carefully avoids watching anything violent (so we won't be discussing the latest bingeworthy Netflix show), who absorbs the emotions in the room and then becomes easily overwhelmed. As a child, I'd been told I was too sensitive. As an adult, I cry too easily. Even with all these feelings, I was no emotion expert. Gradually, I learned.

The more I learned, the more I realized there's still so much we don't understand about emotion. You won't find all the answers here either. My hope is that this book will draw more people into this conversation, especially people working with technology.

How You Fit into This Story

As someone who is somehow connected with technology (for the sake of brevity, I'll call you a designer, but you might consider yourself an information architect, developer, product manager, strategist, entrepreneur, chatbot script writer, AI trainer, UXer, or even UI/UX unicorn), this is your story, too. You are probably an optimist when it comes to technology, at least a little bit. You feel like technology can make lives easier, make tiresome chores go faster, and make the world a better place. I feel this, too.

At the same time, maybe you are concerned with the way things are going. You feel the negative impact of technology in your everyday life. Or maybe you've been tasked with making something that started, or somehow ended up, at odds with living well.

So how do we sort out this paradoxical way of making technology? One way is to consider the invisible layer of experience. We've spent a lot of time and effort on the cognitive layer of technology, but less so on the emotional layer. The way we live in this new world, powered by the latest greatest technology is not rational, not by half. So why wouldn't we reconsider the emotional?

Perhaps you wonder why you should read yet another book about design and emotion. Don Norman's *Emotional Design* (Basic Books, 2005) is filled with wit and wonder, and the "robot chapter" is more relevant than ever. Aarron Walter's Maslow-inspired hierarchy (*Designing for Emotion* [A Book Apart, 2011]) is near ubiquitous. It might seem like we have this whole emotional design thing locked. We don't.

A lot has happened in the past decade or so when it comes to what we know, and we don't know, about emotion. And technology aimed at deciphering emotion in new ways, some intriguing and some deeply misguided, is gaining momentum. Emotional design needs a reboot, too.

What if you're a skeptic? I get that. You might think emotion is a people thing, not a tech thing. You might think tech is a neutral space, a means to an end. Or maybe you think emotion is just some marketing nonsense. This book is still for you.

Maybe it's the Midwest in me talking, but I'm a pragmatist. Technology can't help but shape who we are as individuals, as societies, as a species because it usually does. It's not always obvious or evident, of course. And it's much easier to see in retrospect.

AI isn't the first technology to make a sweeping claim about consciousness, nor will it be the last. Just think for a moment about the compass and the crane, the loom and the lightbulb, the sewing machine and spacecraft. All technology that enables us to *do* new things is technology that enables us to *feel* new things.

Experiencing the world in a new way shapes our inner lives. So, even if you consider yourself a rationalist about technology, I'll ask you to acknowledge your own emotional response to a book about emotion and read on.

We have an opportunity to rethink our approach to designing technology, by which I mean designing everything, really. In this new era of wearable, companion, ubiquitous, maybe-soon-ingestible technology, how will we design for emotional well-being? That's the big question for this little book.

Here's the Short Version

This book is a little strange for an O'Reilly book. It's not a book all about cool new technology—that is, The Promise (or Peril) of Emotion AI. AI that detects some aspects of human emotion will be big business, no doubt. Emotion AI will practically force us to design for emotion in new ways. It will change how we conceptualize emotion. It will require us to think deeply about ethics. And it is coming on quickly.

Part of my motivation in writing this book is to get more people thinking about emotion AI while there's still time to get ahead of it. But emotionally intelligent design isn't just about new technology that will auto-magically reveal hidden truths. That's not what the technology can do. And, more important, that's not how emotion works.

It's not a book filled with step-by-steps or code snippets or design best practices. Although there is a method to this madness, I approached the book as a way to draw together new research about emotion, new technology that engages with emotion, and new design practices. Think of it as a new way to consider something age-old.

Each chapter follows a certain path. I begin with a mashup of emotion wisdom and design method, giving a bit of background about each. Then, I consider how to bring them together, based on experimentation in my own research and experience with corporate and startup clients. So, the first part of most chapters is background, the second half how-to. Here's how it breaks down chapter by chapter:

Chapter 1: Our Emotional Relationship with Technology
Our relationship with technology isn't always, or even mostly, rational. While we zigzag from utopian dreams to dystopian nightmares, we rarely acknowledge the emotional impact. This chapter is a call to action for emotionally intelligent design.

Chapter 2: The History and Future of Emotional Design
Without an understanding of history, it's difficult to work toward the future. So, in this chapter we look at the history of emotion, how it's been translated through design, and how new tech is going to transform it once again. This chapter moves from Aristotle to AI, from sentimental education to sensors, from whales to wearables. Well, you get the idea.

Chapter 3: Designing, with Feeling
How might we bend our current practices toward emotional intelligence? With a mix of design thinking, mixed methods research, and emotion tech. Rather than come up with a completely new model, the idea here is to build on what's already working.

Chapter 4: Cultivate Human–Machine Harmony

Let's talk relationships. Not "building a bot" or "creating a character bible," but thinking about how we will be increasingly living our lives with artificial friends. Framing our experience as a relationship changes the design process. Here, you'll find a way to gauge whether your tech should have a personality, how much is enough, and how to evolve the relationship.

Chapter 5: Crafting Emotional Interventions

Digital well-being is often framed as taking a time-out from tech. A good start, but we could take it further. By blending well-being interventions with the grand tradition of design patterns, this chapter identifies positive interventions and negative antipatterns.

Chapter 6: Forecasting the Future with Feelings

What do affective forecasting, prospective psychology, and speculative design have in common? Each gives us a way to *feel* the future. In this chapter, we look at how to bring more emotion-sense to envision technology a decade into the future or more.

Chapter 7: Toward an Emotionally Intelligent Future

This final chapter looks at the implications of emotionally intelligent technology. Emotion impacts public policy, law, organizational culture, and society. We pause here to consider what will come next.

You'll notice throughout that I keep the concepts of emotion and feeling, and even sentiment, loose. Some experts make a distinction between emotion as physical, instinctual, and basic, and feeling as perceptual, constructed, and complex. Others don't. Either way, it's complicated by the social and cultural layers of emotion. It's kind of like that nature/nurture argument. I try to tease it out where I can, without stressing about it too much.

Likewise, you might find my use of emotional intelligence a bit unusual. Emotional intelligence comes in a few different flavors, but basically it comes down to understanding emotion in multiple dimensions. For now, that's a very human enterprise. Soon, machines will be in on it, too. For me, both humans and machines together will formulate a new kind of emotional intelligence.

Feeling Forever Grateful

Writing this book was cathartic, exciting, frustrating, and humbling. It involved video chatting through bad hair days, half-read books lying face-down all over the house, lying awake in the middle of the night, scribbled notes in my chicken-scratch handwriting, equal parts coffee and wine, oh, and lists—lots and lots of lists.

At the heart of it all, generous, kind, brilliant people offered their time and wisdom in wonderful ways.

Thanks to all the people who shared a little bit of their lives with me, as participants in interviews, studies, and social experiments. Your generosity will have a long reach.

Thanks to my reviewers, Lane Goldstone, Anne Marie Léger, Sylvia Leotin, Cynthia Savard-Saucier, Alastair Sommerville, and Mark Wyner for thoughtful commentary and tactful correction.

Thanks to sages who shared their work with me as I put together the book, especially Ben Bland, Elizabeth Buie, Rana el Kalouiby, John C. Havens, Simon Jimenez, Anya Kamenetz, Georgia King, Lucie Lemire, Andrew McStay, Taniya Mishra-Linger, Gawain Morrison, Dorian Peters, Anna Pohlmeyer, David Ryan Polgar, Caroline Sinders, Rob Strati, Lillian Tong, Marco Van Hout, Ben Virdee-Chapman, and Trevor von Gorp.

Thanks to Angela Rufino, my exceedingly patient editor at O'Reilly, who stayed with me through several different versions of this book.

Thanks to my colleagues Tony Alongi and Diana Sapanaro, who picked up so, so much slack for me.

Thanks to my parents, Andrea and George, who have provided loads of support over the years.

Thanks to my brother, George, who never ceases to surprise me with a fresh point of view.

Thanks to my spouse and partner, Steve, who made this book possible in all kinds of ways.

Thanks to my luminous daughters, Grace, Lizzy, and Eleanor. They are the inspiration for nearly everything in this book and in my life.

And thanks to you for reading, and hopefully, sharing your stories in the future.

Our Emotional Relationship with Technology

TAKE A MOMENT TO imagine what your home will look like in 10 years. Maybe you imagine living in *that* house. You know the one. It's a pristine space—all curved lines and smooth, white surfaces. Objects are minimally designed with intelligence embedded deep within, or maybe with a projected layer of augmented reality. You might imagine wandering from one behaviorally and emotionally optimized choice to the next, occasionally enlisting the help of a chatbot here or a robot companion there. Or maybe you don't have to imagine.

In 2015, Target launched *Open House* in San Francisco. Part retail space and part lab, the project uses interactive storytelling as a way to help people picture the smart home of the future. Open House, designed by Local Projects, is arranged like a 3,500-square-foot home that just happens to be filled with internet-connected everything. The products are present day, from a kitchen with smart coffee pots to a bedroom with a Withings smart baby monitor to a living room outfitted with Sonos speakers and a Nest thermostat. With transparent walls lit by Philips Hue lighting and sensors that detect your presence, the house pops up conversation bubbles above each product.

FIGURE 1-1
Clearly, the quintessential home of the future (source: Target)

Beyond crafting a tangible future for purchase, Open House reveals a vision of ease and convenience, running on an invisible layer of technology. On the surface, Target is promoting what technology of the near future can do. Look a little closer and you can sense something else. This future is about how we feel.

More and more, we assume that the good life runs on technology. As designers, developers, and makers, we take care in crafting experiences that make life easier. Yet, we don't devote as much attention to how technology runs much deeper. In this chapter, we begin by looking at the ways technology is inextricably intertwined with our inner lives and what it means for design.

Inventing Our Best Lives

Depending on how you look, you can glimpse two futures for our lives with technology. Put on your rose-colored virtual-reality headset, and you'll see the promise of unparalleled ease. Scroll, bleary-eyed, through your social media feed and it's a cacophony of voices foretelling the collapse of the world as we know it. What can these future visions tell us about our emotional relationship with technology?

FRICTION-FREE TECH UTOPIAS

Tech utopias are few and far between in science fiction. *Star Trek* or *The Jetsons* and a handful of novels are all we have to bring us from the brink of despair. A positive future world of technology has, however, been vividly imagined for consumers.

Target's Open House is just one version of the home of the future in a long line of future home fantasies. From the 1933 Homes of Tomorrow exhibition at the Chicago World's Fair, to Disney's Home of the Future of the 1950s, to the contemporary Google House of Dubai, future homes invariably feature smart ovens, robot butlers, and beds that make themselves. Food is prepared at the push of a button. Clothes clean themselves. Life is leisurely.

The office of the future has the same glossy vibe. At the office, a central physical space with meditation pods coexists peacefully with flickering screens projecting dashboards on a conveniently placed wall here and there. Remote work, situated in the high-tech home of the future, transports us via hologram.

Visions of smart cities are sprinkled with pixel stardust, too. From moving sidewalks to hoverboards, from flying cars to autonomous vehicles, fantasies of future cities place ease at a premium. We see this future vision spread from city to city—Alphabet's Sidewalk Labs creating a high-tech future city on the Toronto waterfront, and the German town of Duisburg partnering with Huawei to infuse daily living with technology. Outside the city, a dusting of Elon Musk's solar-tiled rooftops might be visible to the trained eye.

At home or at work, utopians' futures look remarkably similar—clean and minimal, the soft whir of subtle technology. And our smart world seems to hum along on universally agreed-upon values of ease to fuel productivity at work and leisure at home. Emotionally speaking, you might say it's serene. But it's difficult to tell; emotions are muffled.

Maybe that's because people only rarely inhabit this future. Homes, workplaces, even whole cities are mostly empty. Colorful lights bounce off slick surfaces, while the robots roll quietly through deserted hallways. A world that's been so carefully calibrated for comfort doesn't engage our participation, making it difficult to imagine the kind of life we might make there.

Or maybe we imagine ourselves in front of that smart mirror (Figure 1-2) that seems ubiquitous—to tech insiders, at least. I like to think of it as the Lacanian mirror phase of technology. We begin to recognize ourselves in the future, but it's a challenge. This future lacks the human touch.

FIGURE 1-2

The smart mirror doesn't make it easier to picture ourselves in the future (source: MirroCool)

DYSTOPIAN FUTURES

Contrast the sparse future of tech utopias with the chaotic clamor of dystopia. Swipe through the news any given day, and you'll hear predictions of smart robots taking our jobs, autonomous cars taking out innocent pedestrians, and mass virtual-reality escapism. Or you might read perilous projections of a near future in which technology harvests all your data, reducing your life's purpose to a few salient data points that are superimposed over security-camera captures. You end the day, staying up later than you intended, to watch just one more episode of *Black Mirror* or *Westworld*.

You can find a dystopian future almost anywhere you click. The relentless repetition of negative headlines comes at the pace of innovation. The vast worlds of compelling sci-fi dystopias are populated with carefully crafted details that fuel our dismal dreams. From time to time, we can spot these fictional futures come true. From TASERs to animojis (Figure 1-3), gadgets created to support a fictional dystopia become a cliché embedded in our all-too-real present day. Falling into dystopian rumination about the coming end times turns out to be effortless, especially when it's been so fully realized.

FIGURE 1-3

When sci-fi futures surface in the present, should we call them self-unfulfilling prophecies? (source: @blackmirror)

Dystopias don't just limit our imagination, they might already be having a real effect in our everyday lives. According to the World Health Organization, more than 300 million people of all ages suffer from depression.[1] Although there are a range of factors that lead to depression, data from the Gallup-Healthways Well-Being Index tells us that unemployed adults are about twice as likely to be depressed as people

---

1   World Health Organization, Depression Fact Sheet, February 2017.

employed full-time.[2] Anxiety about looming job losses might already be contributing to a mental health crisis. Imagine hearing that your job is easily automated, and that you need to reskill with money you probably don't have. For those who have jobs that seem safer from automation, there's a sense of relief tinged with guilt followed by apprehension. It's only a matter of time, after all (Figure 1-4).

FIGURE 1-4
No reason to be smug; automation will come for you, too (source: McKinsey Global Institute)

So, here we are, trapped between a placid future of convenience and a post-apocalyptic hellscape where anxiety-plagued humans have designed their own obsolescence. To complicate things just a bit more, these binary futures play out in our present-day triumphs and trials with technology.

The Present: It's Complicated

Most of us struggle a bit with being human in the digital age. We sleep poorly. Our necks are sore from bending over our phones. Social media quietly chips away at our self-worth while heightening our sense of

---

2   Gallup-Healthways Well-Being Index, "In US, Employment Most Linked to Being Depression-Free," 2013.

collective anxiety. We feel isolated despite being more connected than ever. Study after study tells us that heavy use of technology is making us depressed.

Yet, we can catch a little glimpse of our best selves in each innovation. From fitness bands to smart speakers, from travel tools to productivity apps, technology promises, and often delivers, confidence. Social media often cultivates compassionate action. Skype calls with far-flung friends can be joyful.

Just as our futures are alternately calm and crazed, our present is a whipsaw of wonder and worry. Even so, the triumphs and tribulations of our personal experience with technology aren't typically framed in emotional terms.

STREAMLINING THE WORLD, STREAMLINING US

One way that technology strives to create calm or contentment is by streamlining our lives, especially those aspects that seem mundane. Convenience has emerged as a value, even a way of life. With a promise of effortless efficiency, technology frees us up to pursue what we really want to do, even if we aren't always sure what that is.

Some of us do benefit from home automation and work productivity tools. Amazon's Echo orders our groceries when we don't have time to pop by the store, and Nest turns down thermostats while we're away. Google Docs and to-do apps help us stay organized and get work done faster.

Sometimes, though, the streamlining doesn't quite work as intended. Productivity apps don't make us more productive but give us another app to manage. Work communication tools, from email to Slack, create yet another channel to actively monitor. GPS will give us the fastest route, but it might just end up taking us out of the way. We'll never know, of course, because we forgot how to read maps. Apple Watch promises that we can "do more in an instant." Or is it "fill up every instant with more to do"?

As technology has crept into our personal lives, smart seems a little dull. Google Photos categorizes and organizes our lives by theme. As much as Pinterest might feed our artistic impulses, it does so in a standardized way. Fitness trackers tell us precisely how many steps we've taken but reveal nothing about the journey itself.

Our days can seem like a sequence of answers to questions we out-grew in grade school: What do you like? Will you share it? Do you love it? Likewise, it can trivialize what should be important. When a friend posts of a pet's passing, it's a little too easy to click the sad face rather than to send a note. Thanks to predictive text, emojis, and automated rejoinders, we readily dismiss uncomfortable moments rather than doing the hard work of maintaining relationships.

This quiet efficiency has another unhappy side effect—it streamlines us. In a given hour, you might have an argument with your spouse, feel elated at a small victory at work, experience deep gratification at a note from a colleague, look wistfully at a picture of the beach from last summer, feel excited to set up plans with a friend at a restaurant in the evening. Our technology doesn't acknowledge all that.

Instead, it tends to interpret who we are to fit neatly into predetermined, ad-friendly categories. "Married, currently interacting with two other people; at work with IP address x in location y; likes beaches; favors restaurants near work; booked a hotel last July for four days; one female tagged in photo; face matches user." As much as details keep flowing in, technology somehow misses the mark. These data-verified assumptions prompt offers and suggestions and impersonal personalizations that threaten to reduce us to a shadow of ourselves.

Even though some of us may be smugly sipping Soylent, reveling in the efficiency of scientifically engineered nutrition and unmatched ease of preparation, more of us will tire of it. We'll miss the texture, the fla-vor, the effort, and all the interesting mistakes we make preparing our meals. It might feel great to not miss a friend's happy birthday, but does it feel great to have "happy birthdays" stack up like tidy bricks on our walls, only to prompt another round of obligatory liking and thanking? (See Figure 1-5.)

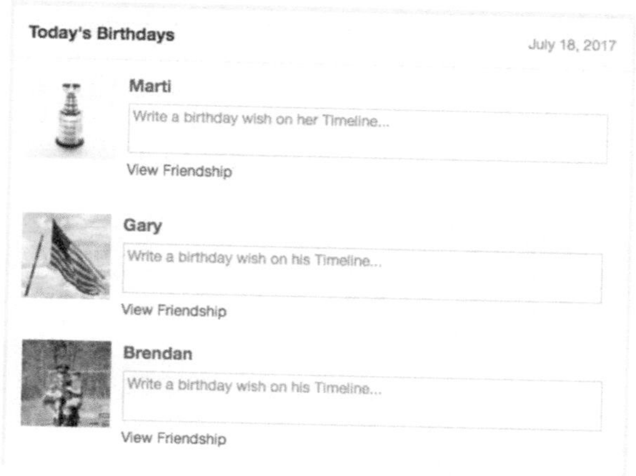

Today's Birthdays   July 18, 2017

Marti
Write a birthday wish on her Timeline...
View Friendship

Gary
Write a birthday wish on his Timeline...
View Friendship

Brendan
Write a birthday wish on his Timeline...
View Friendship

FIGURE 1-5
Making quick work of happy birthdays, oh snap

The cult of convenience fails to acknowledge that difficulty is core to human experience. The joy of a slow journey, the satisfaction that comes from challenges, the confidence that comes from learning through trial and error trump convenience. All our focus on fewer steps hasn't resulted in human flourishing. Perhaps it has even made us more conscious of time.

SAVING TIME, WASTING TIME

When the promise of technology is framed around ease and efficiency, we consider its breakdown in increments of time. Time is the unspoken, but deeply embedded, value. It's so pervasive that we might not even notice it anymore.

One way we frame our bad feelings about technology is as a distraction. This isn't new. Aldous Huxley in *Brave New World Revisited* (Harper & Row, 1958) wrote with dismay about our "infinite appetite for distraction" in the form of news. Years later, Neil Postman attributed our hunger for distraction to television (*Amusing Ourselves to Death: Public Discourse in the Age of Show Business* [Methuen, 1985]). In *The Shallows* (W.W. Norton & Company, 2010), Nicholas Carr writes, "The net is designed to be an interruption system, a machine geared to dividing attention" (W.W. Norton & Company, 2010).

Now, distraction centers on the gravitational pull we feel to our phones. When we are idle, we check our phones. When we are bored, we check our phones. When we can't fall asleep, we check our phones. Distraction takes us away from all of the fulfilling things we should be doing. Hint: those things we should be doing probably don't involve endlessly scrolling social media feeds (Figure 1-6).

にんちん
@carrot666
あまりにも煩いので結局草箱撤去。
んでこのアホは草咥えたままはなさねぇって
いうか、このまま餌食おうとするわ、当然食
えないわけで、マヌケにも程がある……
#うさぎ
Translate from Japanese
RETWEETS LIKES
42,130   50,993
11:32 AM - 22 Dec 2015

FIGURE 1-6

A block of Japanese text and a bunny never fail to spark joy (source: @carrot666)

But, then, what does count? When I read news, am I wasting time because I should be working instead? Is it time misspent if I watch cat videos, but not if I watch a TED talk? Does browsing reviews on Goodreads count? What if I don't intend to read the book? It's difficult to say. Time online is often viewed as a monolith. Even if we admit that all of our time online might not be wasted, we still try to minimize it. Time "offline" is considered intrinsically better.

Distraction is more than a minor irritant, to be sure. What you focus on minute by minute, hour by hour, day by day begins to add up. When our attention is diverted or we simply have too much drawing our attention, we have a hard time focusing on what's important. All these distractions could theoretically ensure that you forget to lead the life you want to lead.

And it's more than distraction. When we feel out of control, it veers into addiction. Internet addiction is a real condition, matter of debate, and widely accepted universal state of mind. Study after study finds a strong positive correlation between heavy smartphone use and anxiety, depression, and other symptoms of mental illness. We can quibble over the details, but the toll it takes is real.

But what are we addicted to, anyway? Is it the phone itself? Some studies make the case. We get pangs of anxiety when separated from our phones. Other studies suggest that we are less focused when our smartphone is nearby. Our brains flood with oxytocin when we hear our phones—we might literally love our iPhones. Even the sound triggers love and loss. The object, security.

Social media, in particular, has been declared addictive in studies and by experts. A friend likes your photo, another friend comments on your post, and we get a kind of rush and then a letdown. Maybe we are addicted to the approval we get?

Or are we addicted to the content, interactions, the stuff of the app? It's difficult to untangle the device from the app from the content. Entrepreneurs study addictive behavior, after all, to help create it. Product teams work hard to engage us, hijacking our time.

Perhaps we are simply addicted to distraction itself. Like gamblers who get in a "machine zone," we are caught up in the rhythm of repetition. An alternate reality flow state drives us toward interactions that are only occasionally satisfying. I wonder if the real fear is that our addiction to machines make us more machine-like.

EMOTIONAL UPS AND DOWNS

When the ideal technology frees up our time, it makes sense to frame the downsides in terms of attention. Tech insiders and the general public have become attuned to the unreasonable demands technology can make on our time. The demands on our emotions, however, are the current that runs beneath.

Our emotional life online can be uplifting—affirmations from friends, genuine offers of help, convivial communities. Once in a while, there's that great feeling of the immensity and connectedness of humanity. Or just the pure joy of being back in someone's life again.

Online, people feel free to explore new identities. The *online disinhibition effect*, first noted by psychologist John Suler (*Psychology of the Digital Age: When Humans Become Electric* [Cambridge University Press, 2016]), means that people don't behave as they would face-to-face. Sometimes this disinhibition can be positive. It can let people feel that they can truly be themselves. But it can also be negative. Bullying and trolling might be attributed, in part, to a false sense of anonymity.

Almost since social media came to be, it's been studied for negative emotional impact. From social comparison to fear of missing out to bullying or worse, social media seems to amplify the worst in us. With all the perfect vacations and beautiful babies and romantic gestures, social comparison has become a daily routine rather than an occasional meditation. Is everyone faking it? Maybe. But then we begin to worry that we're the imposters with everyone else being so consistently brilliant. When we aren't comparing, we feel that pang of missing out on the good life that everyone seems to be enjoying without us.

Empathy online, when we do stumble on it, can be genuine. It feels good to tap a sad reaction or share a cheery gif. It feels like lending support or showing you care. And it does, a little. But we worry that we will begin to prefer diminished substitutes. After all, it's easier to leave a message than actually talk on the phone. It's easier to email rather than call. It's easier to click a heart rather than leave a comment. We worry that we will become streamlined to convey information rather than connect with grace.

Life online, for some of us, requires what I'll call *continuous partial empathy*. Whether it's dealing with harassment on Twitter or offering support on Facebook or shouldering care on GoFundMe, many of us spend our time supporting friends, family, and a wide range of people we might not know very well at all. At scale, it can take a toll on emotional well-being, leaving us drained or stressed.

Many experiences, as currently designed, thrive on extreme emotions. Jonah Berger, in *Contagious: Why Things Catch On* (Simon & Schuster, 2013), found that anger spreads fastest on social network. Negative emotions like outrage and fear activate. Although positive emotions are less viral, pronounced emotions like awe, amazement, and surprise drive engagement, too. This explains why our life with technology can feel like an emotional rollercoaster.

More and more, technology is designed to fuel a cycle of emotions. Whether it's "solving" a low-key negative emotion like boredom with a curiosity-induced headline or conjuring high-intensity outrage for clicks, the behavioral approach to design kills the pain temporarily. And then, if it's successful, repeatedly.

Glance at a notification on your phone, or pull to refresh your email, or endlessly scroll Facebook or Twitter, and you might or might not find what you are seeking. When you do, you get a little burst of dopamine and you feel good. The good feeling doesn't last for long and the false sense of urgency creates a new source of stress. When you don't find it you just keep going anyway. Is the answer opting out?

DETOX, RETOX

Just as our futures are sketched in binary opposition, so it seems our present-day experience of technology ping-pongs between highs and lows. Our approach to this conundrum is predictably binary, too. Experts encourage us to "detox," to take some time offline. Whether it's a no-smartphone family dinner, a weekend off maybe at a Restival, or a vacation without WiFi at Camp Grounded, taking a break restores balance. A detox feels virtuous at first, but somehow ends back where we started: reaching for the phone 200 times or more a day.

Even though it's certainly not a bad idea to put down your device, it's not a successful strategy for balance in the long term. It doesn't create long-lasting change. The Light Phone (Figure 1-7), a minimalist phone with limited features, was funded at light speed on Kickstarter at the same time Nokia 3310 relaunched its iconic "dumb phone." Apps like Flippd and Moment encourage a technology time-out. Google launched, to much acclaim, tools to help us track our time online and occasionally take a breather.

FIGURE 1-7
Minimalist devices still require a "real" companion phone (source: Light Phone)

As much as it might help us become aware of our destructive habits, this will produce new anxieties, too. Dread will likely mount as we warily watch our online intensity indicator move from green to red. The count of hours online will no doubt end in unhealthy social comparison. Nudges to go offline will be met with annoyance.

Design that gives us a breather from a downward spiral into the sixth level of notification hell is a noble effort, but it doesn't get us closer to a sustainable relationship with technology either. Reminding people of their time spent online is more abdication than answer. Detox design ignores the bigger picture—technology silently scripts our conversations and behaviors, and even our thoughts and feelings.

Design Designs Us

Internet critics tell us that our brains are being rewired. Well, of course. Wouldn't it be strange if we were still expected to think, feel, and behave the same way, despite all this new technology?

Even a simple walk through the woods is haunted by the world in our pockets. We might frame our walk with TripAdvisor reviews. We are conscious of notifications accumulating as we walk along. In turn, each step tempts us to check on our health app. The lovely scene demands to be shared via Instagram. There might be some Pokémons to collect just beyond that tree (Figure 1-8). Even if we've left our phone behind, we can't experience that walk without technology. In other words, our existential concerns are underscored by lolcats.

FIGURE 1-8
Pokémon GO frames the modern condition (source: Niantic)

Technology doesn't just frame how we perceive the world, it alters our behaviors. Nest prompts us to rewire our homes to control our comfort. Lyft lets us stay a little longer at that party. Echo encourages us to change the kind of detergent we buy so that we can order it through Amazon. Snapchat scripts our conversations. Facebook shifts how we tackle community problems.

Technology reframes our relationships. It might prompt us to see others too often in terms of endorsements or obligations: posts to like, comments to make, people to follow define relationships in a tightly circumscribed way. But it shapes our relationships in the so-called real world, too. Facebook underpins my own small community, which means we can band together in a power outage or pass on a pair of ice skates with ease.

Technology is tied with our identity. We've become shape shifters, moving between roles we perform for the world and for ourselves. Whether a keynote speaker on Twitter, doting parent on Facebook, or angry anonymous commenter on the *New York Times* website, we try on different roles.

Technology shapes our emotions in ways we are only beginning to understand, too. It creates new emotions, like "three-dot anxiety" as we wait for a text; vemödalen, the frustration of photographing something amazing when thousands of identical photos already exist; or FOMO, the fear of missing out. Then there's that feeling when tech creates emotions that we haven't yet named. As the connective tissue of our modern lives, inside and out, our relationship with technology is emotional.

Why Emotionally Intelligent Design?

Technology has expanded to fill every open space in our lives. And it occupies new spaces that we didn't even realize were there. Yet, we still seem reluctant to acknowledge the emotional layer of our experience. At its worst, technology fills us with rage or unease. At its best, we think technology should be calm, or once in a while, deliver a ping of delight. That's an extremely limited emotional range.

The hyper-connected, autonomous, conversational, increasingly AI-powered devices might be called "smart" on a good day. Sure, they're code-smart, but they aren't people-smart. Technology can't tell whether we feel happy or sad, much less rejected or bored or optimistic or petulant or "hangry." Technology doesn't respond any differently to a soothing voice or crazed screaming (not that I would know, of course). Technology doesn't encourage us to be aware of our own emotions or the emotions of those around us. And that's a problem.

Designers, developers, information architects, content strategists, and now script writers, AI trainers, and countless others responsible for designing technology have treated emotion more like an achievement to be unlocked. Journeys start low and end high. We trace the happy path between human and machine, apprehensively contemplating the possibility of many more unhappy paths. Just in case, we hide a little surprise here and there, hoping to soothe hurt feelings.

New technology is prodding us toward a reconsideration of emotion. Voice humanizes interactions, so much so that therapy chatbots can really help people work through difficult times and home assistants gamely fill in for children's playmates. Social robots dance and play music and pull up recipes while we cook dinner. Virtual reality beckons us to reflect deeply on the lives of others, from the plight of refugees to the experience of solitary confinement. Each imperfectly realized, yet undeniably emotional.

THE NEW EMOTIONAL DESIGN

The next wave of tech will venture further into emotional territory. Smart speakers, autonomous vehicles, televisions, connected refrigerators, and mobile phones will soon be able to read emotional cues. Your fridge might work with you on stress eating. Your bathroom mirror might sense that you're feeling blue and turn on the right mood-enhancing music. Your email software will ask you to reflect before you hit send. The most meaningful technologies are very likely to be the most emotionally intelligent.

Ready or not, those of us working in tech need to not just acknowledge the complexity of emotional experience but find new ways to design for it.

Emotion has already become an organizing principle for design in other contexts. Cities from Bogota, Columbia, to Somerville, Massachusetts, have been using happiness as a method to guide urban planning. Architecture has long considered how the shape of a building can inspire anything from a moment of awe to an emotional climate of civic engagement. Creating convivial warmth in our homes, whether by seeing if objects "spark joy" or create a sense of hygge (the Danish concept of inviting coziness), is a full-blown trend.

What's key to all these movements is that emotional resonance is not a gift we bestow on the world with design. It's made by designers and people from all walks of life together. It doesn't take just one shape, it takes many shapes. It doesn't take us out of the world, it gives us new ways of being in the world.

Something as complex as emotionally intelligent design can't be summarized into a quick list of features. We can't add it as a step in the process: empathize, define, ideate, prototype, test, and—ta dah!—social and emotional well-being. It's not a set of tips to polish the experience. What you'll find here is not a hierarchy or a diagram or a handy set of quick-hit methods.

Instead, I'll propose this: emotional intelligence as a way to change our perspective on design. More than anything, the latest thinking on emotion helps us to see the world in a new way. As we go along in this book, we pause to consider a broad range of research on emotion—from emotional intelligence to happiness to personality models to affective forecasting. And we combine that with movements in the design world, including value-sensitive design and speculative design and our own tradition of emotional design.

Think of each chapter as a way to intentionally tune in to emotion in a new way. At the beginning, or the next beginning (some might call it the end), or somewhere in the middle, these exercises can help build emotionally sustainable relationships with the technology.

Let's start.

[2]

The History and Future of Emotional Design

IMAGINE IT'S A FRIDAY afternoon a few years in the future. Your voice assistant provides a few restaurant suggestions based on not just your past experiences, positive and negative, but also on the emotional climate of current customers. Each movie review you scan is accompanied by an emotional graph showing the rise and fall of audience feelings. As you head out, your car senses that you're a little tense and takes over the drive.

As technology is calibrated to become more sensitive to emotion, design must become more attuend to emotion, too. Designing for emotion, despite its relatively recent entrance into our repertoire of techniques, has evolved in the past decade. Even so, the driving assumption is that people start in some state of unhappiness which we "solve" through a series of shared conventions. Delight is a momentary blip, a saving grace for an awkward moment. If we're lucky, repeated exposure to delight accrues in layers to form a bond that lasts.

In this chapter, we consider emotional design. affective computing, and the latest, sometimes conflicting, theories of emotion. Then, we look at how the new wave of emotionally intelligent machines might move our field toward a more complex and nuanced consideration of emotion and design.

All the Feels, in Theory

William James asked the question "What Is an Emotion?" in 1884, and we still don't have an answer. In everyday life, we know what we experience, of course. We can usually tell whether someone is angry, we know what it means when someone is sad, we think we understand when someone says they are happy. But when you ask people to explain emotion, the concept unravels.

The idea that our internal workings can be distilled into just a few emotions is central to many aspects of everyday life. Evolutionary psychologists suggest that six emotions—happiness, sadness, fear, disgust, anger, and surprise—are expressed by everyone all over the world in much the same way. In this view, emotion begins to look like a simple reflex triggered by an external event: you see a bear, your pulse quickens, you feel frightened, and you run. Or, if we are talking about life online, you see an adorable baby goat, you smile, you feel joy, and you tap the heart. That's only one theory.

EMOTION AS PHYSICAL EXPRESSION

Theories about universal emotion date back to Aristotle, who divided emotions into pleasures and pains. Philosopher René Descartes comes up with six passions in his treatise *Passions of the Soul* (1649): wonder, love, hate, desire, joy, and sadness (Figure 2-1). But we can attribute a lot of our current thinking about instinctive, physical, universal emotion to the Victorian era.

FIGURE 2-1
Some universal emotions seem to transcend time (source: Charles LeBrun)

Charles Darwin studied the expression of emotions in humans and animals, mostly through observation of facial expressions and gestures. In *The Expression of Emotions in Man and Animals* (1872), Darwin wrote that like other traits, emotions evolved over time as a physical response to outside stimuli. He proposed three principles for emotional expression:

- *Serviceable habits*, such as furrowing a brow to prevent light from getting in your eyes, which becomes associated with remembering. You furrow your brow to try to see your memories.

- *Antithesis*, an expression that takes hold because it is the opposite of a serviceable habit, like shrugging your shoulders in contrast to something more aggressive.

- *Nervous discharge*, habits like foot tapping due to a build-up of excitement or a yell that comes as a release of anger.

Darwin studied the work of contemporary French physician Guillaume-Benjamin-Amand Duchenne, even including Duchenne's photographs of facial expression in his own book. Duchenne believed that human faces could express 60 universally recognizable emotions, which he deciphered by applying electrical currents to facial muscles (Figure 2-2). As squirm-inducing as the experiments might be, Duchenne did uncover what muscles of the face form a true smile (aptly named the Duchenne smile).

At the same time, Darwin was skeptical about going too far with universal expression. He wasn't so sure there were 60 of them; in his own "kitchen table" experiment showing photographs of facial expressions to friends and family, he thought there were many fewer.[1]

---

1 Ferris Jabr. "The Evolution of Emotion: Charles Darwin's Little-Known Psychology Experiment," *Scientific American*, May 24, 2010.

Plate III

FIGURE 2-2
Joy, assisted by electrical currents (source: Guillaume Duchenne)

1

4

2

5

3

6

Darwin's evolutionary model of emotion focused on the physical responses that are a crucial part of our emotional repertoire, translating it to universal expression. This approach inspired a series of theories about the universality of emotion. First, was the James-Lange theory. Developed independently by psychologist William James and physician Carl Lange, the theory goes like this: we have experiences, and as a result, our autonomic nervous system creates physiological events such as muscular tension, heart-rate increases, and perspiration. Emotions happen as a result of these detected physiological changes, rather than being the cause of them.

In the late 1920s, Walter Cannon and Philip Bard theorized that the experience of emotion happens at the same time as the physiological. This is called the Cannon-Bard Theory. In the 1960s, another strain of evolutionary theory by Stanley Schachter and Jerome Singer (you guessed it, called the Schachter-Singer model) said emotion was two-factor: a combination of physiological arousal and cognitive interpretation. Whether sequential or simultaneous, evolutionary psychology concluded that emotion was physical at the core, and physical and psychological were linked.

In the 1960s, anthropological research began to explore the idea that a few basic emotions could be universally understood through facial expressions. Researcher Paul Ekman asked people in different countries to match photos of facial expressions with emotions. Although there was variation, people from the United States, Brazil, and New Guinea matched images in similar ways about 58% of the time. And so, these six emotions—happiness, sadness, anger, surprise, fear, disgust—became known as basic emotions that all humans recognize. Some researchers might say there are more or less, but the idea that emotions are biologically innate and universal to all humans took hold.

From that research, Ekman created a Facial Action Coding System (FACS), a taxonomy of human expression in the face (Figure 2-3). Happiness, for instance, is 6 (cheek raiser) + 12 (lip corner puller) to varying degrees of intensity. Human coders, after studying a 600-page manual covering various combinations of the 44 action units, are able to tell the difference between an insecure and involuntary Pan-Am (fake) smile and a sincere and voluntary Duchenne (genuine) smile. For the layperson, *Emotions Revealed: Recognizing Faces and Feelings to Improve Communication and Emotional Life* (Times Books, 2007) promises help in deciphering emotion.

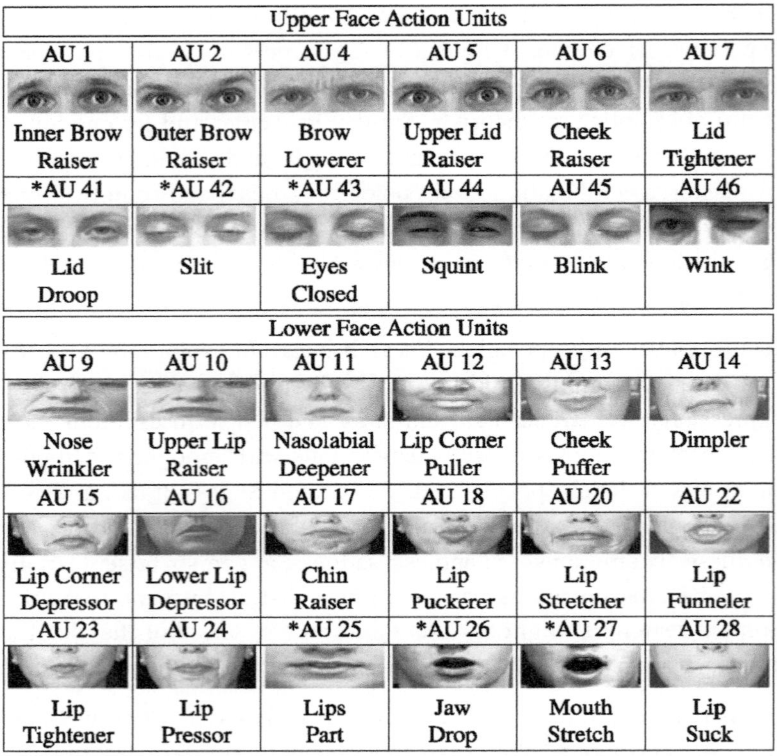

Upper Face Action Units					
AU 1	AU 2	AU 4	AU 5	AU 6	AU 7
Inner Brow Raiser	Outer Brow Raiser	Brow Lowerer	Upper Lid Raiser	Cheek Raiser	Lid Tightener
*AU 41	*AU 42	*AU 43	AU 44	AU 45	AU 46
Lid Droop	Slit	Eyes Closed	Squint	Blink	Wink
Lower Face Action Units					
AU 9	AU 10	AU 11	AU 12	AU 13	AU 14
Nose Wrinkler	Upper Lip Raiser	Nasolabial Deepener	Lip Corner Puller	Cheek Puffer	Dimpler
AU 15	AU 16	AU 17	AU 18	AU 20	AU 22
Lip Corner Depressor	Lower Lip Depressor	Chin Raiser	Lip Puckerer	Lip Stretcher	Lip Funneler
AU 23	AU 24	*AU 25	*AU 26	*AU 27	AU 28
Lip Tightener	Lip Pressor	Lips Part	Jaw Drop	Mouth Stretch	Lip Suck

FIGURE 2-3

Coding human facial expressions lends itself to machine coding (source: FACS)

Today the legacy of that research is everywhere. Used by the FBI and the CIA, it's become a way to detect lies. If you Google it, you'll turn up the Tim Roth emotional scale, or the universal emotions demonstrated by the lead actor of the TV show *Lie to Me*. It shows up in Feelings posters you see in schools. It's the basis of the Pixar film *Inside Out*.

And it's being encoded into our machines (more on that in a minute). It's easy to see why; emotion broken down into elements of an equation translates well to code. But universal expression of emotion is just one theory of emotion. So, before we begin encoding it in every technology we possibly can, let's consider the rest of the emotion landscape.

FEELINGS AS PERCEPTION

For a while, that base set of six classic emotions—happy, surprised, afraid, disgusted, angry, and sad—held fast. Increasingly, there's less agreement about what counts as an emotion and what doesn't. Studies have emerged claiming as few as four: happy, sad, afraid/surprised, and angry/disgusted. In 2017, a new study proposed 27 categories.[2] This new set of emotions ranges from more nuanced versions of the basics like admiration, adoration, awe, envy, excitement, and horror to some surprises like aesthetic appreciation, triumph, nostalgia, and empathetic pain. Why so many more? The answer might be in how emotion was studied.

Previous studies of emotion focused on the physical expression of emotion through observation, often in a social context. Now, feelings are being studied in all kinds of other ways—yes, even asking. One study combined short video prompts and self-report. Other studies involve art, storytelling, or other narrative prompts to encourage people to share their perception of emotion.

Now, emotion and feeling and even mood are terms often used interchangeably (this book is no exception). Neuroscientist Antonio Damasio, in *The Feeling of What Happens: Body and Emotion in the Making of Consciousness* (Mariner Books, 2000), draws a distinction between feelings, which are "inwardly directed and private," and emotions, which are "outwardly directed and public."

More than a mirror of our soul, emotions can signal what we want to happen next. Your best disgusted face might not show you are disgusted but instead signal that you're not happy with how a conversation is going. It's not surprising. After all, we've invented all kinds of ways to signal emotion when we are not face to face: emoticons in email, emojis in text, and hearts or gifs on social media.

Our feelings, Damasio argues, are mental experiences of bodily states and require a level of consciousness that other animals lack. They require a sense of identity or self. But it's not so easy to separate emotion and feeling. Neuroscientist Lisa Feldman Barrett argues in *How Emotions Are Made: The Secret Life of the Brain* (Houghton Mifflin

---

2   Alan S. Cowen and Dachter Keltner, "Self-report captures 27 distinct categories of emotion bridged by continuous gradients," *PNAS*, September 5, 2017.

Harcourt, 2017) that we constantly construct emotions. Based on years of research, she's found that we have pleasant and unpleasant bodily sensation, sometimes triggered by the environment, sometimes not. There's in-the-moment experience of emotion, there's also experience that accrues over a lifetime. This is how we constantly create and re-create emotion.

Think of it like this. The emotion of happiness is a concept. You might learn that certain sensations are associated with it. It also changes as you go along in life. Each experience of it expands what goes into the concept for you (Figure 2-4). The more you learn to appraise that emotion, the better you are at managing it. The more nuance you can add to it, the more you develop emotional intelligence. You don't acquire all this knowledge in a vacuum. The cultural and historical dimensions have a role, too.

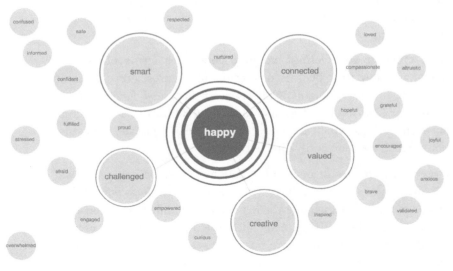

FIGURE 2-4

A single emotion contains multitudes

EMOTION'S CULTURAL LAYER

Cultural historian Tiffany Watt Smith traces the trajectory of emotions over time in *The Book of Human Emotions* (Profile Books, 2015). She argues that past generations probably didn't experience emotions in the same way that we do. For instance, in the 17th century, you might suffer from nostalgia or homesickness so much that it could cause serious illness or even death. Now those feelings have been downgraded to something much less serious.

Emotions are complex systems comprising culture, language, and context. Even if there are universals, emotions certainly aren't as basic as we once thought. Anxiety might accommodate fear and worry or shades of envy. It might manifest in all kinds of ways, from agitation to sleep issues to repetitive behaviors. If we were Czech, we might add *litost* to that bigger concept of anxiety, which is a state of torment caused by the site of one's own misery. And we can now certainly add "three-dot anxiety" (that little lurch of anticipation we feel when we see someone is typing) and cyberchondria (anxiety caused by excessive Googling of health conditions) to that anxiety concept.

The connection between feeling and language, and the urge to describe amorphous emotion with precise words, has been the focus of linguists too. With this in mind, Tim Lomas collected words for emotions across cultures in his book *The Happiness Dictionary: Words from Around the World Help Us Live a Richer Life* (Piatkus 2018). Even though it's tricky to isolate words from their cultural context, the work is a catalog of the emotional variation. Much of it is cultural. For instance, Lomas noticed a pattern among Northern European languages for terms that describe coziness, like *koselig* in Norwegian or *gezellig* in Dutch, whereas Southern European cultures have more emotion words for strolling outside, including the French *flâner* and the Greek *volta*.

There's a reason why we are drawn to these collections of untranslatable words for emotions and maps of uncharted emotional territories (Figure 2-5). Beyond a fascination with fellow humans, having more emotional concepts at our disposal develops our emotional intelligence, too. But is emotional intelligence only a human experience? Now scientists are reconsidering animal emotion, too.

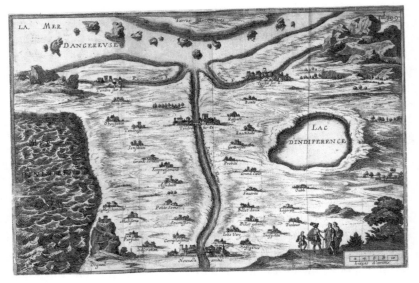

FIGURE 2-5

A map of tenderness charts a lost land of emotion (source: François Chauveau)

EMOTION IS NOT JUST HUMAN

If you have a pet, you might suspect that your cat, dog, or chicken has an emotional life. We humans might feel conflicted about the idea of animal emotion. One the one side, some argue that animals don't feel emotion, and especially pain, in the way humans do. At the same time, emotions are considered instinctual. Maybe there's something about emotion that seems *too* animal.

Charles Darwin, when he wrote *The Expression of Emotion in Man and Animals* in 1872, proposed that emotional expression communicates and motivates in creatures of all kinds, reading emotional expression in a dog's simple tail wag (Figure 2-6). Cross-species affective neuroscience, pioneered by Jaak Panskepp, looks at how mammals experience emotion. In *Affective Neuroscience* (Oxford University Press, 1998), Panskepp explains that people don't have a monopoly on emotion. For one, rats experience emotional contagion: when one was in pain, another experienced pain, too. Humpback whales appear to show empathy, rescuing seals from killer whales. Magpies have been observed carrying out something like a funeral.

FIGURE 2-6
The tail as emotional marker (source: Charles Darwin)

When crayfish receive an electric shock, they become more fearful and anxious according to the research of biologist Robert Elwood, which was enough for Switzerland to outlaw boiling lobsters alive.[3] More recently, researchers at the University of Cambridge were able to detect levels of pain in sheep using facial coding similar to FACS. Biologists have developed FACS for chimps, horses, and dogs, too.

Researchers haven't just focused on how animals experience emotion but also how they might understand human emotion, too. In experiments similar to Ekman's, psychologists showed photographs of happy and angry human faces to see whether horses can read emotion.[4] It seems that they can. So can goats. Dogs have an emotional range that's at least equivalent to a toddler and may broaden their range over the course of their lifetime. Current sentiment technology will likely reveal more about animal emotion (Figure 2-7).

---

3   Karen Weintraub, "The Swiss Consider the Lobster. It Feels Pain, They Decide," *New York Times*, January 12, 2018.

4   Virginia Morell, "Horses Understand Human Facial Expressions," *Science Magazine*, February 9, 2016.

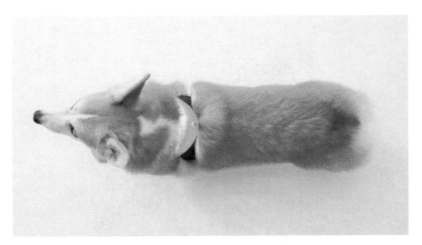

FIGURE 2-7
Dog mood detectors assume that dogs have emotion (source: Inupathy)

This aside about animal emotion isn't just nice to know. It might just help us to think more deeply about nonhuman emotion. Animals experience emotion, but probably not in the same way that humans do. Some animals have the capacity to develop emotional range. Others participate in social rituals to work through emotion. The animals that live with us begin to detect human emotion and adapt to it. Some animals respond to human emotion, even adapting their behavior. When I hear all this, I think robots.

AN EMOTIONAL AWAKENING

Inquiry into emotion is undergoing a kind of renaissance. Even without much agreement on what emotion is, it has a stake in everything. Some approaches focus on a few basic emotions, others on an extensive collection of emotions. Emotion is linked with the body and the brain. It is crucial to attention, perception, and memory. Emotion motivates and prioritizes. Emotion might well point to what we value.

Universities are creating centers for the history of emotion. Anthropologists are exploring new cultural implications of emotion. Neuroscience is finding that emotion is more than just a simple trigger to impulse mapping. Philosophers debate the ethical force of emotion. Scientists are gaining understanding of emotion in other species. Emotion has come to be recognized as absolutely fundamental and beautifully complex.

Design has followed a separate path, coming up with its own theories about emotion. In the past two decades, there have been several approaches to designing for emotion. Unlike the study of emotion, which is growing to accommodate new discoveries about emotion, design has progressively narrowed its view of emotion, almost to a vanishing point.

Emotional Design and Technology

Emotional design, as it's currently practiced, is minimal. We typically don't design for emotional experience at all, preferring ease or productivity or convenience as North Stars.

We know that emotion is important, though. It drives decisions. It motivates us to action. It builds bonds. Negative emotions can mean that people are frustrated enough not to complete what they started, too bored to stay engaged, or disappointed enough to switch brands altogether. Positive emotions not only diffuse problems, but potentially increase engagement in the moment—as a flow state or meaning making—and build attachment in the long term.

Each framework for emotional design implicitly embraces this idea. Reduce negative emotion first, and then surprise and delight. Hopefully, happy moments turn into happy memories, building a cycle of positive emotions. Yet, when we look at the emotional climate of the internet, it's clear we've cultivated outrage, anxiety, anger, and *schadenfreude*, too.

Emotion is a blind spot for design. In theory, we've substituted behavior for emotion. In practice, we've oversimplified. Even so, there are ideas we can build on. Let's review the different approaches to emotional design so far.

FOUR TYPES OF EMOTION

Although design has long recognized the emotional dimension of products, theory has been a fairly recent development. Patrick Jordan, in *Designing Pleasurable Products* (CRC Press, 2002), was one of the first to consider it at length. Based loosely on anthropologist Lionel Tiger's work on pleasure as a biological mechanism for survival, Jordan identifies four types of pleasure that factor into product design.

- *Physio-pleasure* is sensory, tapping into touch, appearance, sound, taste, and smell—the smooth feel of the iPhone, for example.

- *Psycho-pleasure* is cognitive, associated with the usability of the product, like setting up a meeting successfully or managing your budget.

- *Socio-pleasure* is grounded in relationships with other individuals, associated with communication either as a channel like social media or a conversation starter like a meme.

- *Ideo-pleasure* comes from ideas, often drawn from cultural history or personal values, like a product that reduces your carbon footprint by tracking your energy usage.

These four archetypes describe different types of experiences rather than a framework for every emotional experience. That would come next in Don Norman's work.

THREE LEVELS OF EMOTION

In his book *Emotional Design: Why We Love (or Hate) Everyday Things* (Basic Books, 2005), Don Norman writes that "attractive things work better." At a basic level, this means the aesthetics are just as important as function. Universal principles, like the *Golden Ratio* or the *Rule of Thirds*, inform our innate sense about whether something is beautiful. It might be that there are design elements, like saturated hues, harmonious sounds, symmetrical objects, sweet tastes, and rounded shapes that give us joy, as Ingrid Fetell Lee writes in *Joyful: The Surprising Power of Ordinary Things to Create Extraordinary Happiness* (Little, Brown & Company, 2018).

It's more than that, though. When people feel better about a product, they will overlook negatives and assume favorable outcomes. In other words, a positive response smooths over the rough edges in the experience. Folk wisdom tells us that maybe it will make people more loyal to the brand as well.

Rather than focusing on different types of emotional experience, like Jordan, Norman posits that people's emotional responses to design correspond to the three levels of information processing in the brain—*visceral*, *behavioral*, and *reflective*. To be successful, design should appeal to all three levels:

- The visceral level is almost like a reflex response. Norman argues that a visceral response to design is hardwired and might apply even across cultures and people. The impulse to reject bitter tastes, or prefer highly saturated colors, or gravitate toward symmetry are all examples of visceral response. *The visceral level is how the object looks.*

- The behavioral level is the total experience of engaging with an object—how it functions, how it feels to interact, and how it responds. It's what you do, with varying levels of intent. The behavioral level is influenced by visceral reactions, which are largely unconscious, but also by reflection. *The behavioral level is how it works.*

- The reflective level is how you perceive the product, the representation of the product in your mind. Rather than an emotional response based on a gut reaction or an in-the-moment interaction, reflective response is evoked by the design's symbolic meaning. *The reflective level is what it means.*

Emotional Design inspired the design community to consider emotion as part of the big picture. It maps to the prevailing theory of the time—the triune brain—which has an allegorical appeal. It isn't really wrong, but it's an oversimplification.

Even so, Norman's concept of emotional design expands on the idea that emotion is more complicated than pure instinct. The book provided examples of emotional design, from teapots to cars, but there still wasn't a lot of how-to for designers. Process and practice were to come next.

A SINGULAR EMOTION

Aarron Walter's in *Designing for Emotion* (A Book Apart, 2011) and similarly, Trevor von Gorp and Edie Adams in *Design for Emotion* (Morgan Kaufmann, 2012) came up with a hierarchy for emotional design: useful, usable, and delightful. The model loosely mapped to Norman's three levels but also introduced a new influence—Abraham Maslow's hierarchy of needs. Just as Maslow's framework started with basic needs building toward higher goals like love and self-actualization, so too does the most widely used model for emotional design. The design should meet a specific need first, then function well, and then finally add delight. These emotional peaks, if done well, would memorably cement the relationship.

The common-sense idea to take care of the basics first and then think about ways to add good feelings fit well with many designers' workflow. Delight is mostly in the details. Lovingly obsessing over the finer points is an endearing trait of designers, after all. The details might be tiny, but they often strive for something bigger:

Conciliatory

A lot of delight attempts to lighten the mood when you encounter an error. When you search for an emoji in Slack that doesn't exist, you get the cry emoji instead. 404 messages are often the place for a cheerful message, lightening up a moment of minor frustration.

Curious

You might be tempted to call this category pointless fun, but Snap has proven that discovering secret features motivates people to share them. When you discover that Alexa answers "What's your favorite color?" with "Infrared is super pretty," you might get a fleeting sense of delight.

Caring

Some delightful details seem to have your back. When Chrome detects that you are on an insecure connection, it won't autofill credit card details. When you are sending multiple messages to hosts on Airbnb, the name of the host is swapped out automatically to prevent embarrassment. When you try to add a song you already have in a playlist, Spotify shows a cheeky warning.

Celebratory

Delight is nothing if not taking a moment to celebrate quick wins, from everything to adding a pair of shoes to your Zappos cart to successfully launching an email campaign (Figure 2-8).

FIGURE 2-8

It's impossible to speak of delight without referencing Mailchimp

High fives!

**Your campaign is in the
send queue and will go out shortly.**

Delight-spotting websites like *Little Big Details* collect meaningful examples of delight in the wild alongside the more whimsical, such as novelty transitions, skeuomorphic page turns, and the like. Stephen Anderson's *Seductive Interaction Design* (New Riders, 2011) inspired us to take a playful approach. Dan Saffer's *Microinteractions: Designing with Details* (O'Reilly, 2013) guided designers to focus on the finer points. And these small details can make a big difference.

But delight has its downsides. Delight can feel formulaic. Creating a design element, a naming scheme, or an interaction pattern that's surprising and clever can sometimes go wrong, too:

Trivializing

Once in a while, delightful details trivialize something that isn't trivial at all. In a research project on retirement saving, one participant was annoyed by the illustration cheerfully telling him that he had enough saved for 42 days of retirement. He said flatly, "I don't think this is exactly a YAY moment for me."

Obstructionist

Whether unclear naming or distracting animation, too-clever details make it more difficult to actually engage with the product in a meaningful way.

Paternalistic

Although we want products to show that they have our back, it's all too easy to cross the line toward a "we know best" kind of tone. Product Hunt suggesting that you go to bed if you've been browsing for too long might just cross that line, even when a cute cat is in the mix.

Infantilizing

A little childish humor is okay, but we don't want to be treated like children. Compare Waze (Figure 2-9), which is meant to provide traffic navigation for grownups, with Pokémon Go, a game for kids (and grownups). A lot of delightful details try very hard to be funny, but humor is not only subjective, it's contextual. For instance, you might find cute cars fun on your usual ride, but annoying when you start to be guided through a maze of side streets.

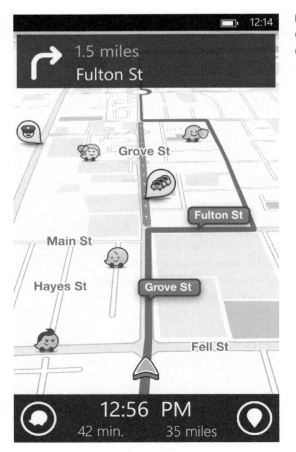

FIGURE 2-9
Charming or childish?
(source: Waze)

The downsides of delight can be much more serious. In *Design for Real Life* (A Book Apart, 2016), Sarah Wachter-Boettcher and Eric Meyer note that tech companies are often willing to invest resources chasing delight over addressing real-life pressure points:

> Apple has no trouble dedicating its smart, highly paid staff to preloading Siri with pithy quips and jokes. That was a priority from day one. Five years later, Apple still hasn't stress-tested Siri for its response to crisis.

Delight will inevitably lose its appeal over time. I remember the first time I noticed the lazy-loading color swatches on Pinterest (Figure 2-10). At first, it was nice. Then, I just expected it. As it became a design convention on Google image search and other sites, it lost a little luster. The half-life of a delightful detail seems proportional to its ubiquity and its frequency.

We adapt, or even come to expect, the things that once gave us joy. It's not limited to design, of course. It's called *hedonic adaptation*. For that reason, delightful details have the most impact along the periphery of an experience—those aspects of an experience we see once, like setting up an account or introducing a new feature or encountering an error.

FIGURE 2-10
The thrill is gone, alas (source: Pinterest)

Emotional design has become synonymous with delight, but delight might have peaked. Just as people adapt to delightful details, designers have adapted to delight. Delight has simply become one technique among many others that set apart good design.

A CYCLE OF EMOTION

Delight paved the way for design's pursuit of happiness. Behavioral design took it a step further, by putting delight at the peak of a cycle of emotion. Nir Eyal's influential book, *Hooked: How to Build Habit-Forming Products* (with Ryan Hoover; Portfolio, 2014), distills behavioral psychology into method. The attention model starts with negative emotions like boredom or anxiety or FOMO (fear of missing out), and then "solves" it—but not predictably and only for a little while—with a little dose of positive emotion.

Variable rewards are a way to sustain our attention by keeping us guessing. As our attention is pulled in different directions, the thinking goes, the more designers need to build in random rewards to up engagement. After you've learned about variable rewards, you begin to see them everywhere you look. When you glance at a notification on your phone, pull to refresh your email, or scroll social media, you might or might not find what you are seeking. When you do, you get a little burst of dopamine and you feel good.

What seems to be happening, though, is that designing to alleviate pain doesn't alleviate pain at all. Instead, it can cultivate a cycle of negative emotion. The good feeling doesn't last. The false sense of urgency creates a new source of stress. And the good feeling might not be that good, after all. It creates an experience that feels addictive.

It's certainly possible to use emotional triggers for positive outcomes. Fitbit, Headspace, Duolingo (Figure 2-11), and a host of other apps show how principles from behavioral design can be used to promote healthy habits through (predictable) rewards. Rewards themselves can boost a good mood and build confidence. Behavior-change apps might sometimes satisfy an emotional need. But so far, the better angels of behavioral design do not always prevail.

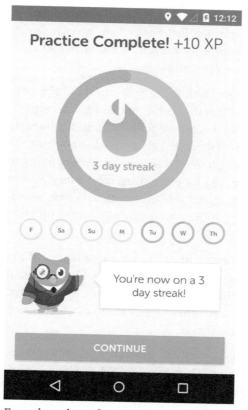

FIGURE 2-11

Behavioral design
has emotional impact
(source: Duolingo)

Even though we frame negative experience caused by behavioral design
as an "attention problem," it translates to an endless loop of emotional
ups and downs. Maybe that's why the proposed antidote to design that
demands too much attention is design that demands as little as possible. The counterpoint to compulsive design is calm design.

EMOTION ZERO

The term "calm technology" was coined in 1995 by PARC Researchers
Mark Weiser and John Seely Brown.[5] As a response to the increasing
complexity and inevitable ubiquity of technology, calm technology was
proposed as an alternative. Rather than monopolizing our attention
and, in turn, causing anxiety or stress or distraction or overstimula-
tion, it moves tech to the periphery to create calm. Modern interpre-
tations like Golden Krishna's book *The Best Interface Is No Interface:*

---

5   Mark Weiser and John Seely Brown, "Designing Calm Technology," Xerox PARC, 1995.

The Simple Path to Brilliant Technology (New Riders, 2015) and Amber Case's *Calm Technology: Principles and Patterns for Non-Intrusive Design* (O'Reilly, 2015) extend the concept for current times with tactics to minimize the insistent presence of technology.

With Google announcing a digital well-being program that helps people switch off, it seems the idea that the best technology is less technology is taking off. Apple and Microsoft have followed suit. It's possible more will follow. Instead of autostarting the next episode by default, for instance, Netflix could prompt you to set a certain number of hours to watch. Facebook could make it easy for you to turn off the feed during certain times of the day. Calm, digital well-being, digital detox, mindful design, humane technology all have a similar aim—turn off tech, tune in to life.

All good. A little restorative time "offline" (note: there is no offline) is fine. But what happens when we go back online? So far, digital well-being hasn't addressed that. Perhaps part of the reason is that digital well-being has framed the technology problem as an attention problem rather than an emotional one.

Calm technology doesn't explicitly mention emotion. It's attention-calm, not emotion-calm. That seems apt. Calm is presented as a kind of neutral state, an absence of strong emotion. The assumption behind calm technology (and now digital well-being initiatives) is that technology plays a purely functional role, or it should. Logically, that makes sense. Realistically, we know that's hardly the case.

NEXT-GENERATION EMOTIONAL DESIGN

This quick tour of emotional design shows that each theory is a product of cultural zeitgeist, from the triune brain to the science of happiness to cognitive biases to mindfulness. Design theory tracks to the latest advances in psychology, social theory, and science. This book is no different.

Among all these theories of emotional design, there is one common thread: emotion, when we acknowledge it at all, is a problem to be solved. That's because emotion has largely been seen as something that gets in the way of our rational thinking. At best, emotion must be soothed. At worst, it can be manipulated. For now, we might think it's best to minimize it.

Whether it's related to how tech is designed or not, minimizing emotion has become an ingrained internet behavior. We don't share feelings; we feel feels. We don't cry because "I'm not crying, you're crying." It's that feeling when any show of emotion is countered with an ironic self-awareness. The emotion is there, but we prefer to rely on distance and denial, partly out of self-preservation.

When we aren't minimizing, we are motivating. The foundational model for emotional design hasn't been based on emotion theory. Instead, we've found inspiration in Maslow's hierarchy of human needs, which is behavioral. In keeping with goal-based, problem-solving design, emotion is treated more often as destination than context, culture, or language.

The next wave of emotional design will be informed and guided by data about emotion. And it will be guided by mostly just one emotion theory. The evolutionary theory of emotion, where emotion is considered instinctual and universal, dominates. Emotion artificial intelligence (AI), also known as affective computing or empathic media, will attempt to make physical expression of emotion machine-readable.

Emotion + AI

Apps and chatbots don't know whether you are having a good day or a bad day, whether you are running up against a big deadline or are about to leave for a long weekend, or whether you spent the last hour laughing with close friends or arguing with your spouse. Although a digital assistant can tell you the weather or an app can remember your favorite song or a cute error message can make you smile, technology doesn't react to changes in your mood. It might be engaging or annoying or even delightful, but it lacks emotional intelligence.

Machines have certainly appeared as if they have feelings. Apple consistently lends a human touch to its products. The Color Classic looked a bit human, with its screen placed high in a tall narrow base to look like a face and its disk drive a crooked smile. Apple secured a patent for the Breathing Status LED indicator in 2003—the gently pulsing light that shows your laptop has moved to a standby state is designed to mimic human breathing rates during sleep. The iPhone's passcode screen is characterized by another human gesture: if you incorrectly enter your passcode, your iPhone will shake from left to right, mimicking a head shake.

More recently, there's Cozmo the robot (Figure 2-12). Cozmo doesn't detect emotion, but it displays subtly choreographed expressions designed to induce empathetic imagination. Likewise, home robots such as Kuri and Jibo imitate human qualities to elicit emotion without sensing it (yet). Chatbots, like Alexa, rely on speech patterns and social conventions to imitate aspects of human conversation. If you tell Alexa that you feel sad, she responds with something like, "I'm sorry you feel that way. Sometimes listening to music or taking a walk or calling friends or talking to friends helps. I hope you feel better soon."

FIGURE 2-12
Cozmo might actually have all the feels (source: Anki)

So, some machines might show a human touch by mimicking emotion. Humanized bots are beginning to shift expectations of tech, but mostly, machines are blind when it comes to emotion. Netflix is sophisticated at analyzing our entertainment preferences but doesn't know what we're in the mood for watching. Interactive lessons on Lynda might track how much a student has completed but not how engaged the student really was.

Emotions are beginning to become a part of our everyday use of technology. Emotional responses like angry, sad, and "wow!" are now integrated into our online emotional vocabulary as we begin to use Facebook's reactions. Twitter's stars transformed to hearts, a better signal of emotion. Emojis lend a creative layer of emotional texture to otherwise flat text exchanges.

But we provide the emotional clues, if we choose, by tapping a heart or a "wow" to send signals to other people about who we are and what we feel. Emotion AI will take it one step further, so that machines will be aware of new clues about emotion.

MACHINE-READABLE EMOTION

Computer scientist Rosalind Picard argued that to build truly intelligent machines, we'd need emotion. In her 1997 book *Affective Computing* (MIT Press), she details the importance of emotion in communication, mapping out the implications for robots and wearables. Her work at Massachusetts Institute of Technology (MIT) develops technology that can read the physical signs of emotions, interpret the emotions, and then take action based on them—whether by reacting, changing its behavior, or nudging our own.

By gathering signals through cameras, microphones, skin sensors, eye tracking, and other means, affective computing can translate emotion. This collection of technologies, now usually called emotion AI, focuses on quantifying the telltale signs of emotion we display, consciously and unconsciously. The list of technologies is steadily growing.

Sentiment analysis notes frequency, arrangement, and sometimes context of words and maps that to an emotional category. It can bundle positive and negative emotion into just two categories, but newer systems tease out five or more basic emotions like happiness, sadness, fear, anger, and disgust. Sentiment analysis, like IBM Watson (Figure 2-13), analyzes not just text, but emojis, gifs, images, and video for evidence of moods, feelings, and emotions. It can gauge customer frustration in chat, detect reactions to a company announcement that could affect market value, or script chatbots in a way that seems more emotionally attuned.

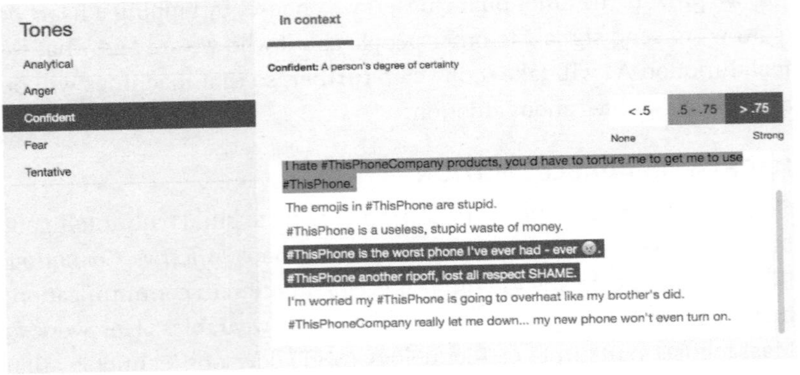

Tones	In context
Analytical	Confident: A person's degree of certainty
Anger	
Confident	
Fear	
Tentative	

	< .5	.5 - .75	> .75
	None		Strong

I hate #ThisPhoneCompany products, you'd have to torture me to get me to use #ThisPhone.

The emojis in #ThisPhone are stupid.

#ThisPhone is a useless, stupid waste of money.

#ThisPhone is the worst phone I've ever had - ever 😡.

#ThisPhone another ripoff, lost all respect SHAME.

I'm worried my #ThisPhone is going to overheat like my brother's did.

#ThisPhoneCompany really let me down... my new phone won't even turn on.

FIGURE 2-13

Watching your tone, literally (source: IBM Watson)

Facial coding reads facial expressions from cameras, video files, or photos. Most affective computing systems are based on Paul Ekman's FACS and interpret five to seven universal emotions from facial expression. Established concerns like Affectiva and Kairos have trained on massive, diverse datasets of human faces around the world. So, these systems can detect "big emotion" or emphatic facial expressions like big grins and pronounced frowns. But they can also identify many more *micro-expressions*, or tiny changes in the face that will eventually become more nuanced. Facial coding is already widely used in ad testing, but it is finding a market in the automotive industry as a way to detect emotion or other states such as distraction or sleepiness that affect safety. On the dark side, facial coding is associated with employee monitoring and predictive policing.

Voice analytics identify patterns in vocal pitch, rhythm, tonality, and intensity of the human voice. Platforms such as Beyond Verbal and Nemesysco put less emphasis on what people say and more on how they say it. Like facial coding, voice analytics could potentially recognize nuances of tone—perhaps even nuances that people might miss. Just as humans do best at reading emotion with face and voice together, most of the emotion-sensing tech is working toward combining face and voice to detect emotion.

Wearables track various biometric markers. Galvanic skin response measures sweaty palms triggered by emotions. Electromyography (EMG) measures muscle activity and tension, which can map mostly to negative emotions so far. Electrocardiogram (ECG) measures the heart's beat and rhythm, which can signal changes in emotional state. Blood volume pulse, skin, temperature, and respiration rate are other physical signs that wearables can detect. Wearables are becoming more widely used for people with Post-Traumatic Stress Disorder (PTSD), sensory-processing issues, and epilepsy as a way to alert loved ones or caretakers. Baby monitors such as Mattel's Sproutling (Figure 2-14) monitor temperature, sleep, environment, and emotion at the same time. Emotion-sensing tech will certainly be embedded in fitness trackers and smartwatches as a way to monitor or share moods, too.

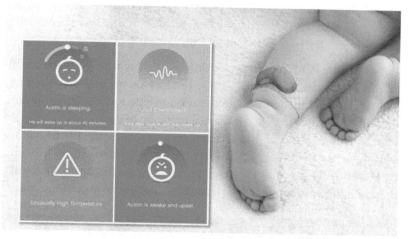

FIGURE 2-14
A no more tears formula (source: Sproutling)

Gesture tracking trains cameras on hands, face, or other parts of the body to detect reactions. Body language and posture can reveal our emotions, even emotions that we aren't aware of ourselves. Nail biting reveals anxiety, or drumming fingers indicate impatience. At a basic level, gesture AI is already used for games without the emotion-sensing layer for now.

Headsets record electrical signals (EEG) along the scalp to measure brain activity, usually through a wearable. The Muse headset is a consumer version of this technology, used for mindfulness practice. This type of emotion detection gets at agitation or calm on its own; or in tandem with other types of emotion AI.

Eye tracking measures gaze patterns, pupil dilation, blinking, and eye movement, which can reveal some clues about emotion and context. It's a crude measure of emotion on its own. For instance, pupil dilation might signal arousal, or excessive blinking could be a clue about nervousness. In combination with facial coding, eye tracking fills in some of the context. What people are looking at, especially if it's something that people are wholly focused on like a movie, may add a dimension to understanding emotion.

Augmented reality (AR), in which the physical world is overlaid with computer-generated graphics, can reveal attention and interaction with digital objects. When combined with other methods of affective computing, like facial coding or gesture tracking, it can reveal emotional engagement. It's more about providing context than detecting.

Virtual reality (VR), in which people react to a synthetic environment, can allow remote viewers to feel into a first-person perspective. Although VR can be combined with biofeedback and other affective computing measures, the focus is the cognitive dimension of emotional experience rather than the physical. Projects range from witnessing life in solitary confinement to simulating the life of an orca in captivity to learning greater empathy for delivering a terminal diagnosis (Figure 2-15). Rather than making emotion machine readable, VR seeks to evoke empathy.

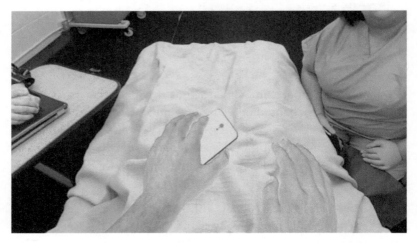

FIGURE 2-15
Rehearsing difficult conversations for better real-life outcomes (source: Embodied Labs)

So, it's clear that emotion AI is a broad category for many different types of technology to detect and interpret human emotion. The industry is projected to grow to $50 billion in just the next five years. The big tech companies like Apple, Google, Facebook, IBM, and Microsoft have already adopted emotion AI in some of their products. Apple purchased facial-coding company Emotient in 2016 and filed patents for mood-sensitive television advertising. Facebook has patents to use facial coding of emotion for advertising. IBM relies on Watson for emotion detection, Microsoft Azure uses emotion products related to computer vision, and Google's Cloud Vision API integrates sentiment analysis. Small- to mid-sized companies like Real Eyes, Humanyze, Sensum, and CrowdEmotion have developed tech that can track these physical markers of emotion.

Where will we use emotion-aware technology? Wherever people have emotions. Basically, everywhere. Table 2-1 lists some of the potential uses.

TABLE 2-1. Wherever emotions can be detected, tech will follow

SECTOR	USE
Advertising and marketing	Optimize the reach and appeal of ads
Art	Engage people in an experience and expand creative techniques
Automotive	Improve safety or create excitement
Education	Engage students and customize learning
Entertainment	Test reactions and increase engagement
Events	Show emotional climate and build communal experience
Fitness	Account for emotion in performance
Finance	Chart emotional climate and provide custom management tools
Gaming	Enhance play and brain training
Healthcare	Diagnose conditions, assist with self-care, enrich therapeutic interventions
Home	Attune the environment to emotional state
Insurance	Assess risk based on mental health
Pets	Assist with training and care
Police and security	Detect lies and identify potential threats
Political organizations	Assess policies and gauge importance of issues

Product research and design	Understand emotional reactions to products
Retailers	Understand in-store behavior
Sex tech	Enhance intimacy
Social media	Optimize the reach and appeal of ads and marketing campaigns
Sports	Hone performance
Urban planning	Gauge citizen emotion
Workplace	Track employee engagement

Companies such as the BBC, Coca-Cola, and Disney are already using the simplest emotion analytics to assess reactions to advertisements, film trailers, and TV shows. Ad agencies are correlating emotion analytics to brand recall and purchase intent. But the big change will come when emotion AI is embedded in products and services.

Initial experiments range from silly to satisfying to sinister. Hershey Smile Sampler is a lighthearted experiment in which people would get a free chocolate for smiling into a vending machine. On the other end of the spectrum, there are products like Brain Power that pair Google Glass with emotion detection to help children on the autism spectrum see emotion.

It's not just experiments, though. So far, emotion AI is already being used in three main ways:[6]

Adjust system response

Here, emotion AI acknowledges emotions and factors them into its decision making. Insurer Humana uses software that detects conversational cues to guide call-center workers through difficult calls. One step further along are chatbots that factor in emotional response to route calls. Automotive AI detects emotion to prevent accidents or road rage. Security software that monitors sentiment in a crowd through facial detection, like CrowdEmotion, or by text analysis on social media is starting to be used to calibrate police presence or response.

---

6   Sophie Kleber, "3 Ways AI Is Getting More Emotional," *Harvard Business Review*, July 31, 2018.

Evaluate or teach emotional skills

In 2013, Microsoft developed Mood Wings, a bracelet that detects anxiety or other emotional states, conveying changes rather whimsically through the flaps of a butterfly wing (Figure 2-16). Similarly, but less whimsically, Philips developed a wearable that monitors the stress level of traders to prevent them from making decisions in the heat of the moment. Recruiting firms are using emotion AI to evaluate facial expression and word choice during job interviews to measure engagement, motivation, and empathy. Targeted emotional learning is also being used in sports to help athletes build awareness and control, in teaching to sort out group dynamics, and in management to build leadership skills.

FIGURE 2-16

Wearing your heart on your sleeve in the form of a butterfly on your wrist (source: Microsoft Research)

Mimic or replace human-to-human relationships

Some bots are designed to not only detect and interpret emotion, but to display emotional awareness. From Karim, the AI delivering social support to Syrian refugees, to the Kirobo Mini, a part of Toyota's Heart Project aimed at making people less lonely, the best of these bots provides emotional support. Microsoft's Xiaoice, Google Assistant, and Amazon's Alexa could detect social and emotional cues to drive purchases. Because personal assistants are connected with advertisers, the potential for exploiting the relationship is real. In a leaked Facebook memo, Facebook claimed it could pinpoint "moments when young people need a confidence boost" by matching ads with emotions like "defeated" and "overwhelmed."[7] On the flip side, it's not difficult to imagine people paying five dollars per month for a feed that makes them feel happier. Consent, paired with intention, can make all the difference.

Emotion AI is just getting started, really. Like any technology, it has positive potential and shadow possibilities. It could help machines seem more empathetic and maybe prompt us to become more aware of emotion. It could also be invasive or manipulative. Let's look more closely at the positives and negatives.

THE POSITIVE POTENTIAL OF EMOTION AI

One day, just after we received our first Amazon Echo, it went missing. Wondering what happened, I wandered through the house to see where it might be. I had my suspicions. As I stood outside my youngest daughter's room. I could hear her talking to Alexa, at first in hushed tones, then with increasing frustration. She wanted to play an audio book and was having a hard time finding her place. "Alexa, fast forward. No, fast forward backwards." Apparently, kids don't know about rewind. "No, no, no, just start at Chapter 1. Ugh, I hate you. Shut up!" Alexa was oblivious to my daughter's rising frustration.

Right now, our devices don't respond empathetically, despite the devoted attention of large teams of designers, developers, content strategists, and the like. Mood-aware technologies could not only mitigate negative situations but also promise to make our lives better in a variety of ways. The potential for emotion-aware technologies, for people, products, and the planet, can be profoundly positive.

It can make experiences more personal

The obvious benefit is that emotion-aware technology can make every experience more personal. It could adjust experience to your mood. Take your Philips Hue lightbulbs, for instance. Rather than adjusting on a timer or on your command, the lights would just know how you feel. Music apps could detect your emotions, comparing against your

---

7   Michael Reilly, "Is Facebook Targeting Ads at Sad Teens?" *MIT Technology Review*, May 1, 2017.

typical patterns, and adapt to energize or soothe. This wouldn't need to be limited to individual personalization. Imagine family bickering reaches epic levels and your social bot lightening the mood.

It can make experiences more exciting

Sensum's platform taps a variety of emotion inputs such as facial coding, heart rate, and breathing in combination with contextual data like weather and location to build compelling experiences. In a recent experiment with Ford, the technology was used to understand and maximize the driver's excitement while driving a performance vehicle. Through a combination of atmospheric sensors, social media sentiment analysis, XOX's biometric wristbands, and VR, Wimbledon and Jaguar partnered to shared visualizations of the emotional climate of the event.

It could keep us healthy

Just as we can track our fitness and physical health, we could track our mental state. Researchers are looking into emotion AI for suicide prevention and mental health support. The Muse headband monitors brain waves for signs of anxiety as a way to train you to manage stress. Emotion AI company Beyond Verbal has partnered with the Mayo clinic to monitor vocal biomarkers associated with stress as well as coronary heart disease.

It could provide therapeutic interventions

Much of the early work in affective computing was centered on helping children on the autism spectrum. For many, communicating their feelings is impossible, sometimes manifesting in sudden challenging events. Because outbursts can be preceded by calm, it can be difficult to detect even by a highly attuned caregiver. Emotion-aware technology can reveal the hidden patterns behind these emotional storms.

For veterans suffering from PTSD, emotion-aware technology can lend support, too. Ellie, an experimental virtual therapist developed at the University of Southern California's Institute for Creative Technologies, analyzes emotional cues through facial expressions, gestures, and vocal patterns (Figure 2-17). For now, Ellie is strictly for diagnosis, identifying veterans who might need help and then referring them to a therapist. Patients admit to feeling less judged talking to Ellie, too. So, they might be more apt to seek out help when needed. In the near future, emotion AI chatbots or virtual therapists will make therapy more widely available to people who need it.

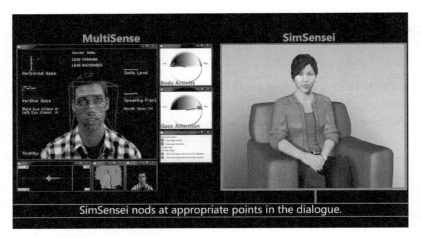

FIGURE 2-17
A virtual therapist that really gets you (source: SimSensei)

It could show care

Japanese company AIST developed PARO, an interactive robot that functions as a therapy pet. Embodied as a baby harp seal covered with soft artificial fur, this therapeutic robot has been found to reduce the stress factor experienced both by patients and by their caregivers. Another Japanese company, Softbank, has developed Pepper, a robot that picks up some emotional cues and responds with care. You can already find Pepper as a greeter in banks, stores, and hotels, but also in medical centers to help patients as they check in.

It could help us learn

In online learning environments, or even in classrooms, it can be difficult to determine whether a student is struggling or when a student is engaged. By the time test scores are lagging, it's often too late. An emotionally intelligent learning systems could personalize the experience, slowing down when it detects confusion or offering encouragement when a student is frustrated.

It could reduce accidents

Driving can be dangerous. Often accidents are often linked with emotion. After driving under the influence, the highest number of automobile-related deaths and injuries are the result of distraction, anger, and sadness—all detectable with emotion AI. An occupant-aware vehicle with Affectiva's automotive AI (Figure 2-18) could monitor the driver for fatigue, distraction, and frustration.

FIGURE 2-18
Worst-case scenario, feelings can kill (source: Affectiva)

It could create safer communities

We might call it instinct or gut feeling, but police rely on their own human emotion detection to read an individual's body language or expression. It's not much of a leap to imagine police using the tech developed by UK firm WeSee, which spots suspicious behavior by reading facial cues in a crowd. Emotions, such as doubt and anger, might be detectable in larger groups of people indicating deceit or guilt. Likewise, lie detection in the legal system is already part human, part machine. Lie detectors will be augmented with emotion AI, potentially making them more accurate.

It could build awareness of cultural differences

Emotion AI systems have access to more examples of more emotions in more places than we ever will as individuals. Most people will never experience reading 10 million faces from all over the world or listen to shifts in tone in 20 languages. Emotion AI will. In combination with empathetic VR experiences, we could make substantial progress in tolerance and understanding globally.

It might help us become more emotionally intelligent

Consistently recording physical signs of emotion means that our apps will be attuned to the signs of emotion in a way that we are not. There might come a time quite soon when our devices begin to understand our emotions better than we do ourselves. It might inject a broader understanding of cultural and social differences into our everyday expression. From this we might be able to learn more about recognizing and regulating emotions in ourselves. We might recognize a broader repertoire of emotional responses.

Existing emotion-tracking tools like Moodnotes can help us keep track of our emotions ourselves. Pair this with automated detection, and we stand to learn more about our own feelings than ever before. The Feel wristband reads emotion from blood pressure, pulse, and skin temperature to detect emotion. Not only could these devices help us to be more emotion-aware, but they could provide some coaching toward emotional well-being as well.

Emotion AI could also help develop emotional intelligence on a social level. Early experiments in sentiment detection, like *We Feel Fine* (Figure 2-19), gave us a glimpse of social media's emotional undercurrent. Understanding emotion at scale in the workplace or in a neighborhood, if handled with privacy and consent, could fuel empathetic dialogue.

Relationships with companion bots might also cultivate emotional intelligence. For all the focus on the downsides of attaching to robots, there are certainly upsides, too. Children's attachments to teddy bears scaffold into an ability to care about people. People's relationships with animals or even plants can foster greater empathetic imagination toward people. Bonds with bots will happen, with as much potential to develop our emotional range as to form unhealthy attachments.

AI that has an EQ has far-reaching potential, much of it for good. Some of it is big picture, like creating a more empathetic society. Much of it is mundane, like being able to hold off on sending an emotionally charged email or suggesting that we take a power nap when our attention drifts. With a technology that's so intimate, there's also danger.

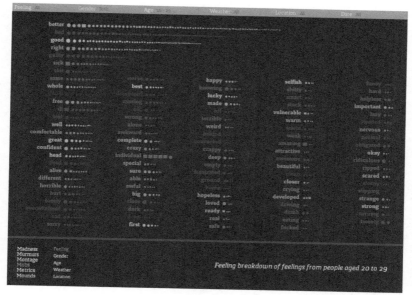

Feeling breakdown of feelings from people aged 20 to 29

FIGURE 2-19

#bigmood (source: We Feel Fine)

THE DARK SIDE OF EMOTION AI

It's easy to go to the dark side when it comes to technology that detects, interprets, and adapts to emotion. Ads that prey on vulnerabilities, workplaces that monitor our mood, or social interactions that are rated all seem like something out of a *Black Mirror* episode. Emotion AI will only be a force for good if we first confront serious negatives.

The sensing part itself is limited

When we are having a conversation, whether actually talking on the phone or texting, we tend to be the most expressive. Otherwise, we don't typically display a lot of emotion on our faces when we are looking at our laptops or our phones. Facial recognition might work well for movies or concerts or ad testing, but its relevance is limited when it comes to our current device use. Voice analysis might be great when we are having an animated conversation, but that's not all, or even most, of our interactions.

As an experiment, I had people use the Moodies app (Figure 2-20) to record tone of voice as each spoke to their voice app of choice. When we speak to our internet things, our tone flattens. As machines themselves become more expressive, this might change, of course. Humans readily pick up social cues through tone of voice, so it's not difficult to imagine that our conversations will become more expressive. For now, though, when we speak to a bot, we speak like a bot.

FIGURE 2-20

When I talk to a bot, I talk like a bot (source: Moodies)

It might skew negative

Positive emotions are relatively undifferentiated: joy, amusement, and even serenity are not easily distinguished from one another in terms of facial expressions given that they all result in a smile. Most commonly used sets of basic emotions include fewer positive emotions than negative emotions. So, emotion research in psychology has predominantly focused on negative emotions, too. The same might end up being true about emotion sensing tech.

The logic behind emotion-sensing makes assumptions

Ekman's facial-coding system, originally designed for human "coders," translates easily to an automated system. But it's only one very limited way of understanding emotion. It assumes that emotion can be observed, that emotion is expressed in universally consistent ways, that emotion can be pared down to a few expressions. Increasingly, emotion AI pairs voice and face to get different inputs, but it's still grounded in the same assumptions.

The intelligence is only as good as the data that trains it

Hopefully, the datasets used to teach the AI are vast and diverse, so the system may end up less biased. Decisions about which emotions to include and detect are still embedded into the system. Cultural differences in how emotions are expressed abound. Many emotions run deep, either invisible or individual. Because most emotion datasets are collected in a certain context or under specific conditions, that data will be inherently limited. Given the proprietary nature of most data already being collected about people, we will need to take great care in gathering meaning from it all.

It privileges in the moment over long-term

Emotions that are strongly felt, accompanied by immediate and discernable physiological and behavioral changes, will register. Less-intense emotion, or complicated emotion, might not register at all or be interpreted incorrectly. Mood will not be easily detectable and doesn't necessarily map to an action. It can start with an intense emotion and dissipate over time, or not. Of course, privileging the most recent and most intense emotion is the way current feed algorithms work, too.

It can assume actions neatly map to emotions

Emotion certainly can drive behavior. Someone you care about is feeling down, so you touch their arm or give them a hug. It can also work the other way around. Behaviors can drive emotions. Actors and actresses who behave as if they care deeply about each other sometimes do actually fall in love. That's why those 36 questions you can ask to fall in love, accompanied by looking deeply into each other's eyes, often have just that effect.[8]

---

8   Daniel Jones, "The 36 Questions That Lead to Love," *New York Times*, January 9, 2015.

When technology can detect emotion, offering guidance seems like a logical next step. It might be that coaching us on crafting sensitive emails or having considerate video chats will help hone emotional intelligence. But actions don't always correspond to our feelings, as Lauren McCarthy demonstrates in her experiment, Us+, an emotionally attuned plug-in for Google Hangouts that directs you to stop talking about yourself or be more positive (Figure 2-21).

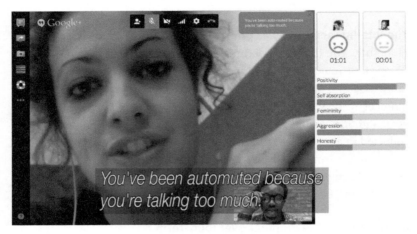

FIGURE 2-21
Emotionally attuned automuting (source: Lauren McCarthy)

Emotions sometimes have no associated action. You're angry, but you're an adult, so you take a breather and move on. Or action can be deferred. You might feel sad, but you have children to take care of and work to do—you'll cry later. The impulse behind emotion-sensing is to prompt people to some kind of action—usually buying stuff or engaging more often. That connection is often too simplistic.

It emphasizes body over mind

In those early Web 1.0 days, moving beyond our bodies toward a meeting of the minds was celebrated. When John Perry Barlow told us that the internet is a "civilization of the mind," we were hopeful for a more humane world. So, bringing the body back into the picture might seem a little strange, or it might seem exhilarating. It's certainly new. And technology loves new.

Emotions do have a physiological component, and emotion-sensing puts that back into the picture. It takes a physical signal and translates it into an emotion. We do that, too. But we are not computers. We do that in an individual way based on our experiences, our memories, our context. Cognitive appraisal, the evaluation we make in the moment and over the long term, is a crucial part of emotions we feel, moods that linger, and attitudes that persist. The latest emotion theory reveals that much of our emotional experience is constructed, but emotion AI doesn't account for that yet.

It might be too granular

Facial coding and tone analysis can detect fleeting expressions that we might not consciously register or might otherwise miss. It might also mean that too much weight is given to emotions that are not all that important. For instance, my teen might feel annoyed and roll her eyes one moment, but then decide to let that feeling go. Emotional intelligence is not just detecting fine-grained or fleeting feeling, it's the capacity to reflect and articulate and evolve.

It emphasizes social performance

Think about a greeter or barista or customer-service agent. Part of the job is always responding with a smile, the joyless show of joy. Emotional labor, or the social performance of emotion, is often required as part of a job. We perform emotion in other ways whether the feelings are genuine or not. Even though it seems like a far-off dystopian future, it's not difficult to imagine that we become trained to perform for the camera. Just as we've learned how to signal emotion through emojis or feel like we need to smile more at a party than we might otherwise, we will certainly adapt on some level. Some of us already feel this pressure to perform on social media. But so far, we aren't performing emotion to the point of faking emotion for anonymous data collection.

It could trivialize emotion

Emotion has already been trivialized with hearts and thumbs ups. Online, we are quick to demonstrate our feelings in broad strokes. It's easy to imagine tech that detects emotion and offers rewards. Recently, IKEA played around with this notion by temporarily renaming products according to most frequently searched relationship problems (Figure 2-22). Perhaps it does reveal the emotional undercurrent to our purchases, but what are the implications of basing it on actual data and making it explicit to retailers or advertisers? Either way, it assumes that our outward emoting mirrors internal feelings and that past actions dictate your current feelings.

| TALK ABOUT THE BIRDS AND THE BEES WITH KIDS Flower box, gray-brown stained gray-brown $30,00 | GET TO KNOW YOUR BONUS KIDS Board game $29,99 | HOW LONG IS A STOMACH BUG CONTAGIOUS Toilet brush, white $6,99 | MY BOYFRIEND IS VAIN Mirror with built-in lighting, white $99,00 | MY CHILDREN DON'T LISTEN TO ME Tambourine, red/yellow $12,99 |

| MANAGING CONFLICT WITH KIDS Ice pop maker, assorted colors $1,99 | SAVING FOR AN APARTMENT Food container, clear glass $4,99 | HOW TO BE A GOOD BONUS PARENT Loft bed with 4 drawers/2 doors, white, blue $449,00 | SHE HAS FORGOTTEN ME Noticeboard, white $5,99 | MY TWINS DON'T SLEEP AT NIGHT Training cup $3,99 |

FIGURE 2-22

Your emotional crises neatly, and flatly, packaged (source: IKEA)

It could be manipulative

Currently, emotion AI has made the most successful inroads in advertising. Now, in one sense, this isn't new. The advertising industry has always been focused on emotion to tap into identity, to persuade, and to motivate. This is a little different, though. Connecting advertising directly to emotion in the moment, or patterns over time, opens itself up to exploitation. Advertising aside, there are many other ways emotion AI could directly manipulate. A suggested purchase based on individual emotion data might qualify depending on the context. Recommendations based on aggregated data about emotion might seem more acceptable, but emotions are contagious. It might not be clear where a trend transforms into purposeful maneuvering. We aren't too far off from this future already when it comes to fake news, which gains its force through sentiment.

It could invade privacy

Emotions are intimate. Although we might perform emotion to express a message, like shock or gratitude or joy, more often our feelings are personal. The biggest fear is that emotion AI might reveal what we'd like to keep private. In *Emotion AI: The Rise of Empathic Media* (SAGE,

2018), Andrew McStay of Bangor University details a survey that he carried out in the United Kingdom in 2015. The purpose was to gauge attitudes toward the use of emotion detection in a wide range of contexts. About half of the survey participants were not okay with emotion detection in any form. Of those who were open to it, 31% wanted to be sure that the information was not personally identifiable.

It could replace human to human intimacy

Machines won't have feelings in the way that humans have feelings. But when they recognize emotion, understand it, express it, and adapt to it, it might be close enough. Relationships with bots and other tech could be like our relationships with pets: another kind of relationship. It's also possible to develop unhealthy attachments at the expense of human relationships. Emotion-aware tech could potentially degrade human relationships.

The big fear around all AI becomes even bigger when it involves emotion, though. After machines have emotional intelligence, will they replace humans? Or replace what we consider to be truly human? Maybe machines won't replicate us completely, but what if we begin to become satisfied with it? These might be far-off possibilities, but with emotion AI already in use, we need initial guidelines.

A Checklist for Designing with Emotion AI

Emotion AI has the potential to help our interactions with technology to feel more natural and to build our own emotional intelligence. At the same time, the potential for exploitation of our emotional life is vast and disturbing. In the near future, we will all need to balance the benefits and drawbacks. For now, here's a checklist to guide some of those decisions.

First, understand the emotional dimension of the experience:

Is emotion a crucial component of the experience?
> The answer here is almost always "yes." Watching TV? Yes. Sports, pet care, mental health—the list of applications for which emotion is essential is obvious. But go deeper. For some applications, emotion is beneath the surface. Banking? Yes actually, money is deeply personal. Healthcare? So complicated. Even so, there will be a range of what's expected and acceptable.

Will emotion tech add value to the experience?

Consider what emotion data, if any, you truly need to improve the individual experience. Then, consider again by thinking through that impact at scale on collective experience in a variety of social, cultural, political, and environmental contexts.

Is that added value worth the benefit?

The experience might have an emotional aspect, but it might also be true that people don't want your organization mixed up in it. Alas, people won't always fully grasp the value until they've experienced it. So, you'll need to consider analogous experience. Don't confuse value to the business with value to the individual. You must have both to proceed.

Is the emotional experience detectable?

Most emotion AI detects only physical traces of emotion enacted in a social context. Consider how people will show emotion. If it's visible by voice, face, words, or gesture, would one or two inputs inform or mislead? If it's not detectable, should you really?

Can you accommodate complexity and ambiguity?

Emotion AI won't capture complex emotion, conflicted emotion, or conscious emotion. Emotion displayed might not be emotion experienced. Just because an emotion is detected once at a certain point, this doesn't mean that it won't change. Bottom line: if you choose to collect data about emotion, it is not the only emotional factor in the experience. Acknowledge what you can't capture.

Then, define what truly matters:

Is it as minimally invasive as possible?

If you decide to collect emotion data, collect only the emotional data that is truly needed. Default to storing only what's needed for as short a period of time as needed. Default to using anonymized emotion data in aggregate. Make sure that anonymized data does not track back to individuals. With those defaults, you can then debate what else is relevant from there.

Have you developed informed consent?

Informed consent briefly and clearly explains what will be captured into the product. No long terms and conditions. No bundling with current terms and conditions. Ideally, it would show what the proposed system will do and what data it will collect before people sign on.

Do you have a plan for when it fails?

Consider potential danger to an individual, to groups, and to the planet. What happens when it's subverted by bad actors? Or when people are just having an off day?

Are you accounting for legal implications?

Study analogous instances given that the law hasn't caught up to the tech. Start with the EU's General Data Protection Regulation (GDPR). Consider human and animal rights laws, too. Don't just leave it to your legal team.

And design with emotional intelligence:

Can you (loosely) follow social conventions and norms?

Consider how emotion is detected and interpreted in a human-to-human context. Use that as a guide, but be aware that conventions and norms shift, too. Consider how norms and conventions might shift, and whether the gains outweigh what might be lost.

Has your platform of choice been trained on a diverse dataset?

Emotion AI registers facial expressions, tone of voice, and gesture differently depending on how it's been trained. Emotional expression, the part that's detectable, has a cultural and social dimension. Ask about the dataset and how it's evolved and how it will continue to evolve. Have a set of scenarios to discuss and test.

Is it possible to use more than one input?

Platforms that use more than one input, like facial coding and voice analytics together, will be more attuned. They also offer a failsafe if one input is less accurate or reliable. People rely on multiple signals, so use that as a guide.

Have you given people agency?

Give people as much control as possible over their own data. Nudge them to review at regular intervals. Give people meaningful choices to adjust the experience, including opting out at any point, ways to express emotion that aren't automatically collected, emotion categories that people use to define themselves, and ways to adjust the sensitivity of the system.

Have you involved a wide swath of people in the process?

Hopefully, this is a given. The next chapter looks at some ways to understand emotion that we can easily add in to our existing processes, too. Test its implementation with people who you personally care about: your family and friends.

This checklist can help you to determine whether emotion AI is ethical, viable, and valuable to the experience. Assume that people care deeply about the privacy of their emotional experience and are cautious about trusting systems that track emotion. That doesn't mean that people won't want to engage with technology to make sense of their emotional life. But it's critical to get this right when we are dealing with something so intimate.

Human + Machine = Higher Emotional Intelligence

Emotion AI prompts us to reconsider emotional design. Will emotion-sensing technology lead to emotionally intelligent design? Probably not at first; maybe not at all. Feelings are complicated and hopelessly entangled with identity and experience and context. Not to mention emotions are mixed up with sensory perception and cognition and behaviors. Recognizing a few canonical facial expressions alone is not going to magically make us more sensitive. Just having more technology to identify or interpret emotion won't automatically create a more human experience. Emotion AI will get better, though, especially if we pay attention to culture, context, and more complicated feelings.

Emotion AI could imbue our practice with a deeper understanding for human complexity. It could cultivate emotional intelligence in machines and in people. At the very least, it could help us make the leap from a bare-bones approach to emotion to one that is much more meaningful.

Designing, with Feeling

RUMMAGING AROUND IN THE clutter of handouts that comes home from school, I stumbled on an alarming article in my youngest daughter's welcome packet, "It's Digital Heroin: How Screens Turn Kids into Psychotic Junkies." Although I certainly struggle with parenting in the digital age, I was taken aback by this high-panic pathologization of technology. Naturally, I tried Facetiming my middle school daughter, just in her room upstairs. No answer. Then, I texted my oldest daughter also at home somewhere. At first three dots, and then nothing.

Eventually, I found the same blurred and crooked photocopy in each packet—elementary school, middle school, and high school. When I sampled the opinion of other parents, no one gave it a second thought. When we think about the most vulnerable among us, emotions are laid bare. Smartphones make kids feel stressed, envious, depressed, and inadequate. Everyone knows that technology makes you feel horrible, I was told. But I wasn't so sure.

This was a turning point for me. And, as a researcher, I approached it in the best way I knew how. Thousands of diary entries and hundreds of interviews later, I noticed how difficult it is to find a "good" experience that isn't emotionally complex. A smooth process, once appreciated, was soon taken for granted. Rarely did I see mention of the little blips of delight we diligently design. When people described their highs and lows with technology, it was with mixed emotions. Often the most satisfying tech use tied to something bigger—a better version of themselves, an authentic connection, an engaging challenge, contribution to community. The emotional texture was not simply happy or sad, overwhelmed or calm. It was all of those simultaneously plus many, many others.

Yvonne Rogers, director of the University College London Interaction Centre, calls this technology for engaged living, or "engaging experiences that provoke us to learn, understand, and reflect more upon our interactions with technologies and each other."[1] As a complement to calm technology doing things for us in the background, it's technology that no longer plays a purely functional role but social and emotional roles.

In this chapter, we consider emotional intelligence and its implications for technology. Rather than a new framework, what you'll find in this chapter is a mashup of emotional intelligence and design thinking. Rather than designing for task completion or moving people toward a goal or even building habitual behaviors, it's designing with emotion. But that doesn't mean we'll always design to make people feel a certain way. Here, we look at ways to build emotionally sustainable relationships with technology and one another.

Emotionally Intelligent Design Principles

Emotional intelligence is a gateway to a balanced life. People with high EQ are more likeable, empathetic, and more successful in their careers and personal lives. People who are a bit deficient when it comes to EQ are often unable to make key decisions in their lives, keep jobs, or build relationships. Even setting broad claims and myriad studies aside, it's common sense. If we can understand and work with, rather than against, our own emotions and those of others, the outcome is positive.

The idea that emotion is integral to intelligence is age-old. From Plato to Proust, Spinoza to Sartre, Confucius to Chekhov, emotion is a way to make sense of the world and ourselves. The concept of emotional intelligence, as we know it, has been in circulation since the 1960s. Daniel Goleman's bestselling 1995 book, *Emotional Intelligence: Why It Can Matter More Than IQ* (Bantam Books) popularized the idea at a time when IQ was the prevailing standard of excellence. Emotional intelligence is not just being emotional or feeling feelings, though.

---

1   Yvonne Rogers, "Moving On from Weiser's Vision of Calm Computing: Engaging UbiComp Experiences," in P. Dourish and A. Friday, Ubicomp 2006, Lecture Notes in Computer Sciences, Vol. 4206.

Emotional intelligence is recognizing emotion in yourself and others and managing those emotions in meaningful ways. It's usually summarized like so:

- *Self-awareness*, or how accurately you can recognize, understand, label, and express emotion. Most often associated with self-compassion, self-esteem, and confidence.

- *Self-management*, or how well you can regulate your own emotion, which usually includes discipline, optimism, and resilience.

- *Social awareness*, or the ability to recognize and attempt to understand the emotions of others. Also known as empathy but encompassing tolerance and rapport.

- *Social skills*, or how well you can respond to the emotions of other people. This translates to vision, motivation, and conflict resolution.

Although Goleman's model is the most widely known, it's really a mix of two approaches. The ability model, advanced by Peter Salovey and John Mayer in the 1980s, emphasizes how people perceive, understand, and manage emotions.[2] The trait model, based on the work of K. V. Petrides, says that emotional intelligence develops out of personality traits. Despite the variation between different models, each approach is more about emotional competencies than moral qualities.

To effectively reason, plan, and perform tasks (all things we think of as cognitive), human beings need to have emotional intelligence. It means managing feelings so that they are expressed appropriately and effectively. It means handling interpersonal relationships fairly and with empathy. It affects how we manage behavior, navigate social situations, make personal decisions, and work with others toward common goals. And emotional intelligence, whether you consider it more about personality traits or more about ability, can be cultivated.

That's just what many organizations are trying to do. In schools, social and emotional learning (SEL) is core to many curriculums teaching ways to cope with emotional distress and pro-social behavior. Leading

---

2   Peter Salovey and John D. Mayer, "Emotional Intelligence," *Imagination, Cognition, and Personality*, March 1990.

the way is the Yale School of Emotional Intelligence with its RULER model for emotional intelligence: Recognizing, Understanding, Labeling, Expressing, and Regulating emotion.

Companies take it seriously, too. Emotional intelligence has been identified as a core skill for the workforce in the next 50 years by the World Economic Foundation. Companies from Zappos to FedEx provide leadership training with emotional intelligence as a core component. Organizations rely on tools like Culture Amp and Office Vibe to foster emotionally intelligent workplaces. Starbucks employees learn the LATTE method to respond to negative emotions in positive ways: Listen to the customer, Acknowledge their complaint, Take action to solve it, Thank them, and Explain why it occurred.[3]

So, what would happen if we applied the principles of emotional intelligence to design?

First, it would need to start with the organization. Right now, few organizations recognize how much emotion matters. Those that do tend to make the same mistakes. Many don't factor in emotion at all. Or they rely on weak substitutes, like Net Promoter Score or behavioral metrics. Others go straight for a desired emotion, without trying to understand the context. Or they focus on evoking emotion in the moment, without thinking about the long term. Often organizations focus too much on one emotion, like delight, without thinking about other emotions that create value and meaning.

Then, it would need to be supported with a method that encompasses new ways to recognize, understand, express, evoke, and sometimes cope with emotion. It could certainly bring in new technology, too, employing emotion AI to help sort it out. It would mean expanding our repertoire to account for a more diverse range of emotional experience. Let's begin with a new way of approaching emotion.

ADOPT A NEW MINDSET

Emotionally intelligent design starts from a mindset that considers emotion as intrinsic to the experience, not a nice-to-have extra. Whether we intend it or not, we already design emotion and build relationships.

---

3 Charles Duhigg, *The Power of Habit: Why We Do What We Do in Life and Business*, Random House, 2012.

Where emotional design strives to create products to elicit an emotion, emotionally intelligent design builds emotional capacity. Designing products and services through the lens of emotional experience can make the experience better for everyone. First, a few guiding principles:

Learn from emotion

Empathy is already a critical aspect of design, but that hasn't always translated to emotion. Learning about our emotional life with technology and other products means spending time understanding the full scope of emotion. When done well, it's more than evoking emotion. Emotions are clues to what we value. Fear tells us that something important is threatened. Sadness might remind us of what's been lost. Shame might indicate that we haven't been living up to our own goals. Values, in turn, guide behavior, motivate toward action, and prompt judgment.

It's not a one-to-one mapping. It's not always the same. But it's important that we pay attention whether or not we are in it for the long term. Value-Sensitive Design (VSD), developed by Batya Friedman and Peter Kahn at the University of Washington, intersects with emotionally intelligent design. A core principle for VSD looks at who will benefit and who will be harmed, considering tensions between trust and privacy, environmental sustainability and economic development, and control and democratization. If we are paying attention to emotion and translating what it means, it can work in tandem with VSD to identify values, explore tensions and consider trade-offs.

Embrace complexity

Our inner lives are beautifully complex, yet even the most emotionally intelligent among us tend to translate what we feel into just a handful of emotions. What we need to develop our emotional intelligence isn't fewer concepts, but more (Figure 3-1). Likewise, what we need to design emotionally intelligent tech is to embrace complexity in our work. Think about the most meaningful, emotionally satisfying, personally compelling experiences, and you're likely to find mixed emotions. This doesn't mean making design complicated, but instead creating rich experiences.

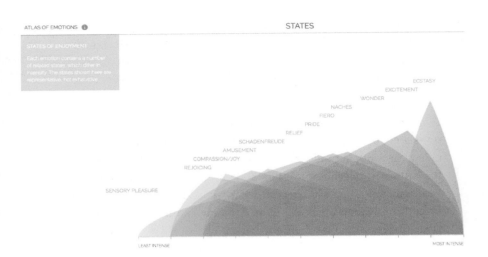

FIGURE 3-1

Core emotions unfold into a spectrum (source: Atlas of Emotions)

Build a relationship

Designing for fun is...well, fun. A pop of joy can certainly make a difference in your day. That's emotion in the short term, and that can be significant. That view tends to focus on the emotion itself as the destination. Emotional intelligence takes a longer view. It means thinking in terms of relationships over experiences. As our products develop more intelligence about us, we will expect more. That means evolving emotional connections over time by studying how emotions, behaviors, and decisions form into lasting relationships. And it means making a leap to consider relationships with products and organizations and institutions as not just desirable for business, but worthwhile for all.

Be inclusive

Psychology has largely been the product of North America and Europe. So much so that more than 90% of psychological studies are WEIRD (Western, Educated, Industrialized, Rich, Democratic).[4] Consider that the preponderance of studies that rely on college undergraduates, and you have just a tiny slice of our

---

4   Joseph Henrich, Steven J. Heine, and Ara Norenzayan, "The Weirdest People in the World?" *Behavioral and Brain Sciences*, June 2010.

psychology. The study of human emotion has mostly evolved out of knowledge of a small part of the world. Clearly, humans share basic physiology and some fundamental needs. We no doubt share some core affect. Whether you argue that we share only a high-level binary of positive and negative affect as some neuroscientists do, or that we share five to seven basic emotions, as evolutionary psychologists argue, it's not the entire story. The emotional texture of our experience is more nuanced. It's on us to bring more diverse voices into the process, which has benefits beyond emotionally intelligent design.

Consider scale

Emotions are contagious. Your emotions will trigger another's emotions, and so it goes. Although it seems like emotional contagion spreads more readily face to face, where we can see emotion, that just isn't the case. There are emotional signals all around us that send emotions ricocheting between people, through communities, in cities (Figure 3-2) and around the world. Reading emotional climate without losing individual nuance and tracing the pathways without losing the thread will be vital to consider emotion at scale.

FIGURE 3-2

The emotional climate of a city, aggregate and individual (source: Christian Nolde)

Picking up emotional signals is just that: signals. Clues about emotions. After all, feeling angry is not the same as flaring your nostrils and yelling. Even if there are patterns in appearance, that emotion might not be felt in the same way. Emotions certainly won't be expressed the same way either. Anger online is expressed much differently than anger at school or at home. Emotions shift in cultural and historical context. Loneliness today is considered much more negative than in times past. Belonging in present-day America shares little resemblance to a similar suite of feelings in Japanese culture. Context changes everything. Without sensitivity to context, there's no real path to emotional intelligence.

With something as deeply personal and wonderfully nuanced as our emotional lives, it's clear that we need to take care. Prioritizing emotional experience is not just a different mindset, it affects how we practice design.

SETTING NEW GROUND RULES

When we focus in very narrowly on someone in the moment of interacting with a technology—a user—our current approach works well enough. Even looking at a customer's journey, hopping from one business touchpoint to another, we might feel comfortable with current methods. But when we expand our view to consider a broader range of human experience, it becomes trickier.

If we look at anthropology, the tension between being a participant and an observer is acknowledged and discussed. That's a healthy conversation for our field to have, too. As an observer, you change the power dynamic. Rather than people framing the experience in their own way and telling their own story, the observer ultimately gets to be the storyteller. As a participant, you lose a bit of that outsider perspective. Either way, you change reality a bit. Let's set some new ground rules.

1. Lead by example

Check your bias

Even trained emotion coders will disagree on which emotion or how much emotion is expressed. People just do not see emotions in the same way. We have unconscious biases that lead us to draw different conclusions based on the same information. The emotions we detect might reflect us just as much as they reflect other people or the system. Machines will exhibit bias, too. Partially because of human bias in creating the system, and partially because of newly created bias in how emotion is interpreted.

Be aware of stereotypes

Women might describe themselves as more emotional, especially when you ask retrospective questions, like "How have you felt over the past week?" But gender differences rarely show up in experience sampling, according to Lisa Feldman Barrett in *How Emotions Are Made* (Houghton Mifflin Harcourt, 2017). Likewise, emotion-sensing tech doesn't always register differences on a gender divide, and the same is true when it comes to race. There's a huge body of research on emotion and stereotypes, which you can pore over. Or, you can simply commit to questioning stereotypes and do good product research.

Let yourself be vulnerable

Some of emotion research is detecting what we normally observe in others—an expression, a gesture, or a tone of voice. It's visible, and it's open to (your) interpretation. If you choose to go further than that, you'll soon learn that it's a give and take. Should you decide to have those conversations, know that you'll need to reveal a bit more about yourself than you might otherwise do.

2. Create a safe space

Participate as equals

Researchers favor the observer position. Implicit is the belief that "people don't know what they want until you show it to them." That mindset doesn't give people nearly enough agency. I'd rather see how we can creatively engage people to shape the future with us. Many organizations are leaning toward a participatory approach already, with design team members as equal participants, not leaders.

Respect boundaries

If we are going to be a little more personal, we need to respect boundaries. All of the same guidelines we have for research already around privacy hold true, of course. We need to hone our skills to listen for verbal cues, whether obvious or subtle.

Training in body language is essential. Knowing your own personal boundaries is a given. As we develop a wider range of participatory research methods, we need to honor any and all contributions.

Think post-demographic

Demographics, whether traditional age and gender breakdowns or behavioral categories like shopping habits, cast people in broad strokes. Demographic or behavioral data inherently aim to predict what people will do in the future based on stereotypes. Besides veering toward caricature, demographic categories are slippery. Gender is a spectrum, age is often unmoored from typical attitudes or behaviors, "techiness" is constantly in motion.

3. Develop a shared understanding

Develop an emotional vocabulary

Emotions are, in part, concepts that we learn. Sometimes, we pick them up as part of our culture; sometimes, we're taught; sometimes, we transmit them from one person to another. Most of us do not excel at talking about emotion, but it's a skill we'd do well to develop. Practice becoming more specific in your vocabulary and adding new emotion concepts to your repertoire. There are endless lists and emotion maps to build a common language, like the Dalai Lama's *Atlas of Emotions*, or T. U. Delft's *Negative Emotion Typology*. Try out an emotion tracking app, like my favorite, Moodnotes (Figure 3-3), to help you develop your own sensitivity.

Offer multiple ways to participate

Design thinking has opened up a new world of collaborative activities around making. Empathy exercises are no longer rare. But let's not stop there. Emotion is often best understood indirectly, which means developing new ways to prompt stories. Emotion is often private and personal, which means balancing think aloud with think alone, group brainstorm with singular contemplation.

Listen empathetically

The best listeners don't just hear; they make the other person feel heard. To understand emotion is to home in on emotional undertones in language. It involves tuning in to body language and nonverbal cues. It might mean mirroring the mood of the speaker. More than just reflecting back, it also means showing care and concern.

FIGURE 3-3

Emotionally intelligent tech needs emotionally intelligent designers (source: ustwo)

What this really comes down to is a shift in perspective. We've created methods to understand behavior, but we've neglected emotion. Behavior can be observed much more readily than emotion. Either way, we see only the tiniest slice of real life. As technology insinuates itself into more facets of our everyday life, we need to facilitate more ways to understand how it affects our inner world as much as our outward behavior.

Design Feeling in Practice

Now that have some new principles for emotional intelligence in design, let's put them in action. Next, we need a method. Design thinking is not perfect, but it's widely practiced and easy to follow for designers and nondesigners alike. And it's readily extensible to new contexts. For instance, Microsoft's Inclusive Design process, under the leadership of Kat Holmes, follows five phases similar to a design thinking process: get oriented, frame, ideate, iterate, and optimize. Likewise, *IDEO's Circular Design Guide* to sustainable design merges Kate Raworth's thinking in *Doughnut Economics: Seven Ways to Think Like a 21st Century Economist* (Chelsea Green, 2017) with design thinking in four phases: understand, define, make, and release.

Here, we merge emotional intelligence and design thinking. Should we call it *design feeling*? Or simply emotionally intelligent design? I'll leave it to you to decide what feels most comfortable. Let's use the following model for design feeling, with the easy-to-remember acronym FEEL.

1. *Find*, understand emotion in multiple dimensions using mixed methods.

2. *Envision*, map emotional experience and generate concepts.

3. *Evolve*, model and build relationships.

4. *Live*, develop ways to sustain the relationships.

You can observe the following as a step-by-step process. Or, you can supplement your current design practices with some of the ideas and activities. The core idea is the same—to design with greater emotional intelligence.

Find Feeling

Empathy is essential to emotional intelligence. The concept stands in for a wide range of experiences, but usually it means both the ability to sense other people's emotions and the ability to imagine what someone else might be thinking or feeling. The split between two types of empathy—affective empathy and cognitive empathy is contentious, though.

In our field, the emphasis has been on cognitive empathy. When we talk about empathy, we usually mean curiosity and perspective taking. In *Practical Empathy: For Collaboration and Creativity in Your Work* (Rosenfeld Media, 2015), Indi Young makes a point of differentiating between the two, finding cognitive empathy more useful for design.

Cognitive empathy gets us only so far, though. All we have to do is look at some of the current tech products on the market to test the limits. For example, the team who proposed a smartphone-enabled vending machine called Bodega designed to replace actual bodegas, almost certainly ticked off "empathy" in their design sprint, interviewing potential customers and possibly looking at behavioral data. And yet the proposed concept lacked emotional empathy.

In other areas of life, cognitive empathy is not enough. If you try to understand another person's point of view without internalizing their emotions, you're still detached. This can manifest in all kinds of ways. It might mean that you can't understand another's perspective. It might mean that you simply aren't motivated to help. It might mean that you don't fully realize the impact of your own behaviors on others. Take it a little further, and you'll find narcissists and sociopaths who use cognitive empathy for their own gain, whether to manipulate opinion or inflict pain.

When you begin to allow yourself to feel what other people feel, that's emotional empathy. It attunes us to another person's inner world. And it even has a physical force, as emotional contagion activates mirror neurons in our brains, creating a kind of emotional echo. Emotional empathy has serious downsides, of course. It can lead to distress and physical exhaustion, so much so that certain professionals experience emotional burnout. Social, medical, and rescue workers can't afford to let emotional empathy overwhelm them, but they'll provide poor care without it. It's not much of a stretch to see how that applies to designers, too.

In truth, we need both kinds of empathy. We need to understand what people are going through and to feel their emotions (to a degree). In some circles, this is called compassionate empathy. Whatever the case, it means expanding our repertoire.

MORE MIXED METHODS

As the first step in a design thinking process, empathy doesn't always home in on emotion. Designers have developed keen observation skills but train their sights on individual behaviors. Emotions are more of an afterthought.

It's not that observational methods can't get at emotion. After all, we observe emotion in others all the time. High EQ is associated with how well you can notice subtle facial expressions and changes in tone and then interpret those signals. Emotion AI is trained to work in the same way, although in much broader categories. But there are limits to observation when it comes to emotion, too.

Observation can reveal truths but sometimes misses subtleties. Technology creates barely detectable shifts in behavior that can't always be easily observed. If you are observing only a few people, you might not pick up on workarounds or adaptations. Because we train our sights almost exclusively on people acting alone, we might miss social dynamics. New gestures or expressions, even given the wonders of AI, go undetected. Emerging contexts of use are not always evident.

Emotion AI is no different in that respect; it's observational, too. Already touted as a "lie detector," it threatens to reveal your emotions, like it or not. Just as polygraphs tracked blood pressure and breathing to gauge stress levels associated with lying, so too does emotion AI. The emotion AI company Human promises real-time lie detection by analyzing faces from smartphone videos and security cameras (Figure 3-4). Coverus claims the same from eye tracking. Usually, the claim is not overt, but the assumptions are the same—smart observation reveals human truth.

Emotion AI is subject to many of the same pitfalls as any observational approach when it comes to the emotional side of experience. It captures physical signals that can be interpreted in many ways. It privileges the social performance of emotion. And it works within a limited context.

A vast expanse of human experience—arguably the most important part—is simply not considered by relying on what can be observed. Observation stays at the surface, so we miss out on how people perceive and interpret and feel. It omits how people make sense of their own experience. It skims over how people make their own meaning.

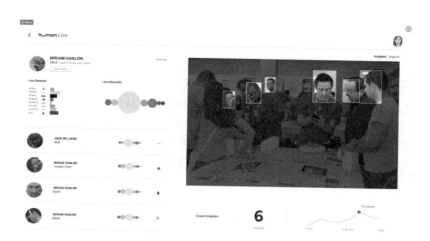

FIGURE 3-4

Can observation reveal our secrets? (source: Human)

The implications go beyond that. By privileging observation to such an extent, we privilege our own voice as designers and developers. We frame the story by choosing the context for observation. We get to tell the story, rather than giving people ways to tell their own story. We then shape the story going forward, based on our interpretation of what we can see.

So, we need to let emotion into research. And we need to work with mixed methods to understand all aspects of emotion. Design has already embraced mixed methods for research. Adding emotion just takes it a bit further.

Start by considering how to understand different dimensions of emotion. Emotions have a physical dimension. Maybe your face heats up or you feel a tightness in your jaw. Maybe you get butterflies in your stomach. Or, you know, maybe you just smile. Then, there's also a perceptual dimension; how we recognize and interpret a feeling, what we call it, how we describe it, and what we compare it to. Our perceptions are grounded in memories and possibly in future projections, too. Some of our social response seems automatic; most of it is learned and highly context-dependent. There's a behavioral dimension. You might yell in anger or frustration—an external behavior. But you could also suppress it or internalize it in another way. Emotional responses change depending on whether you are alone or with others. That's the social dimension. And the unspoken norms, conventions, rules, and even stereotypes add a cultural dimension.

With so much to consider, we need to push mixed methods a little further. For now, some of the methods listed in Table 3-1 are fringe. Not every team has access to emotion-sensing devices and platforms, but you don't really need to. Consider this collection of methods as a frame to build on as affective computing becomes more common.

TABLE 3-1. Emotions manifest across many dimensions

AFFECTIVE LAYER	SIGNALS	QUANTITATIVE METHOD	QUALITATIVE METHOD
Neurophysical	Pulse and temperature, gaze, brainwaves	Wearables, eye tracking, brainwave trackers	Observational research
Perceptual	Core affect, personal meaning	Data over time, aggregate data	In-depth interviews, diaries, metaphor elicitation, therapeutic research
Behavioral	Interactions	Behavioral analytics, satisfaction ratings	Observational research
Social	Facial expression, intonation, body language, language	Facial analysis, voice analysis, gesture analysis, sentiment analysis	Group conversations, paired interviews, co-design activities
Cultural	Norms, attitudes, laws, institutions	Location tracking, behavioral analytics, aggregate data, literature scans	Contextual inquiry, narrative study, co-design activities

That's big picture. Now let's go step by step, starting with the most basic emotions. Even in broad strokes, even with the latest emotion AI, it's not easy to do.

IDENTIFY BASIC EMOTION

Perhaps you've seen Pixar's *Inside Out*? The movie is about five basic emotions: joy, anger, fear, disgust, and sadness. Although the filmmakers considered including a full array of emotions, they kept it to five to simplify the story. Whether you agree that these five are universals or not, these are simply big categories to use as starting points. Think of each as a continent. Within each there are many states, cities, disputed territories, shifting boundaries. Those we'll fill in later through qualitative research. Most designers aren't paying much attention to even these big categories in research yet, but there are three main ways to get started.

First, you can add some emotion awareness to what you already do. We already gather some information about how an individual frames an experience, how they interpret what they see, and how they take action in the context of usability tests. We already observe personal context and daily ritual or routine in ethnographic interviews. An easy place to start is to simply make a point to notice verbal cues, facial expressions, pauses or hesitations, and body language and gesture. In *Tragic Design: The Impact of Bad Product Design and How to Fix It* (O'Reilly, 2017), Jonathan Shariat and Cynthia Savard-Saucier share a list to notice, including sighing, laughing, shifting in a chair, nervous tapping, and forceful typing. Going back to our new rules of engagement, you'll need to be aware of your own biases and expand your emotional vocabulary to make this work.

It's easy enough to add emotion categories to your data collection sheets or logs. If you are running research sessions alone, you can take notes on a simple cheat sheet during the conversation if it's not too intrusive or after the session when you review the recording. If you have a partner, they should record their notes, too. The more people you can factor in to record and interpret, the better.

A simple sort of happiness, sadness, anger, fear, disgust, and surprise is a good place to start, even though it will be imperfect. You can take it a step further, analyzing the words in your written transcript using sentiment analysis or the tone in a voice recording using a tool like Beyond Verbal's Moodies app. In workshops, I've had people try using Affdex Me and Moodies in combination to get a general read on emotion.

Obviously, there isn't a one-to-one mapping between observed actions and emotion. A pause might indicate hesitation, confusion, or interest. Context might give you a clue, or it might not. Quickly swiping through might mean someone is having fun, but it could signal boredom or even anxiety.

Second, whenever possible, give people a chance to comment on their emotional experience. Add a way for people to self-report their emotion whether in-person or online. Even if you consider yourself keenly emotionally intelligent, you'll miss a lot of emotional cues and you'll misinterpret. Outward expression of emotion varies with social context, and research is an unusual one. People vary in their range of expression and intensity of emotion in ways you won't be able to observe.

You can ask directly. Net Promoter Score or satisfaction surveys don't tell us much about emotion. Instead, include questions that give people a chance to express emotion. A simple selection of smile or frown, thumbs up or thumbs down, can lend a basic read to positive or negative emotion. That's a level one emotion signal.

Better still to get a simple range of emotion. YouX (Figure 3-5) is an experimental tool inspired by Plutchik's wheel of emotion.[5] Tools like PrEmo, which rely on images rather than words, work around language barriers. It can get at multiple emotions at the same time and it translates across cultures better, but it still assumes that everyone will be able to interpret facial expression. Follow either approach with a narrative question though and you'll get context to understand the emotion as well as more granularity. Layer in sentiment analysis on open ends, and you'll get a general read on emotion.

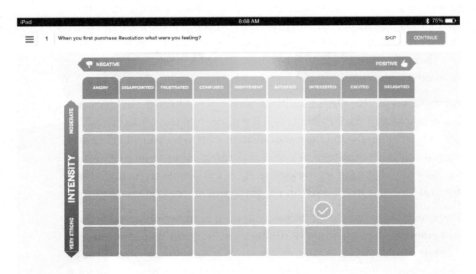

FIGURE 3-5
Asking, with feeling (source: YouX Tools)

---

5   Sarah Garcia, "Measuring Emotions: Self-Report as an Alternative to Biometrics," *UXPA Magazine*, July 2016.

In a follow-up questionnaire or online survey, the most well-rounded approach is to give people a short list of emotions along with a narrative prompt to accompany it. In person, direct questions might not be the best approach. People are not apt to honestly reveal emotion to strangers in a research context. So indirect is best, whether you are prompting conversations between participants or engaging them in design activities.

Third, cautiously consider a tech layer. Emotion AI is able to detect broad categories, 5 to 10 at least. In the near future, it might be embedded in a product you're developing, and you'll be tasked with interpreting those signals to further evolve it. For now, it's probably not. So, one way to get familiar is to begin trying some of the tools. You can certainly capture these same signals using existing research tools. A multimodal platform like iMotions layers together a few different biometrics tools to record facial expressions and tone of voice or heart rate (Figure 3-6). Getting participants in a lab, wearing headgear and sensor bracelets, is not the kind of research we typically do on design teams. Even so, trying it out can lend some understanding to how emotion detection embedded in products might work.

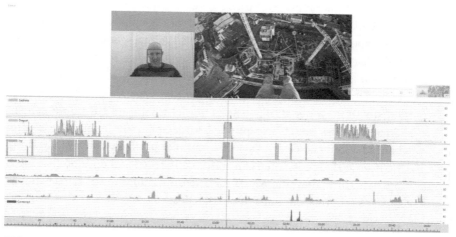

FIGURE 3-6
Peeling back the layers of emotion (source: iMotions)

Platforms that detect emotion don't automatically interpret the results, revealing what it all means. Emotion AI embedded in a product won't either. Instead it will begin mapping broad categories to anticipated behaviors and types of content. Think back to one of our core principles: don't assume too much.

Now that you've started to tune in to emotion signals, you've got an initial read on in-the-moment reactions to a product or service. That's still limited. Next, move beyond broad strokes to understand emotion with greater nuance, and over time.

ADD NUANCE AND TEXTURE

When you heard about Cambridge Analytica, were you mad? Or were you morally outraged, bitterly disappointed, filled with dread? Was the feeling intense? Did it linger? Did you comment online using words like "angry" or "bad," or did you employ more nuanced words like "flagrant violation"? The more finely tuned your feelings, the more adept you'll be at navigating your emotions.

The greater your sense of granularity and complexity, the richer your experience of the world, too. You'll see analogies to wine or perfume. Think of it like fonts. Designers perceive subtle variations in the curvature of a's and j's, the slant terminal, or the spines. People who have less experience might not see these differences but can still distinguish between an oblique and an italic. A novice might be less capable of making these distinctions, perhaps picking out only differences between a serif and a sans serif. Then, there are those who have little sensitivity to fonts at all, just seeing letters in a string on a screen. Those novices won't be equipped to decipher the subtle messaging behind a font choice or to select a font that perfectly conveys a feeling. Novices and experts alike can continue to learn and develop that intelligence. Ultimately, the payoff for discerning nuances in fonts is not as great as for emotion, but you get the idea.

If you're able to make fine distinctions between many emotions, you'll be better able to tailor them to your needs. You'll adapt to new situations. You'll be better at anticipating emotion in others. You'll be able to read the emotion of a group. You'll be able to construct more meaning from other people's actions, too. A finer sensitivity to nuance translates to higher emotional intelligence. So, let's see if we can bring that into design.

Emotion classification can be more art than science, with myriad possibilities. A few basic models can build toward greater nuance:

- The *circumplex model* suggests that there are two main dimensions.

- The *PANA model*, or positive and negative activation model, develops granularity along lines of positive and negative affect.

- The *mixed model*, also known as *Plutchik's model*, is a hybrid of circumplex for intensity (or arousal) and valence (positive or negative) (Figure 3-7).

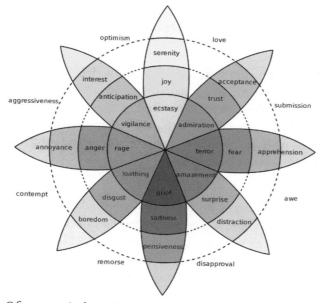

FIGURE 3-7

A mixed model for mixed methods (source: Robert Plutchik)

Of course, it doesn't end there. The *PAD model* adds dominance submission to the other dimensions of the circumplex model. The *Lovheim cube of emotion* is a three-dimensional model combining dopamine, adrenaline, and serotonin with eight basic emotions.

Rather than stress over which model to choose, the key takeaway is to understand a range of emotion. If the most emotionally resonant and sustainable relationships are the most complex, we need to lean into that complexity. Here are a few activities to add to your repertoire that will tease out more detail.

Icon (or screen) annotation

Studies tell us that icons can trigger feelings, but we've probably intuited that all along. Icons have symbolic value. That is, icons often begin to represent a feeling, a value, a person, an action, or a story. A quick exercise I use is to have people sketch or take a screenshot of their home screen or desktop and annotate each icon. You can ask for emotions or values—people often don't distinguish between the two anyway—by prompting them to tell you what each means to them or what role it plays in their lives. Whether you are trying to understand your own app, or an analogous one, or how it might live among the others on a smartphone, this activity can help uncover deeper meaning and even how it shifts over time.

Feeling drawings

Rather than annotating icons or pages or photos with feelings, here you take the reverse approach. Instead, you ask people to draw what an experience feels like. The idea is to have people focus on illustrating their feelings rather than talking about them. Whatever the result, follow up with questions about what they drew and why. You can continue with more drawings too.

Movie making

Movies tap into emotion in a way that is profound and meaningful, but also indirect. Part of this is pure storytelling. Narrative is the superglue that helps us make sense of our lives. Part of this is also the way movies move us through time. In my own research, this translated to having people frame crucial moments with a device or app as a movie and then going back to "watch" these stories, noting the sequence, hitting pause on certain key events, muting the conversation to focus only on actions, fast-forwarding to look at consequences, and finally putting together a trailer to summarize.

Object interviews

Made in cooperation with cultural institutions around the world, the *object interview* series, imagining objects as if they had separate lives, is quite whimsical. What if a vase were teaching French or a bench were playing hide and seek? As our tech products develop more personality and agency, this technique seems more and more relevant. If we consider people and product to be in a relationship, it means lending a voice to both.

Start with a narrative approach in which people tell stories about the product or an analogous product. If possible, start with one that elicits strong feelings (or even use that as a recruiting factor). Have them tell a story about it, show pictures, and draw it to describe that emotion. Then, flip it. Narrate from the object's point of view. You'll get a sense of how emotion builds or dissipates. You'll begin to understand how conversations or interactions support or challenge.

Kansei clustering

Kansei engineering, the Japanese technique to translate feelings into product design, has always seemed intriguing and a bit mysterious. Developed in the 1970s to understand the emotions associated with a product domain, the approach centers on an analysis of the "semantic space" gathered from ads, articles, reviews, manuals, and customer stories. The analysis can be large-scale and statistical, but it doesn't need to be.

In my work, I begin with interview transcripts, diaries, customer stories, and social media posts, but I find just culling emotion words is not very helpful. Love, hate, like, distracted, and angry don't mean much without the context. So, instead, bring it into a follow-up interview or a participatory design activity to fill in that missing piece.

Worry tree

Another technique that I've tried is using a *worry tree*. A little like the "five whys," this technique looks at your anxiety or worry and traces it back to what you can do. You start with an anxiety. Perhaps it's an anxiety caused by an existing technology, like FOMO. Or, perhaps it's an anxiety that your technology is trying to address. After you list the anxiety, the next step in the tree is to list what you could do. If you can do something, you can begin to list how and when. If you can do nothing, well, then you need to let it go.

Sentence completion

Sentence completion is a way to understand emotions and, in turn, values. Suppose that we are looking at a fitness app. You might include some sentences to get at emotions related to fitness, exercise, and healthy lifestyle. Here are just a few examples:

- I feel _____ when I exercise/eat healthy.
- When something gets in the way of my routine, I feel _____.
- The best fitness experience is _____.
- When I think of my fitness/health, I dream about_____.

You might also include exercises that ask about the app directly but emotion indirectly.

- Using [app] is _____.
- To me [app] means _____.
- The [app] makes me think of _____.
- When I use [app], I think of myself as _____.
- When I use [app], other people think _____.

Moving beyond basic emotion doesn't need to be awkward or arduous. We can understand emotion by building on some of the techniques we already use or adding new activities and exercises to our repertoire. At this point, all of this emotional data is still abstract, though. Next, we need to visualize.

MATERIALIZE EMOTION

The finale to the find phase is to materialize emotion. Using technology, where appropriate, or low-tech prototyping methods, the aim is to find new ways to give substance to emotion uncovered in research. Creating a material vision surfaces the meaningful aspects of the experience.

Think of it as a remix of art therapy and participatory design research. Working within the comfort level of individuals and the team, the goal is to make the experience palpable. Making the data physical facilitates further discussion, and ultimately informs the design.

Organizations are already trying this approach in the mental health space. Mindapples provides kits for groups to share their "five-a-day" prescription for mental health. Aloebud is a self-care app that visualizes mental health as a garden. Stanford's Ritual Design Lab installed a Zen Door in downtown San Francisco for the April 2015 Market Street Prototype Festival encouraging people to contribute their wishes as a kind of data sculpture.

Individuals are turning to it as a way of understanding physical and mental illness. For instance, Kaki King and Giorgia Lupi created data visualization to record a history of strange symptoms—mysterious bruises on Kaki's daughter. The idea was not only to help understand the patterns but also to see with fresh eyes something that's difficult to assess. At the same time, it became a coping strategy for processing the illness of a loved one. Laurie Frick's *Stress Inventory* is another vivid example of transforming data she tracked about herself in a tangible form. It's a way to interpret the data and a way to process the emotional impact.

When I run these sessions for clients, we distribute cards with a high-level activity related to building emotional capacity: discover, understand, cope, process, manage, enhance, remember, and anticipate. Depending on the project, there might also be cards that include scenarios or people, too. Most crucially, we create cards that summarize aspects of the data, such as a distribution of emotions words, a core emotion and related emotions, data that connects emotion with values, and so on. Each data card includes the topic, the source, a description, and a visual. Finally, I select materials that cover a range of properties. Materials that lend color like food coloring or paint. Materials like wood blocks that don't have any give and, by way of contrast, materials that are flexible like moldable soap or erasers. Materials that bind together like elastic bands, or attract like magnets, or fit together like LEGOs. The idea is to represent a wide-open field of possibilities.

After an introduction to the activity and the data, individuals or groups choose and discuss the cards. Then, I have participants select a maximum of three materials before moving on to create a material representation of the research data and document their process. In a recent session about e-sports, emotion research materialized variously as a paper chain of people holding hands framed by color-coded translucent windows. It demonstrated how people were coming together for a certain amount of time to share an experience, that would color their view of reality afterward. This illuminated some of the emotional goals for the project while giving us a touchstone for further discussion.

The outcome is to find ways of characterizing and framing emotion, propose new ways of doing things or approaching issues, and gauge people's reactions and responses. Rather than finding a universal color for joy or the default texture for security, which is likely a futile effort anyway, this instead lets us begin connecting physical qualities, features, and functionality with emotional experience. These emotional objects provide a bridge to the next phase.

Envision Experience

Now that we've collected more information about emotion, by documenting the emotions and values at play, we can try to shape this into a strategic direction. Because our emotional life is subject to so much variation, we need to begin by bringing more people into the process.

When we start to treat people as collaborators, we need to make sure that they have a way to contribute in a meaningful way. Our current repertoire of participatory techniques favors extroverts and, like any group activity, tends to privilege some voices over others. It's on us to acknowledge and amplify unique voices. We need time to reflect and to respond critically. We should do everything possible to draw out the imagination of the broader community.

FOSTERING FRESH IDEATION

Ideation sessions, hackathons, design sprints, and co-designs aren't always conducive to open conversation and thoughtful reflection on our inner lives. So perhaps our practices are due for a refresh. One way we can do this is to lend the right prompts, constraints, and opportunities to speak to their unique strengths and capabilities. Here are a few new ways to stretch our practice with a mix of social and less-social activities.

Create intimate experiences

To build communal spirit and encourage associative conversation, think about how to build codesign experiences that create a sense of intimacy. Rather than a conference room, even a hip one with glass walls and fun furniture, create a safe space where people can be a little vulnerable and power dynamics are leveled. The trend toward dinner parties like *Death Over Dinner* (Figure 3-8) or *The People's Supper* is one that has promise for codesign. Alice Julier, author of *Eating Together: Food, Friendship and Inequality* (University of Illinois Press, 2013) finds, "When people invite friends, neighbors, or family members to share meals, social inequalities involving race, economics, and gender reveal themselves in interesting ways." Some agencies, like Frog Design, are following suit with ideation sessions that take a more personal approach, held in homes or at off-the-beaten-path restaurants.

FIGURE 3-8
The best things happen over dinner (source: Death Over Dinner)

Seek renewed inspiration

Technology is not the first field to reinvent, however inadvertently, inner life. Philosophers and filmmakers, artists and architects, painters and poets have long contemplated our emotional world. In a series of pop-up events around the world called *Future Feeling Labs*, I've been doing the same. Each session elaborates on an emotion, like schadenfreude or outrage. We begin with a history through art, literature, and culture before moving on the current culture. Looking toward novelists as we characterize chatbots, or to sculpture as we create new objects, holds promise as intentional inspirations.

Simulate emotional experience

Sometimes, simulated experience can inspire and mobilize. An empathy museum that encourages patrons to try on the shoes of migrants and refugees while listening to their stories can transport you. Empathy kits, complete with augmented reality (AR) headsets and awkwardly shaped lollipops, can be a bridge to understanding autism or dementia (Figure 3-9). Typefaces that simulate the problems faced by people with dyslexia can prompt temporary attunement. Simulated experience gets us only so far. Empathy, emotionally attuned and cognitively aligned, will never be lived experience but it can lend emotional force to abstract problems.

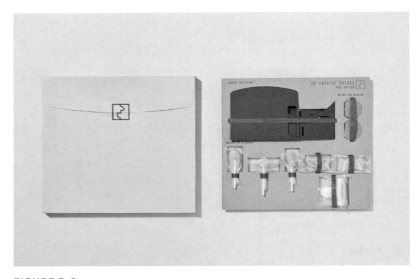

FIGURE 3-9
A tidy kit unfolds into messy emotion (source: Heeju Kim)

Strive for immersion

Let the ideation session become a playing field for exploring different worlds. Virtual reality (VR) certainly has the potential to immerse us in other worlds and introduce multiple realities. But we don't need VR for that. Think of language immersion programs, in which you leave your language and culture behind to enter a new world. Although we probably can't make that drastic of a switch, we can cultivate that feeling that you have entered a new world. It could be a shared ritual that leaves behind the "old world" like when people turn in their smartphones as they check in to *Camp Grounded*. It could mean staying "in character," like you would in a Live Action Role Play (LARP). Anything that brings an element of absorption to the session.

Activate the senses

Sketching and whiteboards are the typical tools for ideation. Unexpected materials seem to foster new pathways for creative thinking. Just as we habituate to what once made us happy, we also feel less than inspired by the usual supplies. At the University of Washington's HCI design lab, pom-poms, pipe cleaners, and popsicle sticks nest in bins alongside sharpies and Post-its. Alastair Sommerville's popular sensory design workshops incorporate scent jars and walking tours. Many teams are experimenting with LEGOs and clay. My favorite supplies come from hardware store bins and fabric shops. Broken toys, party favors, and miniatures can also trigger unexpected creative collisions. The odder the objects, the more people open up.

Add think-alone time

Unstructured time and independent activities leave space for new ideas and critical thinking. *Future Partners*, for instance, makes silent walks an integral part of the ideation process. Even in a typical conference-room-with-whiteboards-and-Post-its ideation session, we can build in time for quiet. We certainly should include ways for people to be alone with their thoughts and then come together again as a group.

Expand participation

Think beyond everyone together in the same room. Why not invite people from anywhere to participate on Twitter or Snapchat? How about leaving a tabbed flyer with a number to call and leave a good old-fashioned voicemail? Future visioning agencies *Situation Lab* and *Extrapolation Factory* have invited anyone interested to call a toll-free number and record their future dream in a voicemail, using that as a foundation toward speculative design. Anything to challenge creative expression while involving more people.

It might sound like we are bringing empathy back into this phase. Yes. Empathy in all the phases. Besides a refresh on how we approach ideation, it has the potential to lend the support of disparate stakeholders. So, what do we do after we have a new frame for ideation? Create an emotional imprint.

IDENTIFYING THE EMOTIONAL IMPRINT

After you've developed a conducive co-design space, use the material-ized research as a bridge to design. Begin with the mix of emotions associated with the experience. What is your product's core emotion? What else is associated with that emotion? What emotion do you want to evoke? What emotions are people expressing? What emotions are unexpressed? Which are the most intense feelings people identify? Which are the least? When beginning, sinking into, and finally leaving your experience, what states are you evoking and in what order? Your research might have answered some of these questions; some might remain. Either way, we can use these answers to begin.

First, you'll create a map of the emotions associated with the experi-ence. Empathy maps connect feelings with thoughts and actions, but the tendency is still to "solve" negative emotions. Instead, let's try to connect emotion with motivation.

Motivation has many models. There's self-determination theory, focus-ing on competence relatedness, and autonomy. There's ERG theory, comprising existence, relatedness, and growth. There are intrinsic and extrinsic theories of motivation. There are goal setting theories. But let's start with the familiar.

In a co-design setting, start with Maslow's hierarchy of human needs. Besides near-universal recognition, it lends itself to easily mapping emotion to motivations, values, needs, bigger goals. You can begin by drawing the pyramid with the five levels of needs: physiological, safety, love and belonging, esteem, and self-actualization. When I do this exer-cise, I use the later model, which includes knowledge, beauty, and tran-scendence. To break out of hierarchical thinking, I don't always use a pyramid (Maslow didn't originally, either). It might be more difficult to consider those higher needs when basic physical and safety needs aren't met, but every human life will still be shaped by higher needs, too. At scale, it's dehumanizing to suggest otherwise. From there you can sort the emotional knowledge you gathered in research, according to needs, to see where strengths and weaknesses lie.

Sometimes, I use a four-world-style model, based on a pared-back model of emotional well-being (Figure 3-10). The matrix is a blend of Daniel Goleman's model of emotional intelligence and recalls Patrick Jordan's concept of the four pleasures. Emotional experience can be situated on a spectrum of self-directed or socially directed, pleasure-based or purpose-based, resulting in a four different kinds of experience.

- *Transformative*, experience that facilitates personal growth
- *Compassionate*, altruistic and prosocial experience
- *Perceptive*, sensory-rich experience
- *Convivial*, experience that brings people together socially

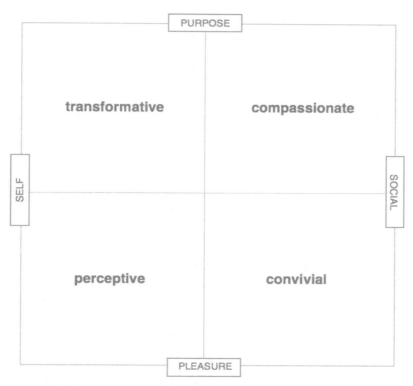

FIGURE 3-10
Four types of experiences to support emotional well-being

Transformative experiences create a context for an individual to grow and find personal significance. These are experiences promising to help you make progress toward a goal, whether it's getting fit, saving money, or becoming more productive. Experiences that help you understand your psyche or your health go in this category, too.

Emotions

> Curiosity, interest, anticipation, vigilance, pensiveness, pride, confidence, inspiration, fascination

Values

> Love of learning, achievement, wisdom, judgment, accomplishment, independence, capability, self-control, intellect, perseverance, prudence, self-respect

Examples: Duolingo, Fitbit, Lynda, Headspace, Mint

Compassionate experiences are those experiences that center on shared purpose, mutual growth, a common cause. Compassionate experiences facilitate giving, helping, and fostering empathetic community, from charitable giving sites to games for good, to civic action.

Emotions

> Acceptance, trust, caring, kindness, sympathy, empathy, respect, consideration, hope, altruism, courage, compassion (counter to contempt, pity, indignation, hostility)

Values

> Fairness, perspective, community, equality, forgiveness, helpfulness, tolerance, citizenship, open-mindedness, integrity, mercy

Examples: Re-Mission, GoFundMe, Resistbot, Be My Eyes, WeFarm

Convivial experiences are social in the way that we most often think about social. These are experiences that emphasize bonding, reputation, shared activities, and conversation. Successful convivial experiences support layered communication, social experiences that engage the senses, mixed reality, shared rituals, and storytelling tools.

Emotions

> Love, admiration, lust, desire, amusement, relaxation (counter to loneliness, shame, jealousy, social anxiety, isolation)

Values

> Friendship, social recognition, harmony, humor, intimacy, trust, nurturing, vulnerability, fairness

Examples: Snapchat, Kickstarter, Pokemon Go, Google Photos, Twitch

Perceptive experiences are sensory-rich with opportunities to play. They can be pure in-the-moment fun, like games or music, but can also help us to savor or wonder.

Emotions

> Amazement, surprise, arousal, tenderness, playfulness, fascination, excitement, amusement, relaxation, relief (counter to confusion, bewilderment, boredom)

Values

> Humor, creativity, zest, curiosity, imagination, cheer, appreciation of beauty, comfort

Examples: Spotify, Monument Valley, Pinterest, Dark Sky, Keezy

Most products are not just one type, of course. An app for good like Charity Miles is both transformative and compassionate. Prompt, a visual diary for those who have memory loss, is both transformative and convivial. Wayfindr might be considered transformative but also perceptive. Skype could be convivial or compassionate, depending on how you use it. The point is not to fit an experience into a tidy box. Instead, it's simply a way to analyze insights and understand strengths.

Let's use Spotify to demonstrate how this works. Listening to music seems to sit squarely in the perceptive quadrant. If you think about making and sharing playlists, well, that is convivial. Perhaps you use Spotify Running to motivate you toward fitness goals. That's transformative. We could easily imagine a Charity Channel or games that work with Spotify to raise awareness of social issues. That would be compassionate.

Ideally, you might try to boost all four quadrants. In practice, this is not always practical or even possible. But we can use the matrix to think through emotionally resonant experience in new ways and determine where to build capacity.

A part of mapping the emotional landscape means considering the emotional role the technology will play in people's lives. Does it enhance an emotion that's already there? Does it activate new emotion? Does it help people process their emotions about the product itself? Or relate to something else entirely? Does the whole experience stand in as a coping mechanism? Has it come to represent an emotional moment, or experience, or even just a feeling on its own? Recall Don Norman's levels of cognitive processing: visceral, behavioral, reflective. Or, you can think about it in the following terms:

- *Source*, the product itself elicits or inspires emotion.

- *Support*, it helps people understand, process, cope, or otherwise handle emotions.

- *Symbol*, the product or experience stands in for a feeling.

As a way to categorize qualitative research or as a way to define features and functionality, these three roles can serve as a guide. More often than not, a product will engage more than one of these core emotional roles. But even then, the emotional signature of each won't necessarily be the same.

DRAWING APT ANALOGIES

You might say you feel empty to convey a lingering loneliness. Another day you may tell a friend that your outlook is sunny to communicate optimism for the future. Or maybe you feel like monkey mind is a good way to describe a persistent state of distraction. After a year of working through social anxiety, you might feel like a turtle poking its head out of a shell. Emotional states inspire little blips of poetry, in an otherwise prosaic existence.

When we try to articulate how we feel, emotion words—even an impressive vocabulary of emotion words—are not nearly sufficient. Instead, we fall back on metaphor. A metaphor is a pattern that connects two concepts. When we are considering emotions, it serves a double purpose: it articulates emotion and evokes experience. Metaphors bring the emotional imprint to life, giving us a rich set of concepts to work with as we design.

Analogy has long had an influence on design. Henry Ford's assembly line was inspired by grain warehouses. Hospital emergency rooms draw from Formula 1 pit stop crews. Design thinking already relies on analogy to develop products. Yes, there is a difference between analogy and metaphor. Metaphor makes a comparison; analogy demonstrates shared characteristics. A metaphor sparks instant understanding, while an analogy often requires elaboration. For our purposes, let's not get too down in the weeds.

So, here we'll develop emotional analogies. This activity works best with a collection of emotion and value words. It's fine to mix them because they will already be jumbled together. Shame surfaced because people felt they weren't able to live up to expectations. Anxiety kept people coming back, increasing each time. Values like presence or generosity, for example, will likely be somehow connected with serenity and admiration. You've probably already stumbled across these connections in your research.

When you are working with metaphor, there are a few combinations that are most useful to inform design:

- Emotion + attribute, for connecting emotion with physical aspects of experience like color, texture, scale, size, material, weight, temperature, luster, age, and depth

- Motivation + interactions, for connecting social and emotional goals like belonging, transcendence, safety, flow, recognition, love, autonomy, and so on with how people will engage with the system

- Value + natural world, for connecting values (or emotions) with the natural world like shadows, changing leaves, a flock of birds, roots, and so on

- Behavior + relationship, for connecting an action or behavior with a relevant relationship metaphor like a friend, parent, physician, or pet

A metaphor-based approach bridges the abstract concepts around emotions, values, and motivations with concrete aspects of design like what the object might look like or what behaviors it supports. It nudges us toward new aesthetics and experiences and away from clichés, too.

TRACING A LONGER JOURNEY

Emotions rarely fall on a neat timeline. When we develop customer journeys, they seem tidy though. The narrative arc feels familiar. It begins with a negative emotion and builds to a positive moment. In reality, that's rarely the case. A journey is alive with all kinds of emotion.

Most contemporary models of emotion include a few components (see Figure 3-11). It goes something like this:

1. Cognitive appraisal (evaluation of an event or object; let's say a repeated misunderstanding by a voice assistant)

2. Bodily symptoms (rapid heartbeat)

3. Action tendencies (speaking more slowly or pounding your fist)

4. Expression (your face is twisted in anger)

5. Feelings (subjective experience of an emotional state, say terror)

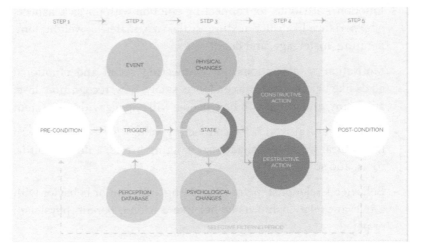

FIGURE 3-11
An emotional timeline within a larger timeline (source: Atlas of Emotion)

Some would add your emotional state beforehand as a factor. Maybe you are already upset or you're in a hurry, which could give some context to your response. Other experts would add your personality traits, and say you tend to be quick to anger. Maybe your mental health history is an issue; perhaps you have PTSD or have suffered some trauma. Most likely, you sift through a personal repertoire of memories as you process the emotion. You've had terrible experiences before, or you just read an upsetting story about a voice-assistant fail. Some of this new experience gets added to the mix; some doesn't make the cut. To make matters more complicated, the next day, even though the voice assistant remains the same, you could have a totally different emotional experience. And then there's the other people in your household...

Well, that got complicated. And it might well be something that machines are better able to map in the far-off future. For now, let's dial it back a bit. Let's think less about the event, or even a single experience. Instead, let's look at the relationship.

Framing emotional design as a relationship hasn't really taken hold, but it certainly isn't new. In *Design for Emotion* (Morgan Kaufmann, 2012), Trevor von Gorp and Edie Adams drew connections between their ACT model (attract, converse, transact) and psychologist Robert Sternberg's relationship phases: passion, intimacy, and commitment. Stephen Anderson, in *Seductive Interaction Design* (New Riders, 2011), modeled emotional experience on falling in love. We'll revisit the relationship model again in Chapter 4 in the context of social bots. For now, let's apply it to the overall experience.

Start with milestones. Every relationship has milestones, symbolic markers that form a kind of ongoing timeline. Perhaps you might think of big milestones, like moving in together or buying a home. It's also small moments, like taking care of a partner when they're sick or sharing a bathroom for the first time, or when you sent a text that only the two of you understood. Your relationship with a brand, product, or experience has these milestones, too. We already focus on firsts, like the first encounter, the first purchase, the first return. Consider other relationship milestones too, whether it's introductions to friends or a deepening commitment.

Then, move on to meaningful moments. It seems obvious to start with emotional peaks and endings. Other moments may be even more important, though. Think about where there is a change in emotion or moments of strong emotion, good or bad. Those are the moments that reveal bigger values, build capacity, create support, form a memory. For example, Garren Engstrom of Intuit speaks about the moment of clicking "Transmit" using TurboTax software. Before that simple click happens, there are hours of mindless drudgery, intense effort, and a fair measure of anxiety. After you've successfully sent your return, you are likely to be flooded with emotion.

Finally, look at the emotional arc. After you have identified milestones and moments, you can begin to develop a narrative arc for each that draws on emotional experience. The first time you felt understood by a voice assistant might move from curiosity ("Can I ask this?") to frustration ("How many times do I need to rephrase?") to surprise ("Wait, that worked!") to relief ("It feels like I can rely on it") to bonding ("Wow, it really does understand me a bit better").

As you move through these exercises, weight, texture, color, light, scale, and other aspects associated with the emotional experience will emerge. Some features will rise to the top, others fade away. Content and tone begin to align. For now, we have an initial plan for a more emotionally experience.

Evolve the Relationship

Developing emotionally intelligent design is grounded in deep human understanding. Rather than looking at experience as a snapshot, or even a progression, we need to shift toward considering how it evolves. It needs to be elastic enough to grow and adapt and change over time.

After you have a prototype, you should continue to do research. You should iterate, as one does. The most successful experiences find ways to evolve the relationship further though. If you've made it this far, you'll have people who love your product or service. Paul Graham of Y Combinator once advised Airbnb to cultivate that crowd, saying, "It's better to have 100 people that love you than a million people that just sort of like you."[6] Airbnb's 100-lovers strategy meant engaging the most ardent fans to shape the community. Likewise, Strava evolved the experience with a small group of avid cyclists who helped it formulate an emotional profile for friendly competition. Strava's team was able to translate the feeling of accomplishment and camaraderie to keep the community motivated.

The 100-lovers approach is one way to develop a bond. But it shouldn't be the only way. The same dangers you might encounter with a panel or a small group of beta testers still apply. It can become an insiders' club. It can be prone to tunnel vision. It can get tapped out. So, you'll want to continually seek out new people. Consider adding people with mixed emotions or those who overcome negatives. Bright-spot analysis is a way to accomplish this.

---

6 Simon Schneider, Armin Senoner, and Danielle Gratch, "What Airbnb and Strava Know About Build Emotional Connections with Customers." *Harvard Business Review*, May 2018.

In *Switch: How to Change Things When Change Is Hard* (Crown Business, 2010), Chip and Dan Heath outline their process for finding bright spots. In every community or organization, there are people whose exceptional practices enable them to do better and feel more. These people might be considered the bright spots. For our purposes, it might mean studying how people adapt a negative experience in a positive way. It also might mean that they've developed a community, embraced a subculture, or adopted a set of behaviors that have shifted the experience.

As you're evolving, you'll be tempted to measure success, too. John and Julie Gottman have studied couples in their Love Lab at the University of Washington. Among other methods, the two rely on affective computing biometrics to monitor couple's facial expressions, blood pressure, heart rate, and skin temperature, all while asking questions about how they met, positive memories, and moments of conflict. Micro-expressions, the Gottmans claim, reveal which marriages will thrive and which will fail. Based on this high-tech approach to relationships, John and Julie Gottman came up with a formula for a successful relationship: five positive interactions for every negative.

Almost in parallel, Barbara Frederickson came up with a 3:1 ratio for flourishing. That is, three positive emotions for one negative. Every so often, you'll hear the idea of a *magic ratio* surface again.

A magic ratio turns out to be difficult to replicate. It's easy to see why. Imagine a person who experiences three moments of joy in a day, another who experiences one moment of joy and two of contentment, and still another who experiences two of joy and one of anxiety. If we subtract negatives from the positives, it would seem the first two people are happier than the third. But emotions aren't quite that mathematically predictable. The broader our range, the more resilient we become.

As appealing as the promise of a simple mathematical equation seems, our emotional life is more complicated than that. But here's what seems to stick. Building capacity to grow, to change, to adapt, to make meaning matters more than tallies of positives and negatives. All that takes time, so as much as we try to actively evolve the experience, we also need to consider how people will live with it.

Live and Reflect

Much of our emotional lives can't be understood at a sprint. We will get better at understanding emotion, creating a framework, and creating and testing designs to support it. But emotional experience is not static. Without a long view, we'll lose the texture.

One way to keep growing is to look at ways to sustain the relationship. Usually, this means getting a fuller rendering of how people are making products a part of their lives. So, if we are looking for emotion resonance, we need to shift from the center to the edges. At the risk of overdoing the acronyms, I use DECIPHER as a shorthand. Here's what it means:

Dreams

> Wishes, hopes, dreams—we might shy away from these topics, unsure of how to proceed. Whether too personal, too aspirational, or just the firmly held belief that people don't truly know what they want, we miss possibilities by avoiding. Yet, aspirations are where people create identity, and identity is the nexus of our inner emotional life.

Etiquette

> We have shared conventions around behavior or expression, but often these are unspoken or even go unnoticed. Almost by accident, research can detect new etiquette (or lack of it)—phone stacking (already defunct), text speak, and ghosting are just a few examples. Etiquette contains clues about how we feel and what we value.

Contradictions

> Another place to spend more attention is where we see conflicted feelings, behaviors, or use. For instance, parents who want to limit their kids' time online yet still rely on devices to fill in gaps while they're working would be a rich area of exploration. Often when we see contradictions between what people say and what they do, we choose to simply ignore the former. The truth is more complicated than that.

Images and symbols

> Icons bring a rush of memories, feelings, and hopes. Apps can stand in for relationships. Wearables can signify membership. We attach to experiences where the experience itself might no longer

be relevant. For instance, I regularly visit a forgotten Instagram of a friend who died years ago, like a pilgrimage. It feels like a little secret and I'll be bitterly disappointed to find it deleted someday. Symbolic relationships often open up emotional memories.

Peaks

Our fondest memories and wishes are often mixed up with the technology. Yet, we might be celebrating the wrong things. Twitter will cheerfully tell us when we've hit a certain follower count, Headspace will let us know when we've reached a meditation goal in a super nonchill way, Facebook wants to celebrate every possible thing with us. We assume a lot. What do people consider peaks? What epiphanies do peak moments spark?

Hacks

As people make a technology their own, many develop work-arounds, adaptations, and adjustments suited to their context and community. We get excited about these hacks but tend to happen upon them by accident, like the ACLU Dash button (Figure 3-12) to channel anger, or when they become popular, like IKEA hacks. Fixing strategies, creative repurposing, and unusual adaptations suggest ways to live successfully with technology.

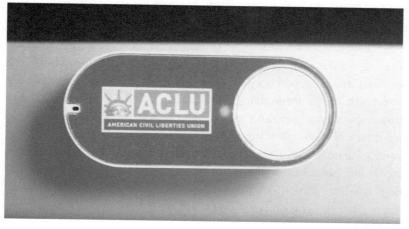

FIGURE 3-12

Hacks creatively cope with mixed emotions (source: Nathan Pryor)

People who push the boundaries to break new ground—the outliers—can guide us toward new possibilities. They might be theorizing new ways to build, experience, or replicate something that already exists or pursuing something entirely novel. It's not just trendsetters who engage in extremes, it's everyone at one time or another. It might be a social practice, a community, or a policy that is unusual but addresses a fundamental human need.

Rituals

Nervous tics, curious habits, repeated behaviors, cherished practices, and other ways people try to integrate technology into their daily routines can guide us toward emotional needs and deficits. When people try to train technology through repetitive actions to be what they want, we need to pay attention.

The DECIPHER model shifts attention toward the aspects of human experience that we miss, discount, or simply need yet to understand. Consider these the signals that will help us understand ongoing relationships, emotions, and values.

Emotional relationships with products in our lives change and grow in value over time. Maybe it's a hand mirror, passed down for years, that once belonged to a great, great aunt. Perhaps it's an old Beetle that you restore with VW Heritage parts. Maybe it's a coffee cup with an interior pattern that develops with use (Figure 3-13).

For me, it's the rocking chair gifted to me by my mother-in-law before my first daughter was born. A chair where I spent hours upon hours with each of my three daughters. Gazing down at their miraculous tiny fingers and breathing in that delicious baby head smell, crying from lack of sleep, pleading with my little darlings to go to bed. Later snuggling up to read *Dragons Love Tacos* and stabilizing the rocker with blocks for hideaways and tending to smushed toes. Laughing as my dogs tried to jump up, only to be deposited right back on the ground. Years later, the chair looks a mess, but there is no way I'll be getting rid of it.

Our emotional relationships with technology, products, and our designed environment become more profound the more steeped they are in complex emotion. Delight enlivens, emotional extremes engage, emotional depth and complexity endures.

FIGURE 3-13

Emotional connection etched in coffee stains (source: Bethan Laura Wood)

Design Feeling Is the New Design Thinking

In the near future it seems a given that emotion will be designed into the experience. The text your phone sends you to say that your purchase won't make you happy, the app on your phone that lets you tune in to your partner's mood before they get home, the robot companion who senses your irritation and adjusts its tone—none can be automated. We will be called upon to design for a mess of human emotion and a range of outcomes. And that future requires developing a greater sensitivity to our emotional lives with technology.

Emotionally intelligent design is a set of perspectives and practices that champion our emotional life. Technology that's designed with emotional intelligence has a transformative power to contribute to our mental and physical health, forge our identities, build strong relationships, and help us create meaning in our lives. The impact of emotionally intelligent design is more than just a change in the products and services we develop: it's a shift in mindset and methods.

Detecting, understanding, and responding to emotion is one of the first things we learn, and one thing we'll never fully master. The practices here are part of a dialogue with past methods and a start at new methods to prioritize our emotional lives.

[4]

Cultivate Human–Machine Harmony

MAYBE YOU'VE WATCHED THE viral video "I'm Poppy" on YouTube. Take a trip down that rabbit hole, and what you'll see is as mesmerizing as it is unsettling. Whether the slight delay between Poppy's lips and the audio, the hint of autotune in her voice, or the silvery sheen of her skin and hair, something seems off. She tells us that she's "from the internet." She has stilted conversations with a mannequin named Charlotte. Charlotte speaks to Poppy in a computerized voice, and Poppy answers with her own kind of "artificial intelligence." Part of the reason, perhaps, that Poppy has piqued collective curiosity is that people aren't quite sure what to make of her; she brings attention to the boundary shift between human and machine.

The line between humans and technology seems like it's becoming blurrier. Social media profiles prompt us to consider how we present ourselves in new contexts. We shuffle through identities more rapidly than ever, moving from anonymous to avatar in a blink. We have real conversations with fake people, or maybe a mashup of chatbot and human—we're no longer sure. Robots that look like people challenge our idea of personhood, relationships, and citizenship.

Technology is urgently insisting that we reconsider what it means to be human. It turns out to be much more complicated than "let humans do human things and machines do machine things." Human and machine things are jumbled together. Although some embrace the potential for new ways of being, the low buzz of anxiety is all around us. We get a glimpse of it in news stories about the future of work and in academic studies about the *uncanny valley*. Warnings from Elon Musk or Stephen Hawking about the coming singularity give pause. We see entrepreneurs scramble to cash in on easy-win human things to disrupt, like scheduling meetings or customer service conversations. Designers cast a nervous glance to AI, not sure if it's a collaborator or replacement.

In a world without hard-and-fast rules about what is human and what isn't, how do we design technology? Machines shape our identity; AI makes this truth more acute. And emotional well-being is nothing if not a quest toward our best selves. Technology will almost certainly influence how we feel about ourselves.

Machines will shape our relationships with other people, whether a screen in between or something more. When it comes to emotional well-being, relationships are nearly everything. Every model of happiness, from Martin Seligman's PERMA to the Ryff Scale of Psychological Well-Being to the *OECD Better Life Index*, centers on relationships. Harvard University's 80-year Grant and Glueck Study revealed that it's not money, career, or status that determined a good life; it's love. Good relationships are associated with better health, greater happiness, and a longer life. Study after study shows that friends are crucial to happiness. Yes, human friends, but very likely artificial friends, too.

So, in this chapter, we consider how to cultivate harmony between humans and machines in a world without strict boundaries anymore. We draw from an evolving philosophical consideration of the relationship between humans and technology. We also consider the psychology of personality and relationships to consider how it might help us humanize technology in a way that doesn't dehumanize humans.

Understanding the New Humans

As designers, researchers, and developers, we are keenly concerned with designing for people. Empathy is the essential underpinning of our practice. So, we cultivate it. We observe people using technology. We challenge ourselves to experience the world in different ways through website prompts (Figure 4-1), workshop exercises, simulations, and maybe even virtual reality (VR). Hopefully, we are hiring diverse teams and building an inclusive process. More and more, we try to divine some understanding from data. Maybe we've even trained AI on social media data using *IBM Watson's Personality Insights*.

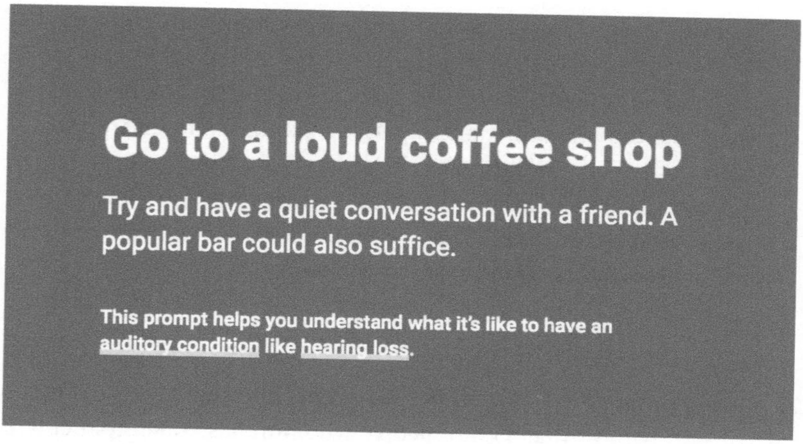

Go to a loud coffee shop

Try and have a quiet conversation with a friend. A popular bar could also suffice.

This prompt helps you understand what it's like to have an auditory condition like hearing loss.

FIGURE 4-1

Empathy prompts nudge us toward human understanding (source: empathyprompts.net)

Then, we create stories from our research called *personas*, characters that we can call to mind and that guide our work. We conjure a kind of design muse to remind us of the real people out there somewhere. It's a challenge to understand people in aggregate or as individuals. Who exactly are we designing for?

USERS VERSUS HUMANS

Well, we design for users, of course. A quaint term from the days when people sat down in front of a machine for a set amount of time. An old-fashioned term for when there was a divide between going online and real life. A limited term circumscribing people by their use of technology. There's life, and then there's this moment when someone is interacting with our thing. And then, for that flicker of an instant, a person becomes a user.

A user is just one small version of ourselves at a moment in time. How do we understand users? We do our best to understand our fellow humans in these moments, usually through a few different lenses. Let's examine these a bit closer:

Broad characteristics

Whether we like to admit it, the starting point is often broad strokes. The business team notes that even though we know our core users are men aged 50 years and older, we are aiming to bring on millennial men and women. The marketing team tells us that customers love Instagram; they are very visual and super tech-savvy. The millennials on the tech team might then be asked to step into the role of instant expert, speaking for an entire generation. A developer or designer chimes in that teens don't care about privacy. Packed into demographics or other technographic or even behavioral characteristics are assumptions upon assumptions that are at best reductive and at worst harmful.

Real people in aggregate

Another way to understand people is to put data from many people together into kind of a puree. We might find that 50% go down a certain path or that 35% of people who purchase one product will purchase another. Or, we might find that our most profitable customers rank highly for conscientiousness on the OCEAN model of personality. That might help us make design decisions. Even though extrapolating individual truth from broad trends in analytics data is dangerously reductionist, we do it all the time. We fall back on averages even though it flattens out experience.

One person

Sometimes, the experience is framed around one person to focus the design discussions. It might be based on a real person we have in our head—maybe a friend or a person we encountered during research. It might be someone we imagine, an ideal customer. It might be someone sketched out in a persona, a blend of imagination and data points. I can easily imagine design teams referencing a character from a VR experience in the not-so-distant future. The user springs to life in a new way, limited by the people the team can conjure up.

Data-double

When we track data for an individual, usually to personalize the experience in some way, our view is trained on a data-double—a mix of past actions, reported demographics, and stated preferences that comes together as a portrait of a person. Sometimes, we get a glimpse of this imperfect replica in the ads served up or social media feeds, but mostly it's hidden. Often, it's how potential partners, employers, benefits officers, and many others get to know us first. Even though we might be loath to admit it, this data-double haunts our design process.

Social performance

We are constantly role-swapping across all channels. Whether we are sampling a slice of life in a qualitative interview or capturing tone of voice in email over time, much of what we gather is a performance of some kind. Maybe we know this in the back of our minds. People are guarded; they aren't always genuine. Sometimes, we are confronted with it through data. If you look at your contacts using Crystal Knows, a virtual email coach, you'll see that almost everyone is an "optimist" or a "motivator" if personality is based only on the tone in their emails (Figure 4-2).

Kyle
View Profile

Amber
View Profile

Corey
View Profile

Martha
View Profile

FIGURE 4-2

If we are all so positive on email, why aren't we happier? (source: Crystal Knows)

Lately, I've been trying out different research methods to learn more about this complexity. Usually, it involves exercises designed for self-reflection—personality quizzes, writing prompts, and paired activities. Then, we attempt to unearth who we are in all kinds of online contexts. The idea is to understand the difference and potential points of disconnect between identities. Here are just a few activities to try:

Unboxing yourself

Every day, we get clues about how big companies and tech platforms frame who we are, but we rarely tune in. In this activity, each person looks at three different memory systems. First, note down predictive text suggestions on your smartphone. Second, list out 5 to 10 ads or types of ads that you see across more than one website. Third, look at reminiscence databases, like Facebook Memories or Timehop. Based on what you find, select only five items (we have a big selection of miniatures and LEGOs) that represent this version of you and place them in a box. Now try designing personalization based on knowing just those items.

This activity can get a little too personal, so I begin with some example browser histories. Often people will volunteer to contribute. Everyone gets a browser history as a prompt to construct a day in the life for that individual, illuminated with a detailed description. If we are bravely using our own browser histories, it's pretty easy to reconstruct a day. You'll see where you've been researching a thorny issue for a project, where you were goofing off, cringe-worthy moments during which you clicked something you wish you hadn't. Use this as an input for personas.

Glimmers of who we are according to the platforms we use are already evident in our daily life. Some of it we craft for ourselves, by adopting different identities in different contexts. So long as we are aware of exactly what we reference when we talk about users, all of these views might have some value as we design. It would be short-sighted not to acknowledge the limitations, though. Identity is shaped by technology in ways that go beyond a consumer in the moment of interacting or an ad target.

HUMANS, ON A SPECTRUM

Humans are forever in a state of becoming. This truth is at the core of the research on well-being. Why else would we try to feel more and do better? Psychologist Dan Gilbert notes that "Human beings are works in progress that mistakenly think they are finished." Sometimes, when we design technology, we forget this though. The goal is to define and narrow, which leaves us at a loss as to how to account for something as fluid as identity.

Humans are more than archetypes and data points. We do have some ways to account for human complexity, however. Ethnographic interviews and empathy exercises strive to render that fullness, but that work can get lost in translation. A glimpse of how humans and technology are coevolving ends up reduced to touchpoints.

Another way to humanize the humans is to acknowledge that we relate to technology in a range of different ways that shapes how we see ourselves and interpret the world. Marshall McLuhan argued that all technology extends our body or mind in some way. For instance, cars extend our physical range so that we can travel farther. Cars also extend our emotional range, by exposing us to more of the world. Good to remember, difficult to model.

For those of us tasked with sorting out these relationships, it helps to get specific about the variations. The work of philosopher Don Ihde, who builds on Martin Heidegger's notion of readiness-to-hand, is a good starting point. In *Technology and the Lifeworld* (Indiana University Press, 1990), Ihde models four ways that technology mediates between people and the world:

Embodiment

When technology merges to some degree with the human, but withdraws as soon as it's removed. A hammer, for example, becomes a part of our hand but only while we use it.

Hermeneutic

When technology represents an aspect of the world, like a thermometer that allows us to read the temperature.

Background

When technology shapes an experience that we are not consciously aware of, like central heating or a refrigerator.

Alterity

When technology is a separate presence, which includes anything from an ATM to a Furby to a RIBA healthcare robot.

More recently, philosopher Peter-Paul Verbeek, in his work *What Things Do: Philosophical Reflections on Technology, Agency, and Design* (Penn State University Press, 2005), identified two more potential ways that technology mediates experience:

Cyborg

When technologies merge with a person to form a single, cohesive hybrid. Think biohacks or implantables.

Composite

When technology not only represents reality but constructs it as well. From radio telescopes to sentiment-based data visualizations, this kind of meaning-making relationship depicts a new view of reality.

We already look at people through different lenses in research, through demographics or data points or stories. If we use the work of Ihde and Verbeek as a model, those profiles might include the following aspects of selfhood:

Hybrid

> With technologies like cochlear implants that enable deaf people to hear again or neuro-implants for deep-brain stimulation, body and technology can be intimately connected. Human and technology approach the world as a combined force. In a hybrid relationship, you might not be aware of the relationship most of the time.

Augmented

> Technology that adds a second layer to the world, anything from Google Glass (Figure 4-3) to Twilio, or even GPS, is augmentation. We are aware of that layer, but it can feel like an extension of our mind or body. The technology augments an ability we already have or fills in gaps. When we talk about technology giving us superpowers, we are often addressing an augmented self.

FIGURE 4-3
The place between hybrid and augmentation is often awkward (source: Google Glass)

Extended

The extended self exists between augmentation and imagination. Rather than just a layer that offers a new view or new capabilities, here our conception of self becomes bigger. Our identity expands. Russell Belk coined the term to reflect the relationship people have with their possessions.[1] Sometimes, this happens through ownership, as in, "I'm an Apple person." Sometimes, an extended self comes to life through use. You might come to think of yourself as a blogger, or even more narrowly as an Instagrammer.

Imagined

From an avatar that we consciously call into existence for a game to a curated identity for social media, this is an identity that we consciously craft. The imagined self can be something that is fashioned intentionally or that develops over time. The focus can be oriented toward other people or purely for yourself. You might think of the imagined self as a subset of the extended self. The *optimized self* exists in this space, too. Part aspirational, part motivational, this version shifts depending on what's being tracked. It's an idealized conception of selfhood, based on quantification.

Immersed

Smart environments perceive a version of our selves. When technology is fused with the world outside of us, it still needs to make sense of us. In the immersion relation, we are represented by the data *doppelgänger* technology detects. Whether a smartwatch reading our stress levels or a website remembering what we shopped for last summer, the world bends toward this version of our selves.

Humans and technology are irrevocably mixed together. Let's think of this relationship on a spectrum. At one end of the spectrum, technology merges with our self; tech and human are a hybrid. Brain interfaces, but also implants and wearable medical devices, might qualify. At the opposite end of the spectrum is an immersed relationship in which technology merges with the world. From sensors in streetlamps to facial recognition built in to security systems, we experience it as clearly separate from ourselves.

---

1   Russell Belk, "Possessions and the Self," *Journal of Consumer Research*, September, 1988.

The middle is murky. Technology can extend capabilities in all kinds of ways, sometimes fading into the background and sometimes not. Often, we flicker between states. You might feel like your phone is part of yourself, a representation of others as voices in your head or a best friend there when you need it.

Technology frames our identity in ways that persist long after we click, tap, or talk. We've internalized it. So much so that it's difficult to say where technology ends and humans begin. At the same time, we cultivate relationships with technology that are externalized, too.

NEW HUMAN-TECH RELATIONSHIPS

When we think about our relationship with technology, we don't think of ourselves on a spectrum where we are part human, part tech. Most of us prefer to think that humans are separate. Paradoxically, this might explain the appeal of humanized robots. It seems like we are happiest when the boundaries are clearly drawn. When a robot looks too much like a human, it's creepy. When it's not clearly separated from us, it's confusing.

As uncomfortable as this boundary shifting might be, we should begin to embrace the mess. I suspect it's the path to better human-tech relationships going forward. Here are a few of the ways it can take shape.

Technology as stand-in

Telepresence robots and gaming avatars might take your place from time to time. It's about to get more sophisticated, though. When Eugenia Kudya lost her friend Roman Mazurenko to a tragic accident, she created a memorial bot. Fashioned from text messages, the AI was enough of a likeness to help friends and family have a last conversation.[2] The result was an app, Replika, that you can use to create a double of yourself, or a very customized friend. UploadMe goes further, creating a second self from your social media and interactions (Figure 4-4). Technology that functions as another you, whether placeholder or fictional character or realistic replica, is a distinct possibility.

---

2 Casey Newton, "Speak, Memory," *The Verge*, 2017.

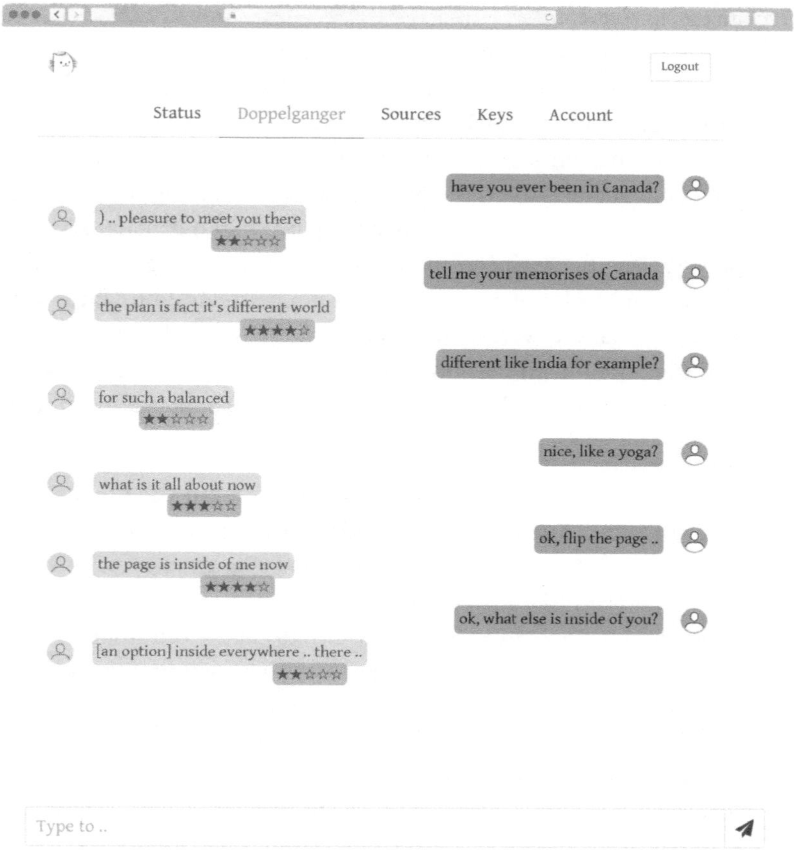

FIGURE 4-4

Your double isn't quite ready to stand in (source: uploadme.ai)

Technology as assistant

Technology that functions as a personal assistant or doubles as an employee fills this subordinate role. You are in charge, and the bot has agency in a narrow frame. X.ai's chatbots schedule meetings, Pana arranges business travel, Mezi shops for you. Google Assistant is billed as "your own personal Google, always ready to help." On a sliding scale of personality, many of these bots keep personality to a minimum, mostly because they exist to smooth over tedious tasks or difficult situations. The tech assistant is part you and part not-you, its role limited by particular tasks.

Technology as collaborator

In this relationship human and machine work together. Jazz musician Dan Tepfer made headlines recently by playing alongside algorithms at a Yamaha Disklavier. "I play something on the piano, it goes into the computer, it immediately sends back information to the piano to play.... Now the piano is actually creating the composition with me."[3] The same trend is happening in the visual arts and poetry. Whether training the AI or a more flexible give and take, human and tech are co-creators. It's not a stretch to imagine this kind of collaborative relationship in many fields, from medicine to design. The tech collaborator is more colleague than personal assistant, but it's a role bound by a set of tasks or specialized field.

Technology as friend (or foe)

No shortage of robot companions await us, from the child-sized, Pixar-inspired Kuri, to the intimidating Spot Mini from Boston Dynamics, to Softbank's family of robots (Figure 4-5). Whether a soft robot seal, like PARO, or a childlike presence, like the robot assistant Jibo, machine-friends seem to sense our thoughts or emotions. Their capabilities are less tightly constrained to a small or specific set of tasks. The machine-friend feels less like you or an extension of you, and more like a friend or family member. Like friends or family members, relationships can go wrong. If our machine-friends don't get us, it might feel like a betrayal. At the same time, we might be a little more forgiving of weaknesses, just as we are for human friends.

3 Nate Chinen, "Fascinating Algorithm: Dan Tepfer's Player Piano Is His Composing Partner," *NPR Music*, July 24, 2017.

FIGURE 4-5

Friends can be a little strange; usually the best ones are (source: Softbank)

Technology as lover

In the movie *Her*, a lonely guy very plausibly falls in love with his operating system. Plausible because it's already happened. In 2006, psychologist Robert Epstein had a months-long email affair with Svetlana, who turned out to be a bot.[4] Research backs up the notion that we could feel a sense of intimacy with a bot. In *The Media Equation: How People Treat Computers, Television, and New Media Like Real People and Places* (Cambridge University Press, 1996), Byron Reeves and Clifford Nass describe a wide range of studies that show how people react to computers as social actors. As soon as bots begin to recognize emotional cues and respond with empathy, it's inevitable that we'll engage with them differently and maybe even begin to fall for them.

Robots might not love us but with so many different kinds of love—from romantic to obsessive, from friendship to transcendent—perhaps it will just become another variation on a theme. No matter your comfort level with this type of human–machine relationship, it certainly is worthy of our consideration as we design technology that will fill in these roles.

---

4   Radiolab, "Clever Bots," Season 10, Episode 1, 2011.

All of these types of relationships can support well-being. There won't be one type of "right" relationship with machines, just like there's not one right relationship with fellow humans. Relationships might be narrowly defined to a task or richly intimate, or something in between. And some will go wrong, and we'll need to know how to spot the warning signs of a relationship gone off the rails.

THE TROUBLE WITH ARTIFICIAL FRIENDS

As we conflate human and machine, confusion arises. One pitfall is the emotional *uncanny valley* or bots that overstep boundaries. Since the 1970s, we've used robotics professor Masahiro Mori's concept of the uncanny valley to explain why robots that look too realistic make humans uncomfortable. I believe we'll begin to see an emotional uncanny valley, a new kind of unease as bot personalities begin to feel too human. In an experiment by Jan-Phillip Stein and Peter Ohler, people were exposed to virtual reality characters making small talk. When people thought that the characters were not voiced by humans, they became deeply uncomfortable.[5] When bots speak or act too much like a human, it creates that same unease we feel when bots look too human.

And then there's *stereotypes*. As a society, we might have been conditioned to expect cheerful female voices in helpful roles. Most assistant apps, including Alexa, Cortana, and Siri (and likely your car's GPS), are all female by default. Not only are we perpetuating stereotypes but we also may be conditioning the next generation to be rude or demanding toward women. Sara Wachter Boettcher, in her book *Technically Wrong: Sexist Apps, Biased Algorithms, and Other Threats of Toxic Tech* (W. W. Norton & Company, 2017), has chronicled the bias baked in to the design of chatbot personalities, tracing some of the problem back to the composition of design teams. Some of this bias might be due to the pressure on teams to make successful products. Marketing teams might insist on "female" bots because people seem more apt to interact. Inadvertent or not, perpetuating and profiting from stereotypes will not cultivate harmony among humans and machines.

---

5   Jan-Phillip Stein and Peter Ohler, "Venturing into the Uncanny Valley of the Mind," *Cognition*, March 2017.

Another complication with creating technology to be a friend is *transparency*. How do we know when we are speaking to a human? Most companies aim for chatbots to seem as human as possible. For instance, Amy and Andrew Ingram, the meeting scheduling bots of X.ai, are scripted for empathy. Xiaoice, Microsoft's natural-language chatbot for the Weibo community, seems so real that people fool themselves into thinking it just might be.

Other bots are actually humans masked by the bot. Facebook's M assistant was only partly bot, with humans filling in the gaps. Pana, the travel assistant, connects with a human after just a few interactions. Invisible Girlfriend, at first, obscured the human behind the chatbot interface (now the company provides conversations "powered by creative writers" but still encourages people to "build your girlfriend"). A faked bot impersonating a faked girlfriend (or boyfriend)—no wonder we have trouble sorting it out.

Perhaps at some point blurring the lines between human and machine might become irrelevant, but we aren't at that point yet. So, we spend our days wondering who to trust. As poet and programmer Brian Christian writes, "We go through digital life, in the twenty-first century, with our guards up. All communication is a Turing test. All communication is suspect."[6] Given that we conflate human and machine in a variety of contexts, from online characters to chatbots, how do we strike a meaningful balance?

Let Machines Be Machines

From a vaguely feel-good affirmation of values, to making tech warm and fuzzy, to giving it a fully formed personality or a life-like body, humanizing technology is a concept that's open to interpretation. Usually, it means designing tech with human characteristics.

Whether physical appearance or personality, an element of humanity builds trust. Humanized robots might partly be a vanity project, too. We're creating them, after all, so why not in our likeness? Even if it doesn't make much sense based on what the machine will do, our impulse is to humanize.

---

6 Brian Christian, *The Most Human Human: What Talking with Computers Teaches Us About What It Means to Be Alive*, Knopf Doubleday, 2011.

All the same, we like it when bots showing the barest hint of humanity fail. As much as we might enjoy the Roomba vacuuming up after our pets, there's a certain charm when it gets stuck. Tutorials on how to make Siri curse like a sailor abound, even though you probably don't need them. The little thrill we get when a chatbot is clueless or a robot slips on a banana peel (Figure 4-6) might be related to the *pratfall effect*, or the tendency to feel more affection toward a person who makes a mistake. But it's a bit different; there's a bit of *schadenfreude* in the mix. And maybe a bit of fear, too. We are drawn to humanized machines, but we don't want them to be too human.

FIGURE 4-6
When robots fail, we might feel sympathy, but it's tinged with glee (source: Boston Dynamics)

So, here we are torn between wanting our robots to be a bit more human and fearing them when they do seem more human. When do we choose to add a human touch? And how much is the right amount?

WHEN LESS HUMAN IS MORE HUMANE

Less is more when it comes the far ends of the human–machine spectrum. Technology embedded in our world or merged with our body doesn't need a personality. It might be funny to think of your cochlear implant whispering in your ear, but the day-to-day reality would be nightmarish. Embedded sidewalk sensors don't need to be brilliant conversationalists, or any kind of conversationalist at all. Not only would that become annoying, but it would likely be a dangerous distraction as well. Whether technology merges with us or merges with the environment, it doesn't require much of a human touch. Here, machines can be machines.

A chip implant is clearly merged with us. A city streetlight is clearly merged with the world. It's not always so neatly differentiated. Might household objects, like your refrigerator or your thermostat, benefit from a little personality? Do wearables such as smartwatches and sensor-laden clothing always need to be so discreet? When a product is newly introduced, the lines are often unclear.

WHEN YOUR ROBOT BECOMES A DISHWASHER

Think for a minute about dishwashers. People dream of robots that will do household chores—I know I do—and there's no shortage of takes on the dishwasher. Robot arms that can load the dishwasher, chatbots that can activate an extra rinse cycle, even a sex robot that also turns on (so to speak) your dishwasher are all possibilities.

We invent robot vacuum cleaners, robot lawnmowers, robot cat litter boxes, but then at some point these robots stop being robots. When these machines become mundane, we no longer add the word "robot." As roboticist Leila Takayama points out in her 2018 TED talk, "What's It Like To Be a Robot?", we simply call it a dishwasher. And if it loses the "robot," that's a clue that it doesn't need to have its own carefully crafted personality.

Although we can't always predict when, or if, a robot dishwasher will become a dishwasher, there are some signals to observe. If you can answer yes to the following, your robot might be on its way to becoming a regular household object.

- *Does the technology automate a background task?* A dishwasher runs while you do other things. Maybe when you get a new dishwasher, you are temporarily obsessed with the new machine, but the enthusiasm wanes. Soon enough, the dishwasher recedes into the background.

- *Does it replace a repetitious task?* Washing dishes is a task that needs to be repeated every day. For most people, it's not a source of joy, at least not most of the time. Unless it's a holiday gathering, washing dishes is not a special occasion. However, repetition can veer into meaningful ritual, with its own set of special practices.

- *Does it replace something that is low affect?* This one is trickier. Even though there might be people who have strong feelings about washing and drying dishes, for many people, emotions around washing dishes are low-intensity or low-complexity, at least most of the time. And if you create a loveable dishwashing robot, those emotions might take hold.

As simple as this model seems, it doesn't always apply. Your mundane task might be my joy. You might long for a leaf-raking robot, while I'd miss the crisp fall air, the colorful leaves, the meditative quality, the interruptions to dive in to a pile of leaves once in a while, and the sense of accomplishment. Leaf raking is not an everyday task, so it's less likely to become burdensome. If I had a leaf-raking robot, maybe I'd prefer it to work with me side by side. But leaf raking also leads us to other questions that we can consider when we think about humanizing tech.

When might it be unlikely that your robot will become a household or other type of everyday object? Obviously, we can start with the opposite of the three previous questions. If it's not automating a background or repetitive task, it might not become a mundane tech product running in the background. If emotions are intense, complex, and conflicted, it might never become a dishwasher. A few other telltale signs can guide us:

- *Is it a rich experience?* An experience that is not only emotionally complex, but sensorially rich as well, might mean that it will never cross over into mundane territory for some people. My experience of fall leaves is rich; for other people it's not.

- *Is it tied to a human sense of identity?* Perhaps you fancy yourself a leaf lover? Your love of fall is an important part of who you are? Maybe it's guided your decision to live in a place where you can experience it?

- *Does it mediate social connection?* Joining a group of leaf peepers or spending time with the neighborhood kids leaf jumping might mean that rakes, leaf blowers, tarps, and all the trappings might not merge into the background for some small and maybe strange subset of people.

Of course, for these kinds of experiences you might not be interested in adding a tech layer at all. Or you might sometimes want the full emotional experience and sometimes not. Sometimes, you just need to get the leaves raked in time for the first snowfall, after all.

When we think about how far to go with humanizing a machine, there probably will never be a clear answer. But we can think about the humble dishwasher. Your robot might already be a dishwasher, or it might become a dishwasher. When that happens, personality takes a backseat.

Plotting the relationship on the human–machine spectrum, we can avoid the temptation to give everything—from your internet-connected coffee pot to your medical tattoo—a brand-lovable personality. If you are designing a travel avatar or a chatbot therapist or a robot companion for the elderly, perhaps you still feel you must develop a personality. Or, perhaps you are getting pressure to make your brand friendly so that people will spend more time or money with your organization. Then go with a light touch.

Humanize Machines, Just a Little Bit

Our relationships with people gradually emerge over time. A good relationship with technology uses the same approach. We don't share every detail of our lives with every person in our lives. In fact, a little mystery is often better. Yet, in our tech relationships it can feel like each actor comes at us fully formed. Whatever the technology, it's a safe bet that it knows things about us that even our partners don't. Engaging with us as a full-fledged personality takes it even further.

So, a light touch means sketching in as few details as possible. This way it lets the *humans* fill in some of the details. They will anyway, after all. I think of Lev Tolstoy's manner of using one detail, like Anna Karenina's plump hands, to characterize without being too heavy handed. Or Anton Chekhov's sisters in *The Cherry Orchard* who emerge gradually through dialogue. You don't need to have studied Russian literature to understand gradually getting to know someone, but perhaps it is something of a lost art with all of us in such a rush to connect.

A light touch, besides supporting humans being humans living good lives, will end up being better for business, too. People tend to ally themselves with brands that speak to their values and resonate emotionally. And they tend to choose brands that they trust. More and more, this will mean gradually growing a relationship recognizing who they are, in a way they are comfortable with, over time.

HOW OBJECTS BECOME HUMANLY

Humans readily attribute personality to all kinds of living and nonliving things. Maybe it means you interpret a meow as an accusation, or you speak to your plants, or you even narrate the thoughts you attribute to your car. The drive to anthropomorphize is strong, even if we don't build a personality. What prompts people toward mind attribution? Let's explore that:

A face, or even eyes alone

Humans are hardwired to see faces everywhere. Our ability to read faces is crucial in helping us distinguish between friend or foe. This ability sometimes extends to nonhumans. The mere presence of eyes cue us to believe that we are being watched, much as a poster with eyes can make us feel watched. If an object has eyes, we attribute a mind to it.

An unpredictable action or movement

We assign a mind to nonhumans when we need to explain behavior that we don't understand. If your computer freezes up or your light switch goes wonky, you might be tempted to describe it as devious or capricious. Clocky, an alarm clock with a hint of a face that rolls around the room if you press snooze, is an example of a product that seems designed to be anthropomorphized (Figure 4-7). Nicholas Epley describes a study in which some participants were told that Clocky would predictably run away, while others were told that it was unpredictable.[7] Those who believed it was

---

7 Nicholas Epley, *Mindwise: How We Understand What Others Think, Believe, Feel, Want*, Knopf 2014.

unpredictable were more apt to attribute some kind of mind to the device. Humans are unpredictable, and if an object is unpredictable it seems human, too.

FIGURE 4-7
So unpredictable that it seems human (source: Clocky)

A voice

People are voice-activated in a way. When we encounter technologies with a voice, we respond as we would to another person. J. Walter Thompson Innovation Group London and Mindshare Futures published a study in which 100 consumers were given Amazon Echos for the first time. The research found that people develop an emotional attachment. As time goes on, the attachment becomes more acute: "Over a third of regular voice technology users say they love their voice assistant so much they wish it were a real person."[8] As we hear machines talk, we respond in a social way, even mirroring the emotional tenor. Voice is not just a shorthand for human; it creates an emotional connection.

A mammal

Species that seem closer to humans receive more governmental protections. People are more likely to donate to causes that benefit animals rather than plants, vertebrates rather than invertebrates.

---

8   J. Walter Thompson Innovation Group and Mindshare Futures, "Speak Easy," April 5, 2017.

The closer the species is to human, the more readily we attribute a mind. When machines look like seals, or puppies, or humans, we are more likely to assign them thoughts, feelings, and agency.

Things we love

We are much more likely to anthropomorphize things we love. The more we like our car, the more likely we are to assign it a personality. This same impulse can lead musicians to consider their instrument a friend. It's why we narrate our pets. And the lonelier we are, the more likely we are to anthropomorphize the objects in our lives. Given that we are facing a loneliness epidemic for certain populations, it seems natural that many people will anthropomorphize technology no matter what.

A backstory

A story fills in the gaps and makes us believe in personhood. *Robot Ethics 2.0* describes an experiment by Kate Darling, Palash Nandy, and Cynthia Breazeal in which they created backstories for some Hexbugs, a tiny bug-like robot, and not others. Then, they asked people to strike them with a mallet. The bugs with a backstory prompted hesitation, even when people knew the stories to be fiction.[9]

It might sound extreme, but we experience this every day. Compare your experience of comments by someone you don't know and someone you know very well. Even when it's ripped out of context, you know the backstory and are likely to be more empathetic to your friend.

Humans do the work of characterization with little prompting, but how to proceed when tasked with creating a bot? In the next few sections, let's go step by step.

CHOOSING A MEANINGFUL METAPHOR

In college, I was a server at a little Italian restaurant. It's all kind of a blur really, except for a few shifts. One of the most memorable was when my favorite high school literature teacher walked in and sat in my section. I freaked out and hid until someone else could cover the table

---

9   Kate Darling, "Who's Johnny? Anthropomorphic Framing in Human-Robot Interaction, Integration, and Policy," *Robot Ethics 2.0: From Autonomous Cars to Artificial Intelligence.* Oxford University Press, 2017.

for me. He was out of context, and so was I. He was a cool teacher and I was (in my mind, at least) a star student, not casual diner and clumsy server. Maybe you had this same feeling when you first started using Facebook. Close friends, an acquaintance from a recent party, coworkers, exes, family members all jumbled up together. It just didn't seem right.

If we must design a personality, we face the first conundrum. Do we choose one role? Or do we let the personality evolve? I think we can find our answer if we look to how much context shifts. Is your technology going to be relevant primarily in one context? Or will it drift to others? The more likely it is to stay put, the better a metaphor might work as a starting point.

Beginning with a metaphor sets expectations for the relationship. Metaphors can be broad: mother, best friend, coworker, pet. It might be better to get more specific, though. Teacher, therapist, accountant, security guard each give people a framework that's familiar. A relationship helps designers to define behavior, create a communication style, even prioritize features. Better still, it can also help evolve the product personality going forward.

A metaphor helps us to consider the following:

- What kind of role does it play in the short and long term?
- What is the communication style?
- What will it know?
- How will it behave?
- What details make it cohesive?
- Where is there room to grow?
- How might it change over time?

The metaphor can guide the relationship, similar to how we might use a persona. The metaphor can be a way to explore what could go wrong, too. A poorly behaved dog, an arrogant boss, an overbearing friend tease out touchy subjects and implicit bias. Even so, a relationship metaphor is still not very specific. Is it enough? If we rely on only a metaphor, it may just veer into caricature.

How might we develop strong bots, loosely characterized? The next step would be to look at its personality.

ADDING JUST A FEW PERSONALITY TRAITS

Personality is a kind of complex, adaptive system itself. Characteristic patterns of thinking, feeling, and believing come together as a whole to shape our personality. The latest thinking on personality recognizes that some traits persist, but many more evolve. When designing a personality is appropriate, then the next step is to assign a few characteristic traits with an eye toward evolving.

The core framework psychologists rely on today is the OCEAN model. Developed by several groups of academic researchers, independent of one another, and refined over time, it helps psychologists understand personality. Also called the Five Factors, this model is thought to have relevance across cultures. Each dimension exists on a spectrum, lending more nuance.

Here are the Five Factors:

Openness

On one end of openness are curiosity, imagination, and inventiveness, and on the opposite end are consistency and cautiousness. Score high on openness, and you might be unpredictable or unfocused; score low, and you might seem dogmatic.

Conscientiousness

Very conscientious means you are efficient and organized. If you are easy-going and flexible, you are probably less so. Too much conscientiousness can veer into stubborn behavior; too little, and you might seem unreliable.

Extraversion

This is sociable and passionate on the one end of the spectrum, and reserved on the other end. Attention-seeking and dominant are the pitfalls on one extreme; aloof and disconnected on the other.

Agreeableness

Agreeableness is the tendency to be helpful, supportive, and compassionate. A little too agreeable, and you can seem naïve or submissive; less agreeable means that you might be argumentative or too competitive.

Neuroticism

Are you more sensitive or secure? High neuroticism is characterized as the tendency to experience negative emotions like anger
and anxiety too easily. Low neuroticism is seen as more emotionally even-keeled.

OCEAN is already in use in bot character guides, I'm sure. Facebook reactions roughly map to OCEAN. Cambridge Analytica (in)famously used it
in the 2016 elections. But there's no shortage of additional frameworks.

We all know, and maybe fervently declare or decry, a Myers-Briggs personality type. Although Myers-Briggs is based on thoughts and emotions, the Keirsey Temperament Sorter assesses behavior types. The
DISC assessment is another dimensional model widely used in organizations, marking dominance, inducement, submission, and compliance.
16PF is used in education and career counseling. The Insights Discovery
Wheel, based on Jungian archetypes, is favored in marketing and brand-
ing circles.

No personality model explains everything about human personality.
The ubiquity of workplace assessments and social media quizzes no
doubt undermines their credibility. The power of personality frameworks to predict behavior is vastly overstated. The result often veers
toward pigeonholing people. As a shorthand for human complexity,
personality frameworks are unquestionably unsatisfactory.

But even if personality frameworks aren't perfect, the infatuation we
have shows that it fills a gap. It prompts insights into our own personalities and our relationships with others. It shows that we view the world
differently from others. A personality framework is better as a starting
point for self-discovery than a finish line. Likewise for bots.

It's tempting to obsessively map out every aspect of a chatbot personality *Westworld*-style (Figure 4-8). But it might just be better for our
relationships if we scale back a bit. Rather than being too prescriptive,
a few characteristics might be more evocative. Because we know that
people will ascribe personalities to objects in the world, it leaves that
space open. People want to be able to grow and change, so the same
goes for our robots.

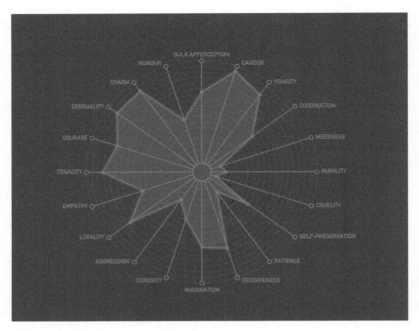

FIGURE 4-8

Exponential personality dimensions, *Westworld*-style (source: silentrob @ GitHub)

Perhaps we should let people select personalities? Personality is probably how people will choose whether they want Jibo, Kuri, or Pepper anyway. The differences in the underlying technology, and even how each one looks, are minimal. Then, how far do we take it? In the game SIMS, players get 25 personality points to spend in five categories. Maybe giving people some agency is appropriate in certain circumstances, especially when the relationship is more imaginary than concrete.

EVOLVING OVER TIME

Even though I admit to scurrying away at seeing a teacher out of context, I don't want to be seen one-dimensionally either. We assign ourselves personality characteristics—compassionate, good at math, introverted— but we also resist those categories. It's more than just pushing back on a stereotype, too. We grow and change over time. When it comes to designing technology, it helps to think of how that role might evolve.

A singular model sticks to one role and circumscribed personality traits. Imagine a health bot that is like a personal trainer. It always plays a motivational role. It might have a personality, but it remains fairly consistent and predictable. Even as it gets to know more about you, it still fits into that same place in your life within the same range of behaviors. As with a real-life health coach or personal trainer, your relationship is bounded by certain context and conventions.

An adaptive model shifts based on context. Rather than playing one role, a health bot might have a core personality that's like a coach but the tone might be more nurturing or tougher depending on the circumstances. As with a human coach, you may appreciate other aspects of its wit and wisdom. Perhaps it helps you set up or keep health appointments, more like an assistant or family member at times. Over time, maybe the coach becomes a friend.

Let's think about your car, for example. The car is in that murky middle where it is partly an extension of yourself and partly a separate entity, so a personality could work. The relationship evolves over time, as does the personality of the car. It recognizes each family member and gets to know each. If we were to truly create a more human model, the car would learn gradually, though, rather than receiving a massive collection of personal data points all at once. There would be gaps, some that would be sketched in gradually and some that would remain a little blurry. The personality of the car isn't the same later in life as at the start, but core elements remain. This aligns with the latest thinking on human personality, too.

As we shift from commands to conversation, our experience of tech will shift as well. Just as we should design to accommodate our own positive growth, we should attempt to design bots that are flexible and adaptable. An empathetic experience is more than a cheerful personality, it's an evolving identity. And that means our relationships will evolve, too.

Build Relationships, Not Dependency

As the tech in our lives learns how to read facial expressions, creatively express ideas, and answer complex, even philosophical, questions, we'll begin to feel as though it finally understands us. We are likely to develop a relationship that resembles the way we relate to friends, coworkers, or pets. We'll develop a meaningful connection.

Developing a good relationship takes time. We rely on our parents' financial advice because our relationship runs deep. We pay special attention to our best friend's taste in music because we have gotten to know them over the years. We trust our doctor based on her years of experience treating us. By studying relationships, we can see that trust builds.

Cultivating a relationship doesn't follow a series of linear steps. A fulfilling relationship is more like progressive transformation for all parties. If just one person (or machine) has more power, if only one grows and learns, if only one adapts, the relationship is bound to fail. Good relationships are about mutual metamorphosis.

Some relationship models are simple. According to anthropology professor Helen Fisher (*Why We Love: The Nature and Chemistry of Romantic Love* [Henry Holt and Co., 2004), there are three stages to falling in love: lust, attraction, and attachment. Friendships, too, pass through stages of interest, attunement, and intimacy. Or in the internet translation, meet someone who is just as crazy as you are, introduce all the ways you are crazy to each other, then build more craziness together, or something like that.

Communication professor Mark Knapp's relational development model is the most detailed, with 10 phases for coming together and coming apart:

1. *Initiating:* Making an impression

2. *Experimenting:* Getting to know each other

3. *Intensifying:* Strengthening the relationship

4. *Integrating:* Identifying as a social unit, a "we"

5. *Bonding:* Committing to each other, often publicly

6. *Differentiating:* Reestablishing separate identities

7. *Circumscribing:* Setting boundaries

8. *Stagnating:* Remaining in a holding pattern

9. *Avoiding:* Starting to detach

10. *Terminating:* Coming apart

Phases 1 through 5 build the relationship, and 6 through 10 describe the decline, but it's not quite as rigid as all that. Integrating, bonding, differentiating, and circumscribing are all part of it. A good relationship is not just a crescendo to blissful union. Coming together and coming apart are the ebb and flow of a good relationship.

MODELING THE RELATIONSHIP

The tendency in tech is toward compression. The relationship arc is often: (1) Hello; (2) Tell Me Everything About Yourself; (3) Here's What You Need. We go from first date to marriage in just a few minutes. We are in a rush to build trust to drive desirable behaviors like a quick purchase or more time spent with the app. What if, instead, a longer relationship arc became the norm? Just as in our human relationships, we'd pass through different stages in our relationship technology, if given the chance. Let's synthesize and simplify to see what a successful tech relationship might look like.

1. (Ambient) Awareness

Sometimes, we get to know other people before we even meet, whether this is by seeing them around the neighborhood or getting a glimpse on a dating app or a story shared by a friend. Through observation, hearsay, or indirect interaction, we start by knowing something about a person. The same goes for our relationship with machines. Starting with a bit of background data is fine; too much becomes creepy.

This includes first impressions, during which we display our best selves while simultaneously trying to detect clues about the other person or machine. Person to person, this can be as straightforward as what you wear or what you say. Or it can be as nuanced as picking up on facial expressions or body language. In the tech world, this might manifest in the care we take with a landing page or the first step of onboarding.

2. (Shared) Interest

In this stage, we get to know each other through exploring shared interests. Interest, in a relationship of any kind, has to be two-sided. We take an interest in a product for any number of reasons. The product must prove itself by showing a respectful interest in us. Because a chatbot or an app or other device seems to recognize and understand us, it builds rapport. During this stage, products can slowly build trust by assisting with small tasks as we learn where it fits in.

Human and machine get to know each other, as many people do, through conversation. Right now, what passes for "conversation" is really something more like commands, texted or spoken in keywords, occasionally punctuated with expletives. For this to really work, we must trust each other enough to move beyond giving commands or exchanging cursory information.

Just as we make mistakes, our devices should be allowed to make honest mistakes like misunderstanding a text or shutting down accidentally. Mistakes that reveal a lack of care though, from data breaches to emotional manipulation, betray trust. The relationship will stop there.

3. (Mutual) Attunement

After a few months of shared experience, we might begin to get in sync. In the current model, the sharing is markedly one-sided, though. So much so that we wouldn't tolerate it in a human relationship. Our devices gather data about our behaviors and emotions, silently judge us, and make predictions that are often way off base or embarrassingly accurate. Sure, they might have such deep knowledge about us that the predictions become better, maybe so much so that it feels caring. It still might not be the best model.

A person who is attuned to another anticipates emotional needs, understands the context, and responds appropriately. Not only do people draw from a range of mirroring mechanisms at a physiological level, we invest enormous effort in trying to resonate. In some relationships, like parenting a toddler, attunement can be more one-sided. In most adult relationships, attunement is gradual, respectful, hard-won, and two-sided.

So, how do we move from out of the parent–toddler phase, in which we are the toddler and our machines the parent? Design for attunement. Just as we reveal information about ourselves to the various devices in our lives, our tech needs to reveal to us what it knows and how it works. Ongoing transparency with room for human agency is the only ethical way to become attuned.

Tech mediates human-to-human attunement already. Strava lets us share our routes, the Hug Shirt transmits an embrace using sensors and a mobile app, the Internet Tea Pot conveys an elderly person's routines to a family member. To develop human–tech attunement, we need to develop that same level of progressive trust.

4. (Healthy) Attachment

Shared experience builds relationships over time. Developing rituals around the relationship can contribute, too. At some point in the not-so-far-off future, some bots and devices will develop convincing empathy by detecting, interpreting, and adapting to human emotions. If the relationship evolves over time, like a healthy human relationship, we can get to positive attachment. Not over-reliance, in which there's a power imbalance, but instead an emotionally durable coexistence.

5. (Sustainable) Relationship

After we attach, that's not the end of things. Relationships change in all kinds of ways over time. Think of the rare 50-year marriage or the unusual friendship that started at school and somehow survived to a 20-year college reunion. Then, think of all the relationships that didn't last. When long-term relationships fail, it's often because a change becomes untenable to one or both (or more) people. On the other hand, successful long-term relationships adapt to accommodate change. Right now, machines are not nimble enough to adapt to us over time while helping us to grow. But, on a good day, I think we'll get to this place.

These phases of a relationship are big picture. There are frustrations and triumphs, challenges and reconciliations, small gestures for maintenance and grand efforts at revival. Some friendships are constrained to a certain context or role; others expand beyond that. Friendships can be intense and then wane and then flare up again or disappear entirely. You might be attracted to people (or machines) like you, or you might seek out opposite but complementary traits. These phases are only a starting point for framing human–machine relationships.

For now, most human–machine relationships barely make it to the second phase. The reasons are complicated. One key reason is that we simply aren't thinking about a long-term relationship, so let's train our human vision on relationship milestones first.

UNDERSTAND MILESTONES AND MOMENTS

Recently, I led a workshop designing cars that care, or autonomous cars that know a bit about our emotions. Cars make an interesting study with which to understand human–machine relationships. Maybe it's because I grew up in the Motor City with lots of family working in the auto industry. Maybe it's just because I like epic road trips despite bouts of motion sickness. But I suspect it's because cars are liminal spaces, between home and work, day and night, personal and public.

Cars, at least in American culture, mark big milestones, too. When you get your license, you get your first old beater. A cross-country move might mean saying goodbye to a car. A new job with a commute often means a new car as well. Having children? Children leaving home? Those occasions are marked with cars, too. Even as we move away from single ownership, this may hold true.

If we are thinking about relationships, these big milestones define the relationship. Introductions, a cross-country move, a new driver, and saying goodbye are the big moments. It's small moments, too, like a bad day or a stressful commute or when the car messes up. It's routines like a daily commute. To give these milestones the attention they richly deserve, I've taken advantage of a few techniques, with a twist.

Relationship timeline

A journey might not be the right framework for a long-term relationship. Plus, it's much easier to see the shape of a journey in retrospect. Looking back on a period in your life, it's easier to make sense of it. It ends up as a story with beginning, middle, and end. The implications seem clear in hindsight. The goals seem obvious. Relationships, when viewed in retrospect, shape us, but while we're living them it's quite a different story. So, a timeline should be flexible.

In workshops, I introduce the adaptation of Knapp's relational model as a starting point. You can simply go with what you know from interviews or other research, too. Discuss how you'll handle key moments in the relationship and how these might evolve over time. Here are a few questions to get started:

- What will we know about each other before we meet?
- How will each actor get to know the other?
- How will each show that it knows the other?
- When will you introduce each other to new people?
- What will change over time? What should stay the same?
- How is trust lost and regained?
- How much should interests grow together—or remain separate?

After you've covered some basics, next move on to the milestones. These are the common relationship builders or busters associated with life events.

Eight milestones

The *crazy-eight technique*, a workshop staple, is easy to adapt for sketching relationship moments. Dividing sheets of paper into eight sections, describe eight relationship milestones. Staying with our car example, maybe it's the first time you picked up a friend in the car or the first time you had a fender bender.

If you have each member of a group creating their own crazy-eight sketches in a workshop setting, have the group come together to discuss the most common milestones and the most unusual. At first, focus on only a few of what will invariably be many possibilities. The impulse will be to find common threads, and this isn't necessarily negative. But I'd encourage looking for extremes and edges, too. Don't stop at just those few; come back later. This relationship is a living thing, which you'll revisit often as circumstances change and new paradigms arise.

After you agree on a few milestones, the group can begin to develop each in more detail. Consider the following:

- Who is a part of this milestone?
- What objects are associated with the milestone?
- What emotions characterize it?
- Are rituals associated with the milestone?
- What forms of expression are acceptable?
- What range of behaviors are associated with the milestone?

When you have a few milestones identified, you'll notice that these aren't just events that happen. They have the potential to change the relationship. That's why you should look at crucible moments next.

Crucible moments

A crucible moment is a defining moment that shapes our identity or worldview or relationship. Often prompted by challenging events like a demanding job, a prolonged illness, a military deployment, or the death of a loved one, these moments are more than that. They are moments of transformation. The crucible moment is a clarifying one, a sudden epiphany or a gradual realization that transforms.

Often crucible moments are associated with milestones. For instance, you might think about the time when you got your first ticket. That's a milestone. But then there's the time when you received two speeding tickets in one day (just theoretically speaking, of course), which led to a change of heart. You (by which I mean me) decided to consciously adopt a more accepting attitude toward being late. That realization, whether made in a puddle of tears at the side of the Garden State Parkway or lying awake in the middle of the night, is a crucible moment.

Now maybe your product doesn't actively participate in that crucible moment. Or maybe it suggests a coping strategy or enhances a small triumph or facilitates awareness. If we are truly designing for emotion, the point is that we care about understanding these moments. Crucible moments, because they are in the mind and in the heart, won't be observable in the data. Empathetic listening is the only way.

Boundary check

Milestones help us build trust and cement bonds. Crucible moments are those moments when product and person come together in a meaningful way. Boundaries can be just as important. Boundaries are the limits we set for ourselves and, in this case, our tech. They protect our sense of personal identity and help guard against being overwhelmed. A few questions to consider as we plot out this relationship would be the following:

- How will you disagree?
- What will you call each other?
- What kinds of interactions are okay and not okay?
- How will you ask for consent?
- How will you know if you continue to have consent?
- What you will share and not share with each other?
- How often will you communicate?

As in every other aspect of our relationship, boundaries are likely to shift over time. Absolutes often as do boundaries that are too vague. Setting boundaries means being specific and direct. Clearly communicating what data is used and how it's used is a start. Giving people agency to set boundaries and reevaluate from time to time is a given for a healthy relationship, with other humans or with tech.

BUILD CIVIC CONNECTION

You'll likely notice that many of the relationship models are focused on making only one person comfortable. Personal assistants, virtual butlers, and bot companions focus on just one person as the center of the universe. The danger is that we create narcissistic products and services, where individuals are insulated from the world with their needs always central and their beliefs always validated. Filter bubbles are just the first manifestation we're seeing.

What if we challenged ourselves to think about the consequences of this approach? Rather than creating one-way relationships in which the machine is a servant anticipating one person's needs, solving that individual's problems, and making them feel good, we need to design for *less* isolation and narcissism. Here are a couple of techniques to try.

Shifting centers

One way to do this is by shifting the primary focus. First, put your individual in the center. Add the bot as a node. Then, begin to fill in the other aspects of the network (Figure 4-9). If we are talking about an autonomous car, perhaps we have the driver or primary owner/renter at the center. The car is a node. Next, we consider passengers: adults and kids, close friends and awkward dates, relatives and relative strangers. Following that, we add other people who share the vehicle, if it's not owned by one person or core group. Finally, add other drivers on the road.

Now move the center. Shift to focus on one of the other nodes in this network. Give that person, or organization or community, the same attention as you would the primary user. Look at how the priorities in both the long term and short term change. Consider how to balance the needs of that primary user with other actors in the network.

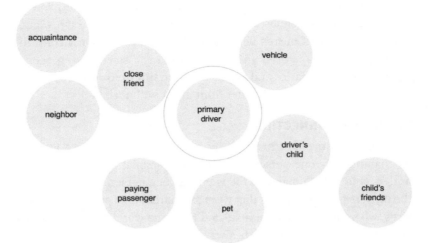

FIGURE 4-9

The circle whose center is everywhere and circumference is nowhere

The network effect

Let's borrow from the principle of emotional contagion for this exercise. Using the same network diagram, list the emotions associated with the one (or two) primary actors for one scenario or one aspect of the experience. Then, start to consider how those emotions might move through the network. Suppose that a car showed care by taking over if the driver becomes sleepy, and the driver felt relief and gratitude. How do those emotions affect passengers? Does it have an indirect effect on the emotional climate of the roadway? Of a city?

Device narration

Role playing from another perspective can sometimes end up hurtful, so this activity takes a cue from social and emotional learning (SEL) prompts. Write a stream-of-consciousness narrative from the device's perspective for a typical day. People talk to their cars. People already lend a voice to their Roombas or treat Alexa as a member of their family. So, this activity comes readily and reveals the quirks, the irritations, and the most beloved aspects of the relationship.

By thinking in terms of networks and giving other actors in the network a voice, we can begin to better understand implications. Rather than creating an emotionally satisfying experience to just one person, we can start to think about the larger social impact.

MAKING IT LEGIBLE

When Google first debuted Duplex making a hair appointment, it didn't reveal that it was a bot to the caller on the other end. With umms and pauses and uptalk, the chatbot caught everyone off guard by seeming just a little too human. By design, it seemed to use quirks like "I gotcha" and "mm-hmm" so that the human on the other end would stay on the line to complete the call. Even if the script was changed, as Google indicates it will do, to something like, "Hi, uh, I'm the Google assistant and I'm calling to make an appointment," it might make people less likely to hang up as they would on any other robocall. I wonder what the humans on the other end of the call feel when they find out they've spoken with a bot.

Bots that try to pass as human have the real potential to manipulate emotion and damage trust. If technology cheapens relationships, tricks us, makes us lose our trust so that we don't know what to believe, it will damage our future selves and our human relationships. And it won't achieve the kind of meaningful role that technology can play in our lives.

A more honest approach might remind us that these devices are actors with human characteristics. Woebot, a cognitive behavioral therapy bot, can be a good model (Figure 4-10). Even though Woebot does seem to remember when you felt anxious, it counteracts that impression by noting what it can't do. By way of introduction, it notes that it "helps that I have a computer for a brain and a perfect memory...with a little luck I may spot a pattern that humans can sometimes miss."

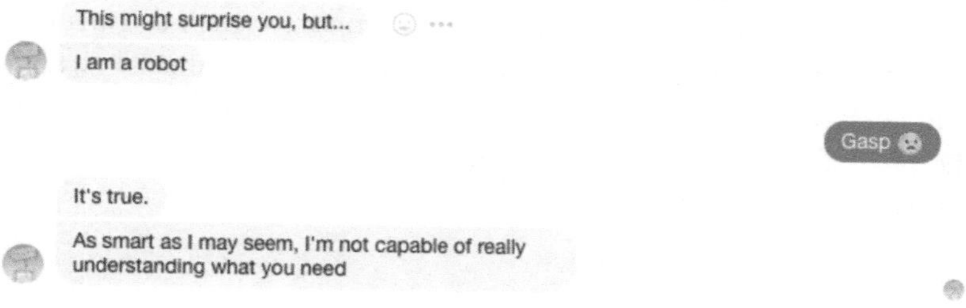

This might surprise you, but...

I am a robot

Gasp

It's true.

As smart as I may seem, I'm not capable of really understanding what you need

FIGURE 4-10
The best bot is an honest bot (source: Woebot)

Humanizing technology is not so much about creating a realistic character or anthropomorphizing bots. Humanizing means giving *our relationship* more human characteristics by cultivating trust so that our interests gradually align, continue with respect, and change together.

Avoiding Automating Humans

Machines are becoming more human-like. Chatbots are going off script, learning with each interaction how to communicate with greater nuance. Robots are using facial recognition to detect signs of emotion in people. At least one robot, Sophia of Hanson Robotics, has been granted citizenship.

Humans are changing, too, in ways we barely register. Tech introduced anonymity into our interactions pre-internet, of course. The fast-food drive-thru makes it easy to forget that we are speaking to a human on the other side of a static-y microphone, so it seems "natural" to bark out orders. Twitchy habits like repetitively hitting refresh are hard to shake. Adjusting your speech to make sense to Alexa or Siri is a given. Let's face it, in some ways, we are becoming a bit more machine-like.

AUTOMATIC FOR THE PEOPLE

Most people wish for more ways to save time and emotional energy. Whether you are slammed at work, or a sleep-deprived new parent, or simply living life as a busy, busy human, there's only so much of you to go around. Wouldn't it be great to have a little help? That's almost the definition of most of our tech today.

Do Not Pay is a legal chatbot that helps people challenge parking tickets and claim compensation for flights. Companies such as Narrative Science can replicate some of the work of human journalists.[10] Arterys can perform magnetic resonance imaging of blood flow through the heart faster than a human radiologist.[11] When AI partners with humans, the result can be feelings of competence.

---

10 Tom Simonite, "Robot Journalist Finds New Work on Wall Street," *Technology Review*, January 9, 2015.

11 Matt McFarland, "What Happens When Automation Comes for Highly Paid Doctors," *CNN Tech*, July 14, 2017.

Often, it's more complicated than that. When it comes to connections, we've tried to scale intimacy. Most of us have moved beyond the Dunbar number, or that sweet spot of 150 people that anthropologist Robin Dunbar says is the maximum number of stable relationships we can support. Keeping up with the constant connectivity does not come naturally.

Rather than culling relationships, we keep them. This means that we rely on automation to extend our reach because we don't have the bandwidth to support conversational depth. Sometimes it's transparent, or nearly so. I know that "personal" email newsletter isn't personal. I've learned that your LinkedIn invite is canned. No worries. It might not be too much of a stretch to get used to automated customer care conversations, after all.

But that certainly won't be the end of it; we like easy, and the connections keep coming. The more we streamline, the more we stand to lose in our relationships. MIT professor Sherry Turkle explains, "Getting to know other people, appreciating them, is not necessarily a task enhanced by efficiency."[12] We try anyway, though. Cut-and-paste platitudes, canned email templates, and predictive emojis make our communication go more smoothly. More and more of our interactions are automated, with a hint of authenticity (Figure 4-11). Tech ethicist David Polgar refers to it as "botifying" humans.

Soon enough, we might be tempted to automate more communication. Think about Facebook's compilation videos presenting friendship slideshows, likely chosen for how much you've reacted to one another's posts. They evoke intimacy while aiming to provoke engagement. It's a glimpse of how the feelings we show can be conflated with the feelings we experience. Just as we lose the ability to navigate cities without GPS, we might begin to lose the ability to navigate our emotions.

---

12 Sherry Turkle, *Reclaiming Conversation: The Power of Talk in the Digital Age*, Penguin, 2015.

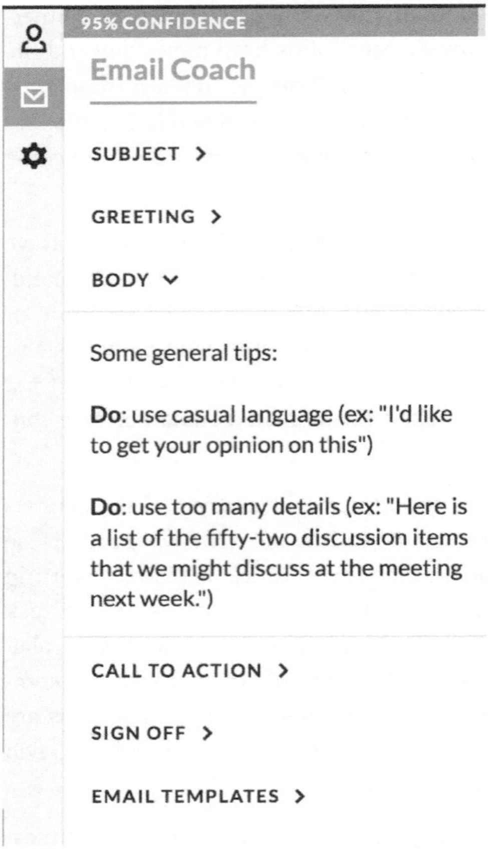

FIGURE 4-11
Better to coach than to automate (source: Crystal Knows)

How can we avoid driving humans to be more machine-like? Brett Frishman and Evan Selinger propose an inverse Turing test to determine to what extent humans are becoming indistinguishable from machines (*Re-Engineering Humanity*, Cambridge University Press, 2018). Perhaps we can test our designs prerelease for how much they might "botify" human identity and connections, those critical elements for our emotional well-being. Or, it might be a checklist like this:

- Is human-to-human communication replaced with human-to-machine or machine-to-human or machine-to-machine communication?

- Are human-to-human relationships being excessively streamlined?

- Are people compelled to speak in an oversimplified manner for extended periods of time?

- Is it unclear when people are communicating with a bot?

- Did the human consent to communication with or through a bot?

- Is an emotional relationship cultivated purely for the gain of the organization?

If you answered yes to any of these questions, you might just be mechanizing humans. Each answer opens up a world of ethical issues that the industry is confronting. Ethical implications aside, automating intimacy isn't likely to sustain relationships. Knowing that meaningful relationships are core to emotional well-being, it's clear that the more we automate ourselves, the less happy we'll be.

New Human–Machine Relationship Goals

IKEA's Space 10 future-living lab asked 12,000 people around the world how they might design AI-infused machines.[13] The results are a study in contradictions. Most people wanted machines to be more human-like than robot-like. At the same time, most still preferred obedience to other characteristics. People are paradoxical; it's one thing that makes us human, I suppose.

It's easy to debunk the survey. The questions offer simple, binary choices. Do you prefer "autonomous and challenging" or "obedient and assisting"? Um, no. Surveys, in general, don't offer the opportunity to think through implications or reflect on contradictions. We are simply humans, mechanically answering the questions put in front of us. Even so, the results show that "human" is the ultimate measure of success.

In our rush to humanize, though, we still don't fully understand what's human ourselves. We know human cognition is quite distinct from machine cognition. Human life, vulnerable to disease and possessed of innate instincts, is not mechanical. Human emotion is profoundly different from anything a machine can detect. Yet here we are, designing a new class of beings.

When people interact with a bot, they will form a relationship whether we design a personality or not. Rather than serving up a fully formed, light-hearted personality, we need to leave room for empathetic

---

13 IKEA Space10, "Do You Speak Human?" May 2017.

imagination. Rather than one-sided relationships, we'd do well to consider rewarding complexity. Rather than replicating humans, we can complement them.

For now, the list of household bots is short, but it will no doubt grow many times over. Within a decade, virtual and embodied bots will live among us, getting our coffee, teaching our children, driving us about. I hope they will also be engaging us in meaningful conversations, making us aware of our emotions, holding us true to our values. Maybe even writing beautiful poems or creating thought-provoking art.

If we design our bots with only an eye toward a function, we might be more productive. Or, conversely, have more leisure. But if we design them to be emotionally intelligent, we might just make progress in areas that are crucial to our human future—connection, care, and compassion.

[5]

Crafting Emotional Interventions

LIKE MANY PEOPLE WHO live in colder climates, I struggle with seasonal affective disorder. Having blown through some of the typical advice, like special lighting and fresh air, I was looking for something new. That's when I came across Koko, a crowdsourced approach to emotional well-being (Figure 5-1). Koko asks you to choose a topic of concern, like work or school or family, and to write your worries about a worst-case outcome. When you click "Help rethink this," your request goes out to a community. Community members—some trained in cognitive behavioral therapy techniques, some not—swipe through each card to see if they can help. It offers a few prompts like, "A more balanced take on this would be...," or, "This could turn out better than you think because...," for those who want to help. Comments are moderated in real time and an algorithm watches out for trigger words that can signal a need for a more serious intervention.

Accepting rethinks helped steer me away from dark thoughts. After a while, I began offering some advice when I felt I could. The app not only helped me build resilience by rethinking stressful situations as a helper, but offered a sense of empathetic community, too.

Koko is only one of many sleep trackers, therapist bots, anxiety coaches, and mood monitoring apps that help us pursue emotional well-being explicitly. Technology as a mental health intervention is becoming accepted practice. That makes sense because we know there's a lot we can do when it comes to designing our own happiness.

FIGURE 5-1

Crowdsourced
interventions create
an empathy buffer
(source: Koko)

Happiness is not all genetics, not even by half. There are about a million things you can do to be happier, but most of us don't do any of them. In *The How of Happiness* (Penguin, 2007), Sonja Lyubormirsky calls these intentional activities interventions: "In a nutshell, the fountain of happiness can be found in how you behave, what you think, and what goals you set every day of your life." Interventions can be a big dramatic break. More often, interventions are more like small changes that reframe our attitudes or actions. Activities that can shake us up a little so that we can feel a little bit happier every day.

In this chapter, we take a cue from the idea of interventions. In psychology, the concept spans *cognitive mediations* to *behavioral nudges*. Interventions are used in healthcare to prevent bad health-related behaviors and promote good ones. Interventions to prompt a psychological or social shift are already in wide use in architecture and urban design, too. Let's first look at how many of us try to craft our own interventions when it comes to tech use.

Strategies for Living Digital

Think about your day so far. <pause> I'll share mine. Maybe it will sound familiar. It's still early in the day. I've refreshed my Twitter feed more times than I can count, ultimately leading me to a review for a book I'd like to read, then over to Amazon to purchase that book, then to Goodreads to note that I started it. It helps me keep track, but someone might be interested. I briefly entertain a fantasy about the fascinating discussion we might have, inserting various people I know into the slot of potential readers.

Rather than diving in to reading the book right now—I have to get to writing, after all—I decide to get in touch with several friends from grad school to remind them of this author's first book, which we had discussed on Facebook at one point. It's been a while and I wonder what's happened to a former professor from those years. A quick Google stalking session later and I can breathe a sigh of relief—still alive! After checking email, naturally, I go upstairs and find the actual print copy on my bookshelf and set it on my desk. Time for a snack. I'm eager to try that smoothie I saw in my feed (ha!) and then I'll really be able to settle in for work.

Even as tech makers and internet evangelists, we feel conflicted. Is our time wasted or productive? Is technology addictive or creative? It feels like it can be both, but how to find the right balance? Perhaps we can learn from the strategies people use every day.

RULES AND TOOLS

Recently, I asked almost a thousand people to share their mantras or personal guidelines for using technology. They shared some internet truisms like "Don't read the bottom half of the internet" and some more forward-thinking ideas like "You shouldn't have to talk *like* a robot to talk *to* a robot" (which inspired the "speaking to a bot" experiment discussed in Chapter 2). By far, most of the mantras were about finding balance, like "One hour offline for every hour online." Anya Kamenetz, in her book *The Art of Screen Time: How Your Family Can Balance Digital Media and Real Life* (Public Affairs, 2018) sums it up neatly: "Enjoy screens. Not too much. Mostly with others."

People use a combination of rules and tools to live up to their personal guidelines. Apps that monitor time online or limit time on certain apps act as personal interventions. Plug-ins like OneTab that convert your tabs into a list, or simply choosing not to restore tabs when your browser crashes, is a sort of self-care. Low-tech rules for screen-free meals or detox weekends are even more common.

Beyond aspirational guidelines, we've developed coping mechanisms, too. We've had to. People are using Facebook to showcase suicides, beatings, and murder in real time. Twitter is rife with trolling and abuse. Fake news, whether created for ideology or profit, runs rampant. The internet loves extremes. A clickbait headline, a provocative post, a half-exposed image. People look, the algorithms are trained, and so the internet supplies more of that. To counter all these very real and negative feelings, we have emojis, memes, irony, and dark humor. And we duck for cover under anonymity and fake identities—so much so that there are more 18-year-old men on Facebook than there currently are on earth.

Certainly, people also push the limits of technology to make their own happiness. Witness the sublime creativity of Amazon reviews for Tuscan milk and Bic Pen for Her and horse masks (Figure 5-2). People will always subvert designed spaces, from street art to ASCII art. They will empty their cache to see if they get another 10 days free, set up real accounts to be fake and fake accounts to be real, and try any manner of workaround available. That's being human on the internet.

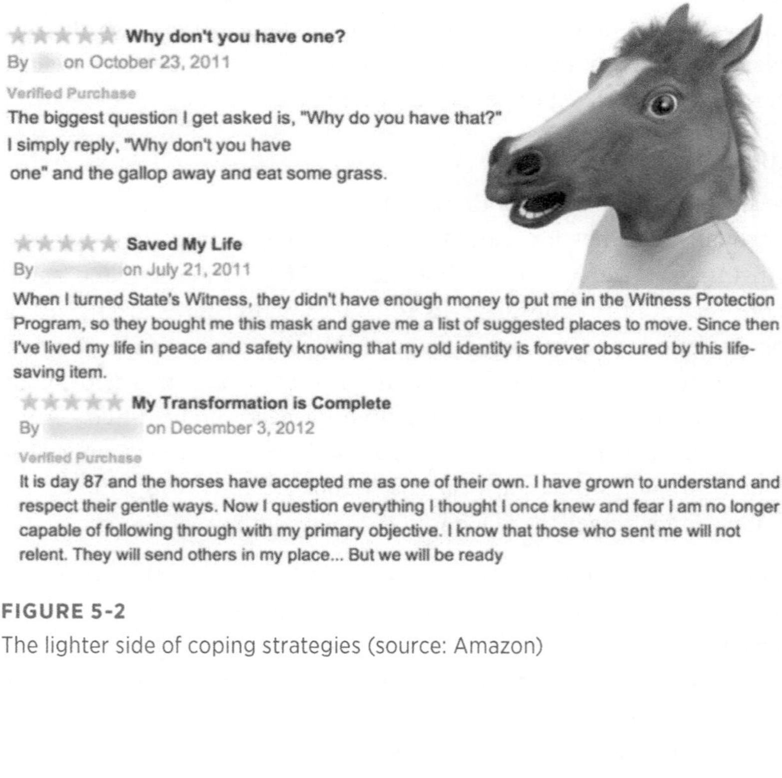

★ ★ ★ ★ ★ **Why don't you have one?**
By　 on October 23, 2011

Verified Purchase

The biggest question I get asked is, "Why do you have that?"
I simply reply, "Why don't you have
one" and the gallop away and eat some grass.

★ ★ ★ ★ ★ **Saved My Life**
By　　 on July 21, 2011

When I turned State's Witness, they didn't have enough money to put me in the Witness Protection Program, so they bought me this mask and gave me a list of suggested places to move. Since then I've lived my life in peace and safety knowing that my old identity is forever obscured by this life-saving item.

★ ★ ★ ★ ★ **My Transformation is Complete**
By　　 on December 3, 2012

Verified Purchase

It is day 87 and the horses have accepted me as one of their own. I have grown to understand and respect their gentle ways. Now I question everything I thought I once knew and fear I am no longer capable of following through with my primary objective. I know that those who sent me will not relent. They will send others in my place... But we will be ready

FIGURE 5-2

The lighter side of coping strategies (source: Amazon)

Sometimes we engage in a little magical thinking. Think about athletes' pregame routines or the elaborate sleep rituals weary parents try out for cranky babies. More often, magical thinking is an irrational response to gain a moment of control. In the context of technology, we see this in the ways that people try to game algorithms to adapt them. People might try to like a certain type of post, or delete old posts, create more posts, unfollow and refollow in an attempt to change what they see. When it doesn't work as expected, it can lead to feelings of futility.

Personal guidelines and finely tuned coping strategies get us only so far, though. It's fine to put responsibility on ourselves for how we choose to live with technology. But obviously, design should take some of the responsibility, too. Technology demands our attention in ways we don't always anticipate or intend. It requires emotional labor educating, placating, soothing people we know well and people we don't know at all. And it shapes our experience in ways we don't fully understand, so much so that we develop our own folk theories about how it all works, whether inside or outside the industry.

Individuals design interventions by setting ground rules for behavior or relying on coping strategies to get us through each day online. Interventions can also take place on a larger scale. *Nudges* are one of the ways sociologists, politicians, and economists have already tried.

JUST A LITTLE NUDGE

We slip up all the time. We eat the donut, we forget to take our medication, we don't save for retirement. Technology doesn't always help in that regard. Automated payments let us buy things a little too easily, games encourage kids to spend real money on virtual things friction-free, autoplay sets binge watching in motion. Until recently, most phones didn't even offer a driving mode to prevent us from killing ourselves by texting in our cars.

Nudges, a construct from behavioral economics, guide behavior toward better choices. A nudge, according to Richard Thaler and Cass Sunstein, is "any aspect of a choice architecture that alters people's behavior in a predictable way without forbidding any options or significantly changing their economic incentives."[1] The ideal nudge guides people to positive choices without eliminating choice altogether.

Better defaults, such as retirement accounts that minimize the effort toward participating and contributing, can help. Motivators that take advantage of social norms such as reciprocity, relatedness, or coherence are another common type of nudge. Badges, metrics, and motivational messages, like the Nest Leaf (Figure 5-3), reinforce positive behaviors without making you feel too bad when you slip up.

FIGURE 5-3
Wasted energy gathers no leaves (source: Nest)

Even so, nudges are tricky to employ. Nudges should be for the good of the individual rather than the good of the "choice architect," but with the pressure of super-fast growth, that balance is difficult to achieve. Nudges can be distasteful, such a highlighting an option for travel insurance that is nearly impossible to collect. Or they can be disastrous, like the mortgage industry encouraging people to take out loans they couldn't afford. Designers and developers find themselves caught between nudging for the good of the individual and nudging toward business goals all the time. Often, those two directions are at odds.

---

1 Richard H. Thaler and Cass R. Sunstein.,*Nudge: Improving Decisions about Health, Wealth, and Happiness*, Yale University Press, 2008.

Other complications abound. The good of the individual is always situated in a larger context of the good of society, and not all nudges are good for both. Then factor in the biases and quirks of the nudgers themselves. Who gets to decide what is a positive outcome? And how do we gather evidence that the outcome was indeed positive? And for whom? And, of course, we are famously bad at predicting outcomes. And outcomes are difficult to predict because systems are dynamic.

Well, that escalated quickly. But if we can set all that aside, perhaps there is something worthwhile. In truth, we must base our decisions on something, and those decisions will have an impact on well-being. Whether we actively create a nudge or not, stimuli are embedded in our environments already. If you look around, you'll not see much that hasn't been designed. Any designed object provides a script; we can avoid it or improvise, but the impact is real.

A nudge is one kind of behavior change intervention, often compensating for a deficit by relying on a deficit (usually, a cognitive bias). Interventions don't just guide us away from negatives, though. They can move us toward positives, too.

EMOTIONAL WELL-BEING INTERVENTIONS

Self-help books are full of ideas about what people can do to become happier, ranging from practical to cringe-worthy. It's only relatively recently that research has developed strategies with science behind them.

Psychology professor Sonja Lyubomirsky proposes 12 intentional activities, validated through extensive testing, to support well-being. These activities include expressing gratitude, cultivating optimism, avoiding social comparison, forgiving, savoring, and experiencing a flow state more often, among others.

Following this lead, the New Economics Foundation proposed five evidence-backed ways to support personal well-being: connect, be active, take notice, keep learning, and give. Likewise, mental health and emotional well-being apps like Happify apply interventions to boost well-being. Happify's STAGE model—Savor, Thank, Aspire, Give, and Empathize—supports activities in each of these core categories. These models aren't just created in a vacuum. Happify's model, for example, is backed by an exhaustive collection of research for each of the principles.

Interest in the idea of interventions is not limited to personal well-being, however. The design world has begun to create interventions as a way to amplify positive experiences. Sustainability consulting firm Terrapin Bright Green recently introduced patterns of *biophilic design*. The relationship between the built environment and nature can be developed to reduce stress and cultivate community. Knowing this, the firm identified patterns that can support the well-being, ranging from visual connection with nature to spaces that support refuge or inspire a sense of mystery.

Happy City, Charles Montgomery's consulting firm, uses lessons from psychology and public health to design happier cities. Dense, mixed-use, walkable spaces build trust and reinforce a sense of community. Apartment buildings with convivial common spaces, rather than computer rooms, build friendships. Building on these patterns, the firm's work takes the form of interventions, like pop-ups around a warm cup of cocoa to build neighborhood bonds, or one-day events to transform parking lots into green spaces or intersections into piazzas.

The Delft Institute of Positive Design, led by Anna Pohlmeyer and Pieter Desmet, features a long list of positive design interventions, from designing for mood regulation to savoring experience. In their book *Positive Computing: Technology for Well-Being and Human Potential* (MIT Press, 2014), Dorian Peters and Rafael Calvo suggest the idea of design interventions to support motivation, self-awareness, mindfulness, resilience, gratitude, empathy, compassion, and altruism.

Positive interventions make us happier in all kinds of ways—injecting creativity by stimulating the senses, enhancing agency over our environment, or prompting more meaningful social interactions. Whether clear prompts or subtle patterns, these interventions can be designed.

Interventions with EQ

Inspired by what I've observed in diaries, design dinner parties, and data, and illustrated with examples from my research, I've assembled interventions that roughly follow the tenets of emotional intelligence.

- Self-awareness (appreciation, self-compassion)
- Self-management (focus, flow, resilience)
- Self-catalyzing (motivation, creativity, hope)

- Social awareness (empathy, attunement, tolerance)
- Social skills (generosity, gratitude, forgiveness)
- Self-transcendence (wonder, compassion)

I'm cheating a bit by bundling together vital activities for the sake of brevity. This is not an exhaustive list. Many of the patterns overlap, because what is conducive to focus turns out to be critical to appreciation, or what is foundational to generosity evolves out of empathy. And not all of these activities are relevant to every experience.

So, what you'll find here is a mix. Be aware of the negatives and stop exploiting them. Employ nudges to compensate with caution. And use positive interventions to help people flourish.

Self-Awareness Interventions

Most of the time we're busy. We try to multitask. We aim to get things done. That means we aren't paying enough attention to the good things. The simple act of identifying something good and then appreciating it fills us with optimism, dampens our desires for more, and deepens our relationships with loved ones.[2] When we express our gratitude to someone, we get kindness and gratitude in return.

The internet is basically the opposite of "stop and smell the roses," though. Recency and speed are valued above all else—in how we interact and how we develop experiences. For instance, today's meme is listing 10 bands and then having your friends guess which one you haven't seen. Rather nice in that it strengthens relationships through appreciating a moment, often spent together. Too bad we will have long forgotten it by the time this book makes it to print.

It's not just the cult of the most recent, of course. The ephemeral quality of digital life works against appreciation. When was the last time you clicked through all the photos on your phone? The sheer number can make reviewing seem an insurmountable task. Many are not worth remembering in the first place (or maybe that's just me). Then there's social media feeds and news apps and the trail of abandoned technologies we leave behind.

---

2 Martin Seligman, "Empirical Validation of Interventions," *American Psychologist*, July–Aug 2005.

Yet, the ability to appreciate in all its forms—savoring the moment, engaging in rosy retrospection, and anticipating the future—is at the heart of happiness. Building emotional awareness through reflection prompts us to craft stories, make meaning, and form connections. Let's look at some design interventions to stimulate appreciation.

POSITIVE SELF-AWARENESS PATTERNS

Right now, design pays a lot of attention to in-the-moment experience. If we are thinking about emotion at all, it's likely to be how frustrated or happy people feel when they're directly engaged with the product or service. Interventions that spark appreciation would help us to savor a moment or expand its significance but also call up a memory or anticipate an event. Following are a few patterns to support positive self-awareness:

Memory prompts

Emotional memories build resilience. Regular immersion in our memories is a critical part of what can sustain and console us. We're always trying to make future decisions in the hope that it will make us happy, but your past has guaranteed points of happiness. Apps like TimeHop or Facebook's Memories attempt to prompt reminiscence. These apps work well as a way to turn remembering into a scalable, consumable, trackable product, but not so well for actual reminiscence. And, of course, they can go horribly wrong by reminding us of things we'd rather forget or just posts that weren't meant for remembering. The kernel of the idea, though, has potential, perhaps with more ways to control the prompts.

Digital–physical bridges

Bridging digital and physical cultivates awareness of both. Pokémon GO certainly seems to fit this pattern, not just by hiding objects to find, but by creating moments to discover new places and new people. Traces is another good example of a bridge. Traces is part messenger, part surprise-gifting service that lets people leave digital messages at physical locations for their friends to pick up with their smartphones.

Sensory burst

Activating the senses heightens awareness. The more stimuli we have to process, the more we pay attention. The new sights, sounds, and smells of a rich experience encourage us to savor. Experiences that engage the senses, especially in a world of screens, might encourage appreciation. Project Nourished's virtual reality (VR) dining experience, which combines a VR headset, aromatic diffuser, gyroscopic utensil, and 3D-printed food is an over-the-top example (Figure 5-4). Everyday sensory examples are games like Tinybop's Plants or TocaBoca's Toca Lab.

FIGURE 5-4
Virtual eating, real sense activation (source: Project Nourished)

Reflection points

Pauses that encourage us to take a moment to think, feel, or celebrate. We can probably think of silly examples of celebrating because it's a typical example of delight, like the burst of confetti when we finish a module on the Happify app. But it can be more than a quick burst: it can be a moment to reflect, too. For a time, LinkedIn's mobile app designed a way to review just a few status updates at a time and then build in a pause. Nike+ Run Club prompts runners to reflect on their run with pictures and notes. Even slowing down to take a picture of your food on Instagram has been found to help people enjoy their meal more.[3] Perhaps in the future, we should be prompted to pause more often.

---

3   Claudia McNeilly.,"The Psychological Case for Instagramming Your Food," *The Cut*, March 7, 2016.

Happy trails

Anticipating a happy endpoint builds appreciation. Endings are rare in our experience of tech. Back in 2014, when I was really starting in earnest to test new ways of understanding experience, one activity I tried was to have people draw what they remembered of a favorite website or app. You would think it would be easy to roughly sketch something you use all the time. But people didn't remember that much besides buttons and checkboxes. And most people drew the beginning of the experience. Hundreds of times over, even with different prompts, like "draw what you remember" or "draw what's most important," I got app icons and home pages, as illustrated in Figure 5-5.

FIGURE 5-5
All beginnings and no endings

We are missing endings, and that's a shame when it comes to appreciation. We are more apt to remember endings. The snapshot model of memory, developed by Barbara Frederickson and Daniel Kahneman, tells us that people judge the entirety of an experience by prototypical moments, privileging the peak and the end. Often there isn't a marked ending to many tech experiences, but when there is an ending it's often a low. Paying for a purchase, rating a driver, and even being asked to share are closure experiences, benefit of the business more than an individual or a community. How else can we try to create happy endings?

Surprises such as a discount code or a donation, especially when they aren't contingent on a share or a like, can create a positive last impression. Even when we simply imagine something coming to an end, we are better able to appreciate it, too. IKEA Place, the augmented reality app that helps you to place the furniture in a room and build it, builds positive anticipation of a projected ending. Thinking more broadly about endings might help us when it comes to appreciation.

Because many of our experiences don't have clear endings, we instead can reinforce happy associations. For example, Intercontinental Hotels Group launched an iPad app that gives guests the chance to re-create their favorite meals. Booking.com shows you your next potential destination, so that if you are spending two days in Lisbon, Porto might be your next destination. Maybe beginnings are the new endings.

SELF-AWARENESS ANTIPATTERNS

Positive interventions help us to develop a new appreciation for both the novel and the mundane, which can cultivate self-awareness. On the flip side, experiences that cycle us through the same experience, again and again, numb us to appreciation. Here are some examples:

Ludic loops

An action linked with an intermittent, variable reward leads to thoughtless repetition. The ludic loop lulls you into a state in which you are perfectly content to do the same thing over and over again. Anthropologist Natasha Dow Schüll, in her book *Addiction by Design: Machine Gambling in Vegas* (Princeton University Press, 2012), first identified this pattern when studying how people become entranced by slot machines in Las Vegas. Pulling to refresh your Twitter feed, swiping on Tinder to see whether you got a match, and obsessively opening up Instagram to see if you got more likes are all examples of interactions that work on the same principle as a slot machine. Cycling through apps, moving repetitively from Twitter to Medium to email, would certainly qualify too.

Metrification

Reducing all the key parts of the experience to numbers feels mechanical. There's no question that counting steps or tracking sleep can have health benefits. At the same time, it can encourage us to be perpetually dissatisfied. In his book, *Irresistible: The Rise of*

Technology and the Business of Keeping Us Hooked (Penguin, 2017), Adam Alter calls this metrification. We aim to beat our last goal. We head outside for another quick walk to make our quota for the day. We constantly crave more followers or likes. We compete with ourselves and with everybody else. It's a game that's impossible to win. It can motivate, but it can also mechanize.

Successful self-awareness interventions slow down time to let us reflect on ourselves and enjoy the good qualities of life. Sensory engagement, mixed emotion, and novel experience help get us to that place. But being aware of yourself and your experiences is only one aspect of emotional intelligence. After we're aware, we need to find ways to regulate emotional life.

Self-Management Interventions

Our attention is a scarce resource, and yet every app, every website, every device demands its share. Our experience of technology is about much more than time, it's about creativity and adaptability and meaning making. Even so, we should look at how we spend attention. The ability to focus is closely tied to emotional well-being. From Linda Stone's work on task switching, to Mihaly Csikszentmihalyi's concept of flow to Cal Newport's writing on *deep work*, a similar principle holds true. This might explain the recent interest in mindfulness and how it relates to technology use.

Mindfulness, or the practice of present-moment focus and awareness, has been linked to reducing stress, enjoying greater life satisfaction, and making wiser decisions. Mind wandering can detract from happiness—there is research aplenty on that, most notably by Matthew Killingsworth.[4] The idea behind modern mindfulness training is that we can decrease stress and increase well-being by changing our relationship to an experience.

Mindfulness is often touted as the antidote to technology overuse. There is no shortage of books devoted to applying mindfulness to technology, whether using technology to become more mindful or using it in a mindful way. From Wisdom 2.0 conferences to focus apps like

---

4   Matthew Killingsworth and Daniel T. Gilbert, "A Wandering Mind Is an Unhappy Mind," *Science*, November 2010.

Forest (Figure 5-6) to digital detoxes, the idea of being more mindful of our use of technology is starting to take hold. What if we could factor some of that thinking into the creation of technology?

FIGURE 5-6
Focus or the tree dies (source: Forest)

POSITIVE SELF-MANAGEMENT PATTERNS

Interaction Design 101 says that good design removes friction. We smooth out the rough edges of experience so that there is little possibility of failure. Smart products learn about us, recognizing patterns in our behaviors to anticipate our next move. The goal is to save time and effort.

Frictionless design can be overwhelming, though. As designers, we need to pay attention to this yearning for *mental whitespace*. Just as design whitespace gives us the space to focus while looking at printed page, mental whitespace encourages us to pay attention to our own thoughts and feelings. Only with the space to reflect and synthesize can we get creative and make ideas our own. A few patterns follow:

Optimal stops

Endpoints that are inserted into a process can get us back on track. We don't have time to process our experience. As a counterpoint, some experiences are building in pauses. For instance, Etsy tested infinite scroll and found it left people feeling lost. People needed a boundary to mentally sort through results. Medium doesn't rely on a feed; there's a finite number of posts on the landing page.

The Quartz mobile app reveals a finite number of stories per day (Figure 5-7) and lets people choose how much detail they want for each story, allowing individuals to pace themselves.

FIGURE 5-7

Go in-depth or just get the gist (source: Quartz)

Speed bumps

Intentionally slowing people down keeps them focused on the task at hand. Sometimes, a little friction can be a focus intervention. A speed bump might minimize risk. In a sign-up or payment process, this takes the form of a confirmation dialog. It might also prevent a mistake, the way touch ID prevents an accidental purchase on your phone. A speed bump might delay an action so that you can reconsider, too.

Summary views

A synopsis so that you can decide whether to go further. Think about Twitter's While You Were Away feature. Rather than feeling frantic about catching up after being away for a day (or the last few hours), this summary gives us the opportunity to decide whether we have caught up or truly want to spend more time. Better still would be a way to understand and shape what we are shown as a summary, whether through a simple rating as we go along or a setting that we are prompted to revisit every so often.

Do not disturb

> *A feature that lets you check out for a while or detects when you are likely to want to do so.* Plenty of standalone apps, like Offtime, have been introduced to help us focus for a while by tuning out tech-based distractions. Still other apps such as Slack have a Do Not Disturb mode that you can select as needed—kind of a descendent of email vacation notices. Apple recently added Driver Mode to iOS 11, as shown in Figure 5-8, detecting when you might be driving to automatically mute notifications.

FIGURE 5-8
A time-out, for our own good (source: Apple)

These techniques can give us the mental whitespace to interpret, understand, and add meaning to our experiences. Each involves our attention in a thoughtful way, potentially deepening engagement. This runs counter to current design practices to minimize friction. Rather than prompting people to constantly seek out what's new and what's next, focus techniques draw attention inward. By giving people room to make meaning, the experience potentially becomes more memorable.

SELF-MANAGEMENT ANTIPATTERNS

There are all kinds of antipatterns designed to hijack our attention. Rather than the dark patterns for signups and sales, these patterns are most often found on social media and other experiences fueled by advertising. The following are fairly well known:

Bottomless bowls

Visual cues that transform a finite experience into an endless one. This type of design pattern gets its name from an experiment in which participants were seated at a table, four at a time, to eat soup. The participants did not know that two of the four bowls were attached to a tube underneath the table which slowly, and imperceptibly, refilled those bowls. Those eating from the "bottomless" bowls consumed more than those eating from the normal bowls. Although the research itself has now come under scrutiny, the pattern is still relevant here. If the internet is our soup, the bottomless bowls are features like infinite scroll on newsfeeds and autoplay on Netflix and YouTube.

Cliffhangers

Any feature that compels us to continue out of curiosity about what's next. Cliffhangers are not exclusively digital, of course. A cliffhanger is a plot device that ends with a precarious situation. Combine cliffhangers with full seasons released at once and autoplay, and it's increasingly difficult to come up for air. Not that binge watching is always bad, but it would be better if we felt like it was our decision. Clickbait headlines and cleverly situated images in feeds, in which only part of the image is shown, work in the same way, turning intense curiosity from a positive into a negative.

As product designers and developers, it makes sense for us to take a hard look at how we design for attention. We should lift some of that responsibility from people who are trying to live their lives without putting technology on hold. These focus detractors make it easy for people to spend more time than they might intend to do. Minimizing the use of those design patterns will certainly help to restore focus.

Focus has been the main focus of digital mindfulness, digital well-being, and other related movements. That's a good start, but there is more to emotional well-being than giving us back our time to focus. We also need to be creatively engaged in our lives.

Self-Catalyzing Interventions

Daniel Goleman's model of emotional intelligence includes motivation as a facet. Rather than thinking about motivating people to buy or spend more time, let's look at ways design might encourage people to self-motivate. Creativity is one way to do that.

POSITIVE SELF-CATALYZING PATTERNS

Creativity might not be the first thing that comes to mind when you think of emotional well-being. Research tells us otherwise. Creativity is an act of self-discovery that gives us a feeling of competence. Creativity motivates us to learn and explore. Creativity involves a mix of intense positive and negative emotions—another hallmark of well-being. Most of all, creativity aligns with a deeply meaningful life.

From doodling to knitting to playing a musical instrument, creative engagement contributes to the upward spiral that is characteristic of happiness where one positive builds and expands on another. Great news for me. Now I can justify my obsessions with theme parties, bespoke Halloween costume design, and absurd collections of miniature objects and partially broken toy parts perfect for dioramas and speculative design workshops. But does it apply to technology?

The diaries of highs and lows that started this journey say "yes"; creativity is key. Even though it's not surprising that people wanted to feel smart and respected, the role of creativity was a little unexpected but consistently evident. Not creativity with a capital C, such as writing bestselling novels and devoting oneself to critically acclaimed art, but anything from sharing microfiction on Twitter to creating a cosplay board on Pinterest to crafting a creative Amazon review.

After reviewing hundreds of these examples, I found that certain websites stand out as bastions of creativity—Tumblr, the dearly departed Vine, Reddit, YouTube, and Twitter. No matter the site, some patterns emerge. It turns out that how technology nurtures creative engagement is not so different from creativity in other contexts. Here are a few ways to cultivate creativity through design:

Constraints

> *Boundaries produce boundless thinking.* Research on gaming illustrates that tough obstacles prompt people to open their minds to the big picture and make connections between things that are not

obviously connected. It's called global processing, a key characteristic of creativity. So as much as people might complain about the 280-character limit on Twitter, it prompts creative workarounds. Likewise for Vine's 6-second clips. A good constraint outlines the right number of choices to get started as well as rules to work against.

Identity controls

Creativity flourishes when we can be flexible about identity. Identity is a kind of slider: we move from being anonymous to playing a role to being true to ourselves all the time. And creativity flourishes when people have control over their identity. Although people can feel creative in a variety of contexts online, creative expression peaks when we aren't tied down to a "real" identity. Bitmoji, for example, encourages people to craft personal stories (Figure 5-9). That's probably why Facebook isn't the center of creativity; it's where we share creative ideas that came from Twitter or Tumblr.

FIGURE 5-9

A balance of freedom and control (source: Snap)

Shifting meaning in new contexts is a creative act. It's that heady mix of conflict, clash, and divergence that inspires a fresh approach. Whether quotation, commentary, parody, or homage, remixing is a way to make sense of culture and put our own imprint on it. Reframing to produce a fresh perspective on the source or context was around long before the internet. Remixing has been traced from Shakespeare to Marcel Duchamp's L.H.O.O.Q. to Kutiman's *Mix the City*, all the way to Kermit memes (Figure 5-10) and reblogging on Tumblr.

FIGURE 5-10
You're probably skipping this section, but that's none of my business (source: Know Your Meme)

Chronological feeds

Progression builds reinvention. When remix and dialogue is fundamental to creativity, well, chronology matters. To share and build off of one another, people need to see the progression. Personalized feeds, news, products, and videos make it more difficult to see the evolution and put your own twist on it. Of course, the other problem is that experience driven by algorithms is geared toward our past behaviors, ideas, and tastes. That can limit creativity as well.

SELF-CATALYZING ANTIPATTERNS

Creative engagement follows four stages: preparation, incubation, illumination, and verification. Online, maybe it looks something like this: you see a friend's post about Prince and then move on to Wikipedia for a timeline of the artist's life, you listen to your favorite song, you hear something unique and new, and you get the urge to pull together a new playlist on Spotify. We can amp up this process with some of the positive interventions. We can also detract from creativity, if we begin pulling apart this process. Here are a few detractors:

Misplaced automation

> *Filling in the blanks discourages creative thinking.* Autocomplete isn't all that bad when you are filling out a form with repetitive details like address or phone number, but when it comes to autocomplete for comments, images, messages, and emojis, not so much. Automated prompts, when overused, curtail creative communication.

Filter bubbles

> *Limited exposure equals limited creativity.* Personalization has its downsides. Google shows dramatically different search results based on our behaviors and other data, whether you're logged in or not. Facebook's algorithm tailors your newsfeed based on the posts you like and who you interact with, creating a de facto inner circle. It narrows our perspective, producing echo chamber effect. Rather than helping us feel more creative, the result can be the opposite.

Without exposure to broader inspiration from the outside world, creativity languishes. Despite the discomfort of stepping away from what you know, exposure to new ideas sparks questions. Of course, we can unfollow people who are too much like ourselves, talk to strangers, and volunteer. But our designs can support this, too. Buzzfeed added a feature called Outside Your Bubble, shown in Figure 5-11, which gives you a glimpse of what other people are posting and thinking. Although designed to expand our thinking politically, it also can inspire new ideas in other contexts.

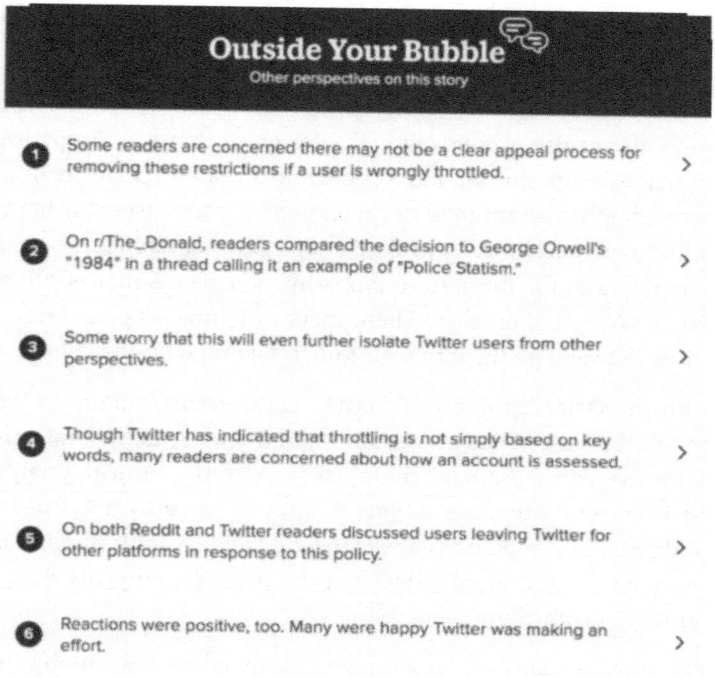

FIGURE 5-11

Better for our creativity and for our culture (source: Buzzfeed)

Despite the general consensus that the internet is killing creativity, technology doesn't need to be that way. Patterns that maximize curiosity, serendipity, and flexible identity can cultivate creativity in any context, motivating us to make our own meaning. Many of the patterns that cultivate creativity intersect with patterns for rapport, tolerance, and empathy, too.

Social Awareness Interventions

In most models of emotional intelligence, social awareness—empathy—is central. Empathy is ultimately an act of imagination. It means viewing the world from another perspective and using that understanding to guide our actions. Considering that relationships are the underpinning of a good life, empathy is enormously important.

Yet we hear conflicting research about empathy. Empathy is waning in young people, a development attributed to the smartphone with varying levels of shrill urgency. Then again, empathy might not be that great anyway according to Paul Bloom (*Against Empathy: The Case for Rational Compassion* [Ecco, 2016]), leading us to prioritize the needs of one person rather than thinking about the greater good.

The arguments are also playing out in the design community. Empathy, foundational to design thinking, has come into question. There are limits to how each of us, working in our own bubble, can reasonably hope to empathize with such a wide range of people. Ethnographic research, our go-to approach for immersive empathy, is a phase that is often skimmed or skipped altogether. Then, there's the uneasy place empathy occupies between going with your gut and going with the data.

I'll go with the Dalai Lama on this issue. Let's reaffirm the need for empathy, of all kinds. What we need now, and always, is understanding, perspective, kindness, and compassion. Affective empathy helps synchronize us with other's emotions. Cognitive empathy helps us to be less judgmental. Empathy is a way toward well-being. It has a real impact on physical and mental health. Even more so, empathy is the underpinning of community.

Although empathy can come naturally to many of us, few among us have reached our empathetic potential. Certainly, we try to cultivate our own empathy as designers, mostly through research. So, how can we design technology to better facilitate empathy among others?

POSITIVE SOCIAL-AWARENESS PATTERNS

Because strong relationships are so critical to happiness, there's no shortage of inquiry into how to cultivate empathy and compassion. A few patterns emerge:

Conversational depth

More time spent in meaningful conversation translates to empathetic understanding. People who engage in discussion about the state of the world and the meaning of life seem to be happier than those who spend their time talking about the weather. It might seem counterintuitive. I mean, staying on the shiny surface could seem less troubling than plumbing existential depths. Because humans have such a strong drive to create meaning and connect with other people, however, substantive conversation does contribute to our sense of well-being.

Conversational depth relies on a push and pull between discovery and synthesis, seeking and coherence. A good conversation is open-ended, emotionally resonant, and distraction-free. And it requires time. Sherry Turkle writes in *Reclaiming Conversation: The Power of Talk in the Digital Age* (Penguin, 2015) about the informal seven-minute rule—that it takes seven minutes for a conversation to unfold.

Conversely, many of our tech-mediated conversations seem built for shallow interactions. Whereas Slack is useful for a quick check-in, it's not great for a sustained conversation; the same goes for other social platforms for which staying in touch, rather than the quality of the conversation, is the endgame. Conversation online suffers not only from a lack of undivided attention and lack of emotional cues, but also from cognitive distortions unique to internet experience. The performative aspect of conversation is inflated on social platforms, too. The sense that you are speaking to an audience changes the tone of the conversation.

We can certainly choose to use social media in a way that supports conversational depth. I use birthdays, the only chronological aspect of the experience, as a reminder to engage in conversation. Many people use FaceTime or Skype to have a conversation, so much so that the American Association of Pediatricians have given the greenlight to video-chat apps at any age. Quora, despite its Q&A format, gets close to this sometimes. However, we could also build technology toward meaningful understanding as opposed to gathering information or broadcasting a message or quickly checking in.

Engaged presence

Engaged presence nurtures affiliation. Whether you're phubbing your colleagues on a video chat or surreptitiously picking up your phone at the dinner table, something about the current design of our favorite technology discourages presence. And yet we know from years of research that engaged presence is what sustains relationships.

For a time, I engaged in a little data collection project in which I sketched people looking at their devices in public places like airports, school concerts, and doctor's offices. I learned two important things: people are not looking at their devices as much as we think they are and many people are happily passing devices between them. Couples, and kids especially, seemed to enjoy a kind of copresence.

Maybe this is where we follow the teens' leads. Some of the most popular apps teens use are geared toward engaged presence. Houseparty is a current favorite in my house to host real-time group chats (Figure 5-12). As much as we might like to complain about Snap or Kik, they can underpin creative, engaged, and, yes, even sustained conversations. Airtime is just one of many new apps springing up that let people share photos, videos, and music in a video chat.

FIGURE 5-12

Conversation isn't dead, it's just shifted (source: Houseparty)

Leaky community

In urban design, well-being emerges from mixed-use blocks. Rather than blank stretches of big-box stores, researchers find that people are more likely to have casual conversation and spend time together when there is a lot of variety. William Whyte discovered, through time-lapse observation, that people cluster around busy entrances rather than isolated corners. When it comes to neighborhoods, people prefer a bit of a jumble.

Whether you call it weak ties or consequential strangers, these porous spaces reinforce empathy at a community level. Pokémon GO faded fast from our collective consciousness, but the most lasting and genuine aspect of its success was as a bridge between neighbors. Suddenly, kids were hanging out in their neighborhood with other kids. People welcomed new visitors to their neighborhood haunts. Similarly, CNA Speaking Exchange pairs Brazilian students with seniors at Windsor Park Retirement Community in Chicago. The program is dual purpose: help students learn English and bring conversation into the lives of the elderly in the United States.

Divergent perspectives

Exposing people to different perspectives can cultivate greater tolerance. In social psychology, the *contact hypothesis* shows that prejudice is reduced through extended contact with people who have different backgrounds, opinions, and cultures than our own. Developed by psychologist Gordon Allport as a way to understand discrimination, it is widely seen as one of the most successful tools for increasing empathy.

KIND's *Pop Your Bubble* project matches people with several individuals who have opposite points of view. It prompts you to follow Facebook users who have been identified as your opposite for geographic location (urban vs. rural), age, hometown, and previously liked and shared content. There's no pressure to like or comment, but even so a personal connection can develop.

Mirroring

Authentic connection relies on mirroring. In *Enchanted Objects* (Scribner, 2015), David Rose envisions an enchanted wall of lights visualizing the moods of your loved ones. That future might not be far off. British Airways recently gave passengers flying from New York to London blankets embedded with neurosensors to track how they were feeling (Figure 5-13). When the fiber optics woven into the blanket turned red, flight attendants knew that the passengers were feeling stressed and anxious. Blue blankets were a sign that the passenger was feeling calm and relaxed. So, the airline learned that passengers were happiest when eating and drinking, and most relaxed when they were sleeping. I wonder about the effect on passengers, given our tendency toward social contagion.

FIGURE 5-13
Happiness is a sensor-warm blanket (source: British Airways)

Although emotion-sensing technology can mirror, it's not the only way to do so. If I am trying to feel connected with my partner across long distances, I might share a heartbeat on my Apple smartwatch. There's even the awkwardly named Kissinger, which sends a physical kiss across a network. Whether it's sharing data about our stress level with a partner or posting images to express joy, technology can facilitate attunement. Empathetic technology, especially when aimed at cultivating empathy between people rather than reinforcing dependencies on products, could be a force for good. Just as often, though, we encounter the negative patterns.

SOCIAL AWARENESS ANTIPATTERNS

Way back in the early aughts, John Suler published the *Psychology of Cyberspace*, in which he laid out several cognitive distortions related to digital identity. More than a decade ago, it was clear that our relationship to one another online was not quite the same as, in the parlance of the time, meatspace. Here are a few examples of those cognitive distortions:

Dissociative anonymity

> *The feeling that you don't need to take responsibility because you are anonymous.* Despite the success of late-night talk show hosts reading out mean tweets, some people feel that they don't need to own their behaviors online. People might convince themselves that their actions "aren't me," which is dissociation in psychological terms. Dissociative anonymity is linked to content vandalism, doxing, cyber-bullying, stalking, and trolling.

This isn't to say that anonymity doesn't have a place. The same freedom you might feel traveling alone in a new city can encourage you to play with your identity. When people can separate their actions from the "real world," they feel less inhibited about being vulnerable. Anonymity can also be a safe space for people who are excluded. And for everyone who wants to experiment with identity once in a while or talk without being tracked.

So, how do we cultivate good anonymity and decrease the bad by design? This is the question most platforms struggle to figure out. So far, there have been a few approaches to counter the downsides of anonymity, trolling, and bullying in general. The Wikimedia Foundation uses supervised machine learning, in which human moderators train AI to filter with more precision. Another strategy is to enlist the public to report harassment. ProPublica has implemented a secure whistleblower submission system. Yet another is to give people more control. Instagram has recently added comment control to let people decide who can and can't comment on their posts. Still, it's a struggle.

Bystander effect

> *A diffusion of responsibility based on the presence of a real or imagined group of observers.* The more we think other people are present, whether visible or not, the more likely we are to assume that someone else will step up, online or off. Just in the past year, people have failed to intervene in livestreamed torture and suicide. But every day we see less horrific examples, too. A lonely cry for help in a Slack channel, where many can help but no individual feels an obligation to respond. The email sent to the group that everyone reads but no one answers.

The antidote to bystander effect might be public self-awareness. When we sense the group is aware of us personally, we are more likely to take positive action. A group of Dutch psychologists led by Marco van Bommel showed that highlighting an online community member's name in red made people more likely to intervene in an online request for help. In brief, you know that other people know you are there.[5] Perhaps it's purely out of concern for reputation, or perhaps it's simply a wake-up call.

Besides just making people feel present, we can nudge a little as well. Quora addresses lonely questions by suggesting individuals who could answer the question, as shown in Figure 5-14.

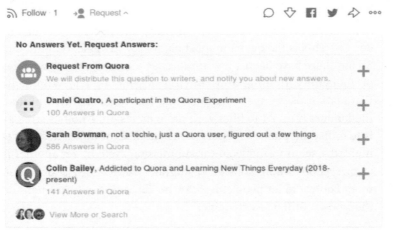

FIGURE 5-14
Gentle nudges for help (source: Quora)

Obviously, people shouldn't be solely responsible for monitoring one another on social media. Social media platforms need to develop more intelligence to detect trolling, livestreaming of crimes, and other abuse. The moderation process needs to be more transparent. Over-reliance

5   Marco von Bummel et al., "Be Aware to Care: Public Self-Awareness Leads to a Reversal of the Bystander Effect," *Journal of Experimental Social Psychology*, July 2012.

on human moderators, who can be traumatized by the work, needs to be addressed. Online harassment has too few consequences, or easily circumvented ones, for harassers and too many for its victims and moderators. That needs to change.

Social Relationship Interventions

When it comes to forging strong social skills, generosity is key. Giving turns out to be better for your emotional well-being than getting. Giving makes us feel happy, so much so that when we give to charitable organizations researchers can actually see the effect. Giving activates regions of the brain associated with social connection and trust; altruistic behavior releases endorphins in the brain, producing a *helper's high*. Besides delivering a bit of a natural buzz, giving is linked with a lot of other positives.

Giving promotes a sense of trust that strengthens our social ties. When we give to others, we feel closer to them and they feel closer to us, reinforcing community. Giving itself promotes a ripple effect of generosity. Researchers James Fowler and Nicholas Christakis found that cooperative behavior cascades on social networks.[6] Altruism can spread by three degrees, so that each person in a network can influence dozens of others.

Giving evokes gratitude, and gratitude builds positive social bonds. People who are grateful are more open to new people and new experiences. Gratitude can even bolster self-control. Like all the other aspects of well-being we've looked at so far, it has a positive impact on physical and mental health, too. So how can we cultivate everyday generosity by design?

POSITIVE SOCIAL RELATIONSHIP PATTERNS

Why people act honestly, generously, and fairly is still something of a mystery. So far, no one has discovered a simple list of variables that predict generosity, yet it seems that we all have a capacity for it. Despite the unknowns, we can draw on some patterns to create generous interventions.

---

6   James Fowler and Nicholas Christakis, "Cooperative Behavior Cascades in Social Networks," *Proceedings of the National Academy of Sciences*, December 28, 2010, p.107.

> *Trying out compassionate action can change minds and encourage altruism.* Games potentially influence altruistic behavior, especially as we start to identify with the game avatar. Games for good, like *The Cat in the Hijab* (Figure 5-15), encourage people to rehearse compassionate action.

APPROACHING NEXT STATION...

FIGURE 5-15
Trying out altruistic behavior, as a cat or not, might encourage more of it
(source: Cat in the Hijab for ResistJam)

VR as a path toward altruism, compassion, and empathy is just starting to realize its potential. Stanford University's Virtual Human Interaction Lab studied how VR can encourage people to be more empathetic to the homeless. The simulation starts in your own home. You lose your job, struggle to make rent, choose items in your home to sell. Eventually, you are evicted and try living in your car. After your car is towed, you try to sleep on the bus, all the while guarding your backpack. Compared to study participants who only read statistics or even narratives about the homeless, people were more motivated to get involved.

But compassionate rehearsals or immersive empathy can lead to burnout and withdrawal. Whether you put on a headset or take part in another kind of simulation, you know that you can step away at any moment and go back to life as it was before. It's temporary. Likely, as the experience loses its novelty, we will feel the force of it even less and need to up the ante. Like all of the interventions here, compassion rehearsals aren't a cure-all but are certainly a promising start.

Mushrooming

Change emerges from cultivating a vast underground of related actions. When I grew up in Michigan, I wasn't sure whether the giant prehistoric fungus that flourished under the Upper Peninsula was myth or reality. No matter, what intrigued me was searching for evidence on the surface. Rebecca Solnit, in *Hope in the Dark* (Haymarket Books, 2016), memorably describes hope as that network of fungus under the surface that occasionally sprouts mushrooms.

Translated to a design intervention, mushrooming means showing how small actions come together to make big change. That's why GoFundMe and Patreon feel empowering. Sites like Spacehack (Figure 5-16), a directory of projects related to space exploration, give people a way to contribute to something bigger by classifying photos taken by astronauts or transcribing logbooks or sharing the discovery of stars.

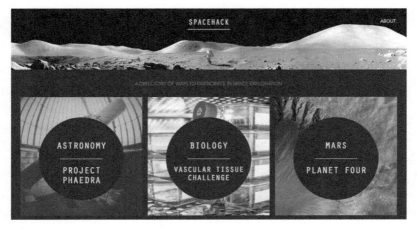

FIGURE 5-16
Hope springs astronomical (source: Spacehack.org)

Positive amplification

Positives beget more positives. If you've ever lived through a natural disaster, you know that most people are calm, resourceful, and altruistic. But you might hear much more about the bad behaviors—looting, violence, and despair. Negatives get our attention, and attention is currency on the internet, for now. Amplifying positive actions, conversely, cultivates hope. At first, Upworthy might have seemed a good example of inspiring posts about brave individual acts. But humans being humans, we habituate to the clickbait headline and gloss over the noble actions. However, stories on sites like Refunite, an organization that tracks missing refugees, and Micos, a microlending platform, haven't lost their power to amplify.

Creative gifting

Spending time choosing a meaningful gift has benefits for the giver and receiver. Considering what makes a good gift can also reveal some possible patterns for giving. Marketing professor Russell Belk has extensively studied the emotional force of gift giving and has found that the perfect gift involves three variables: originality, personal fit, and sacrifice.[7] Here we should look to kids, who are actively and inventively figuring out ways to create meaningful gifts using technology. Whether dedicated Pinterest boards crafted with a friend in mind, a playlist, or a drawing, we can learn from kids who seem more apt to apply creativity to giving. Creativity doesn't need to be handmade, of course, but it shouldn't be a default choice. The more thoughtful the effort and creativity, the better the experience all around.

In the end, almost all giving is good, but some is better than others. Automated monthly giving, a checkbox to add a $1 donation at the end of a checkout process, rounding up dollar amounts to donate to a favorite cause, and starting your shopping at Amazon's Smile page are all convenient ways to give that have tangible benefits for charitable organizations. And all these activities can make people feel good, especially the first time out. As we know, what once made us happy isn't going to last. By automating, we lose some of the positive effect on our own well-being over time. Perhaps that's negligible, though, when we take the big-picture benefit into account.

---

7   Russell Belk, "The Perfect Gift," in *Gift Giving: A Research Anthology* , ed. Cele Otnes and Richard F. Beltramini, Bowling Green University Press, 1996.

SOCIAL RELATIONSHIP ANTIPATTERNS

Just as we don't yet understand that much about what inspires generosity or altruism, we don't know that much about what discourages it, either. Research on the virtues is surprisingly minimal. A few patterns that discourage generosity and social inaction seem to hold true, however. Let's take a closer look at them:

Dystopian rumination

Repetitively going over a dystopian narrative with no potential good outcome. By dwelling on negatives and replaying them, people become stuck in a cycle in which they are reinforcing anxiety or inadequacy. In the climate-change community, this is known as *solastagia*, or the existential distress many people feel about climate change. When we feel that there is no possibility for change, hope wanes. Consider this the tech industry equivalent of solastalgia.

What reinforces this pattern? High-pathos headlines like "When the robots take over will there be jobs for us?" and "Have smartphones destroyed a generation?" leave us longing for times past. We end up relying on coping mechanisms, like cynical posturing or sharing cute baby-animal GIFs, rather than action. Or, our reaction might be to agonize over what we can do without feeling like we are able to accomplish anything. Future Crunch's newsletters and Gapminder's data visualizations are examples of organizations trying to put the negatives in context of big-picture positives.

Heaven's reward fallacy

A pattern of thinking where a person expects rewards for giving. Heaven's reward fallacy happens when a person becomes bitter or angry if they feel a proper recognition was not received. So, although public recognition of gifts or donations is thought to encourage giving, it can paradoxically reinforce this negative pattern of thinking. Think about how leaderboards on sites like Kiva or Kickstarter can make us feel good and bad at the same time. Giving without expectation makes people happier in both the short and long term, but online altruism seems to focus on prompting people to give by ensuring that they will get something. That's something we can flip.

Being part of something bigger than ourselves might be at the heart of generous social relationships. That overwhelming feeling of awe and communion empowers and disempowers at once. So, let's add self-transcending to the traditional categories of emotional intelligence.

Self-Transcending Interventions

Think about a time when you've experienced awe. Maybe you were gazing up at a Georgia O'Keefe painting or looking down into the depths of an infant's eyes. You might have found yourself lost in an inspiring performance of a favorite piece of music. Viewing a solar eclipse for the first time (with the appropriate eye gear, I hope), you might have felt humbled by the vastness of the universe. That sense of awe blurs you a bit at the edges and you feel a sense of communion with nature or other people, or just something bigger than yourself.

Our culture might just be a little awe-deprived at the moment. We spend more time working than we do out in nature or attending art events or participating in religious ceremonies. Our experience of technology doesn't help in that regard. The internet, and all the technologies it pulls together, privileges narrow at the expense of expansive experience.

Awe is an emotional response, usually to something vast that challenges the limits of our current knowledge, by which we transcend ourselves. Awe gives us a sense that time is abundant and endless. And that seems to have all manner of tonic effects on well-being, including increased feelings of connectedness, heightened awareness of the strengths of others, a better sense of perspective on priorities, and an impulse toward altruism.[8] Feelings of awe can also have an impact on how we spend, too. Rather than spending money on products, we'll spend on experiences. On social media, awe is the one emotion that keeps pace with anger for viral effect.

---

8   Melanie Rudd, Kathleen D. Vohs, and Jennifer Aaker, "Awe Expands People's Perception of Time and Enhances Well-Being," *Psychological Science*, December 2010.

No wonder that awe is one of the 10 positive emotions according to Barbara Frederickson's research[9] and transcendence is one of Martin Seligman's 24 character strengths.[10] All this sounds like a potential antidote to what's wrong with technology's pace, but our experience of the internet might be more Aww than Awe (yes, there have been academic studies of the effect of cat videos on happiness in case you were wondering). We might wonder at the latest new technology, but it isn't quite the same as contemplating our spiritual connection to the universe. So, what can we do besides immerse ourselves in Shots of Awe on YouTube? Here are some ideas:

Serendipitous intimacy

Serendipitous intimacy is a term I've come up with for a moment of random, maybe sudden, authentic connection. Like Sonja Lyubormirsky's *random acts of kindness* intervention, it's sometimes associated with a helper's high—that amazing feeling we get when we've helped in a real way. Be My Eyes, an app that draws together sighted people with those who have impaired vision, is my touchstone example (Figure 5-17). The real-life equivalent would be gatherings like *Tea with Strangers* or *Death over Dinner*, perhaps.

Serendipitous intimacy is more than random closeness; it's that plus meaningful communication. That's what separates, say, the CNA Language School from Chat Roulette. It's experiencing the vast wonder of humanity in an intimate moment.

---

9   Barbara Frederickson, *Positivity*, Harmony Books, 2009.

10 Christopher Peterson and Martin Seligman, *Character Strengths and Virtues*, Oxford University Press, 2004.

FIGURE 5-17
Wonder not at the tech itself, but at communion (source: Be My Eyes)

We can find wonder in intimate connections, but more often we think of it as a view that's big picture—really big picture. Just last fall, as I was checking in to the Web Summit conference, I struck up a conversation with another speaker at the desk. We chatted about the conference a bit. Then, I asked what he was speaking about. Oh, he just happened to be an astronaut and was talking about NASA. No big deal. If I'd had my wits about me, I might have asked about the experience of seeing firsthand the reality of Earth in space. Lucky for me, I caught Michael Massimino's talk later, during which he mentioned the overview effect right after he talked about sending the first message on Twitter from space. Maybe that's an awe spiral.

Overview effect

A profound cognitive shift in awareness that induces a sense of wonder. The wonder of seeing Earth as a tiny, fragile ball of life hanging in the void becomes a deeply transformative experience of unity with nature and universal connectedness. The overview effect is experiencing the vast wonder of humanity by taking it all in at once. Because we can't all travel to space just yet, how can we facilitate the emotional power of the overview effect through design? IMAX theater, virtual reality, or immersive games might temporarily facilitate this particular kind of wonder.

Synesthesia

A crossed response of the senses that confounds and intrigues. The most common form of synesthesia is grapheme-color synesthesia, in which people perceive individual letters of the alphabet and numbers to be tinged with a color. Other synesthetes commingle sounds with scents, sounds with shapes, or shapes with flavors. Small children seem especially prone to it. The perceptual mashup can be overwhelming, but it can also bring a sense of wonder. I'll offer the iTunes music visualizer as exhibit A—a blend of music and visuals, a strangely mesmerizing early-day tech experience that cultivated a transcendental state. The Fantom app, released by trip hop artists Massive Attack, is a current example (Figure 5-18). The app encourages people to remix sound with other inputs from sensors and accelerometer in a sensory mashup.

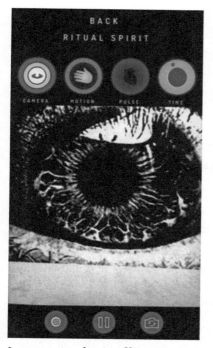

FIGURE 5-18
Synesthetic remixing
(source: Fantom)

Just as synesthesia offers up new associations, well-placed randomness can also foster that sense of awe. Unexpected juxtapositions encourage us to bring together new associations and see the world writ large. Sometimes, we can achieve this by stumbling around the internet on our own; sometimes it's expertly crafted.

We are only just beginning to consider technology and awe. Anthropologist Genevieve Bell has considered spiritual practices facilitated by technology, ranging from virtual confessions to texting messages at the Wailing Wall in Jerusalem. Elizabeth Buie of Northumbria University in Newcastle, England, has been studying how technology can facilitate transcendent experiences. In the *Enchantment of Modern Life* (Princeton University Press, 2001), philosopher Jane Bennett considers all manner of wonder in everyday experience.

The positive interventions to try, and the negatives to avoid, are just a start at identifying design patterns that we can use to support emotional intelligent technology. These factors overlap and intersect in all kinds of ways. Much more work is needed to develop practices that we can adopt. In the meantime, we can begin to assess the impact.

Track Progress

For those who like to track progress, a simple rating system can help. Here, the inspiration comes from well-being measures that track progress on multiple factors. If we have some factors that we know have a positive or negative impact, we can also assess how well we are achieving those goals.

Start with the model here, grounded in emotional intelligence. Or consider another like Happify's SAVOR. Or develop your own. For each, we can track three (or five, if you want to get more specific) levels:

Negative (active or passive)

> A negative impact on physical, emotional, or mental well-being is detected, either on the level of an individual or collectively. To get even more granular, you could distinguish between two levels of negative impact: actively pursuing a negative impact (usually for a business reason) or passively by inadvertently employing a pattern that subverts well-being for a lot of people.

Neutral

> Known negatives are phased out or not used at all, but positive strategies are not employed for the value either. In other words, it doesn't detract, but it doesn't add much either.

Positive (explicit or implicit)

A positive impact supports social and emotional well-being. Here, there could also be a split between products: those for which the core purpose is supporting well-being, and those for which well-being is implicit.

If you plotted these factors on a chart, it might look like Figure 5-19.

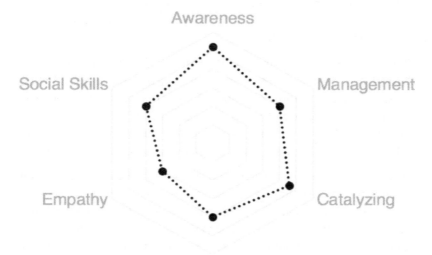

FIGURE 5-19

The contours of an emotionally intelligent experience

Of course, we want to embrace all of these factors when we are developing new technology, but it might be that different types of experiences have different shapes. The intent is not to be reductive, but to make progress toward removing negatives at minimum and planning for positive outcomes. This applies not just to products explicitly designed for mental and physical health, but to all tech, from social media to wearables to news sites to workplace applications.

The first goal is to move out of the negative zone, which probably won't be easy. Why? Because some negative patterns are good for business. And further complicating matters, some negative patterns might not be negative to everyone all the time. People are inventive in how they bring technology into their everyday lives, as we all know. So, consider these guidelines more than hard-and-fast rules.

Interventions Bolster Emotionally Intelligent Design

A lot of the best thinking about design for emotional well-being has emerged from the design of cities, from Jane Jacobs' work in New York City to Christopher Alexander's pattern language for building to Terrapin Bright Green's biophilic design. There is no formula for a happy city, but it has to include the right elements—mixed-use blocks, green spaces, fewer cars, and more bike paths. And that's not enough. It all needs to work together.

The interventions here are a way to lay the foundation, no matter the experience—nonprofits, government organizations, big corporations, or scrappy startups. And none of these interventions necessarily require permission from the top down to enact. Perhaps these micro-level interventions will prove even more effective than a macro-level statement of values and the more recent introduction of regulations.

After all, many big companies and other organizations have grand mission statements that are sometimes at odds with their actions. Corporate social responsibility departments often find themselves trying to offset the compromises made to mission. As individuals, we find ourselves at a loss about how to change minds, whether our own or those of others. What if we balanced sweeping statements with small goals? By putting these small changes into our repertoire, we can make tech more emotionally intelligent.

[6]

Forecasting the Future with Feelings

IMAGINE IT'S 10 YEARS ago, and I tell you about an idea for taking photos that disappear after they're viewed. Maybe I add a detail, like there would be virtual "stickers" that you could put on the pictures or that you could write on them before they disappeared. Meh. Polaroids had their day already, hadn't they?

How many of us would have predicted that Snap would have such emotional force? And that Polaroid would make a comeback, too? If there's one truth about happiness, it's this: human beings are terrible at predicting it. We overestimate how happy we will be on the weekend and we underestimate how happy we will be on Mondays. We think that we'll be happy when we have more money, even though that is consistently not the case. We make these same mistaken predictions over and over again.

Emotional intelligence is a bit of a time hack. When you're overcome with regret, you're paying too much attention to the past. When you are feeling distracted, you're not appreciating the present. When you worry, you're dwelling on an unpleasant future. Negative emotions not only signal some bigger-picture frustrations; they can also spiral into despair in which the future feels hopeless. By shifting attention to the past, present, and future in a positive way, you can effect real change.

In this chapter, we mix techniques from affective forecasting, prospective psychology, future foresight, and speculative design. Paying attention to emotion can guide us toward a fulfilling future. So, let's try a little emotional time travel to help us to make better design decisions for our future selves, and our future society.

The Trouble with the Future

One definition of design, and one that is especially true of designing technology, is that design creates the future. Quite literally, we develop objects to exist in our future lives. At a high level, we see our role as designing a better future. But, day to day, we focus on a very near future in quite a particular way.

Design thinking (or its close relations like human-centered design, user experience design, and human–computer interaction; let's not quibble) has made our lives easier and more comfortable. It has enabled organizations to provide products and services that function with less friction. It encourages customer empathy. Design thinking has developed solutions from mobile payments to self-driving cars. We use problem solving for good, too such as 3D-printed prosthetics and LED lights for the developing world. Design thinking has become a shorthand for a mindset and a method that creatively solves problems.

Lately, we've been running up against its limitations, though. Although it offers a repeatable creative process for designing commercial products that benefit an individual in the moment, it's not the only way or the best way to build an emotionally sustainable relationship or to encourage positive transformation in the long term. Let's consider just how we get stuck.

THE PROBLEM PROBLEM

Listen closely and you'll notice that conversations about design often come back to problems and solutions. Whether we are talking about autonomous cars or fake news or world hunger, we tend to see the world as a series of discrete problems to be solved. We zero in on an unpleasant state and then fix it in the short term.

Design thinking offers a method to address tightly focused problems like a thorny moment in the checkout process. It also applies to big-picture issues, like shaping a platform to educate homeowners about the risks of flooding. Even the way we structure design thinking in the organization—as a sprint—rushes us toward the short term. We get rid of the problem for now, and then on to the next problem.

Except that sometimes we create that next problem. Solving an individual problem can sometimes cause another problem for that individual. You might feel bored and a little lonely one afternoon, so you start watching a streaming video service of your choice. It's entertaining, it fills up that empty feeling, and it's so easy to keep going. The more you binge-watch, the more isolated you might feel. Rather than solving your boredom and loneliness, you're caught in a cycle.

Perhaps our problem-solving creates a larger societal problem. Smartphones increase access to information, which seems to quantifiably increase well-being, but they add a tremendous amount of waste to the environment. Ride-sharing services make it easier for individuals to get rides, but make it more difficult for taxi drivers to earn a living wage.

Beyond that, the mundane everyday problems that we are solving might inadvertently erase foundational elements to emotional well-being, like personal growth and community building. Getting groceries is such a bother, so instead we create a digitally enabled convenient option. All good, until we look at all the other things that might be missing. Flipping through cookbooks together, conversations about what to purchase, inventing new meals because we don't have everything we need, and casual conversations with neighbors at the store are just some of the little things lost from solving the grocery problem.

Another problem-solving tactic we fall back on is giving already acceptable experience an upgrade. You have a photographer, but wouldn't an aerial drone view be cooler? You use the surface of your refrigerator to display a drawing or share a shopping list, but what if it had a screen for that? You know it's important to stay hydrated, but couldn't it be easier to keep track with a smart water bottle (Figure 6-1)?

FIGURE 6-1
Smart water bottles
follow a classic upgrade
approach (source:
Hidrate Spark)

Upgrades often address problems for a tiny, affluent segment of the population. If you need an app to find a great restaurant, we've got you covered. If you're a single mother, or an unemployed veteran, or barely making a living wage, you're unlikely to benefit from the upgraded experience.

It's not that eliminating problems, or even upgrading experiences, is a bad thing. But it often addresses one small piece of the puzzle, which means that it might stir up new problems or miss systemic ones. It favors solving a problem in the present, thinking less about the long-term impact of those quick solutions. And it tends to start with a solitary user rather than a system of intimately connected people, communities, environments, or cultures. At its worst, a problem-solving mindset can create an atmosphere of ambient dissatisfaction, in which everything begins to feel like a problem.

THE NEW NORMAL OF PRODUCT DESIGN

Whether we eliminate an unpleasant reality or upgrade an experience that is already quite good, we quickly adjust to the new normal. This idea, called *hedonic adaptation*, says that we have a thermostat that maintains a certain comfortable level of happiness. For each of us, our set point is a little different, but it means that even with highs and lows, we come back to that set point.

When that shiny new solution soon becomes same old, same old, designers and developers are tasked with the next improvement. And so goes a parallel universe hedonic treadmill for designers and developers, in which each new release is welcomed with appreciation for a brief moment before it becomes standard fare. Of course, this makes it extra difficult to look past the next version, much less 10 years out.

The limits of problem solving aren't the only constraint we confront when we try to design for a further future. Automatic thoughts can color our beliefs and actions in negative ways. Called *cognitive distortions*, these are exaggerated thought patterns that perpetuate anxiety, depression, or other mental disorders. Cognitive distortions can translate to magnifying bad news or minimizing positive moments or jumping to conclusions. And it turns out that certain strains of cognitive distortions are particularly common among tech entrepreneurs.

CONFOUNDED FOUNDERS

Michael Dearing of the Stanford d.school met thousands of founders over the past decade, investing in seed-stage tech companies and advising startups. Over time, he began to notice and document distorted patterns of thinking common to this group. Dearing identified five recurring cognitive distortions based on his experience:[1]

- *Personal exceptionalism,* in which the person sees their work or life or actions outside the bounds of their peers, permitting negative behavior.

- *Dichotomous thinking,* which sees genius or crap and nothing in between.

- *Correct overgeneralization,* by which universal judgments are made from limited observations but are seen as correct.

- *Blank-canvas thinking,* which prompts people to believe that life is a blank canvas for their own original work of art.

- *Schumpeterianism,* based on Joseph Schumpeter's theory of capitalism as creative destruction, which leads people to see only the positives of disruption and too easily accept collateral damage that goes with it.

If you've worked in tech, these distortions might look familiar. And they run the full spectrum from Uber's myriad missteps to SpaceX's inspirational rocket launches.

Given that these are the filters that influence the tech industry, it's easy to see how disruption came to be considered a universal good. Now, these cognitive distortions can certainly lead exponential change with the right idea in the right circumstances. Unfortunately, they can also lead to disruption without much care for consequences. Hubris rather than humility can result in disregard for long-term, far-reaching implications.

So, it's not just methodological gaps but psychological barriers that must be overcome when we design a better future. Problem-solving steers us toward the short term; distorted thinking shifts attention

---

1 Michael Dearing, "The Cognitive Distortions of Founders," *Medium*, March 26, 2017.

away from long-term consequences. Artificial intelligence (AI) might make it even more difficult to move forward because it tends to warp time to create a near future that looks like the recent past.

THE TECH TIME WARP

In graduate school, I'd eagerly drive home for the holidays, excited to show my family how much I'd changed. I'd cultivated new friends, I'd learned about big new ideas, I'd discovered new music. But as soon as I walked in the front door, everything reverted to what it once was. Through no fault of their own, my parents didn't know about the new me. They still treated me just as they did when I lived at home. Of course, that makes sense. That's when they last knew my day-to-day habits, what I liked to eat, or the types of books I read. Even so, I dearly wanted them to acknowledge the new (better) me.

After arriving home, I found myself falling back into old routines. I watched TV, in contrast to the new me, who displayed a wall of broken TVs as an ideological statement. I dutifully recited my grades to distant relatives, rather than engaging them in debates about existentialism. Expectations from the recent past haunted my present and shaped expectations for my near future.

AI can create this same effect, capturing trends in our behavior (and soon our emotions) from the near past and projecting them into the near future. We already see glimpses of this phenomenon. I'll see an ad for that connected water bottle. LOL, that's "book research" me. There are posts with animal rights stories. That's on the mark. Then, there's the ad for the Quip toothbrush, which I can maybe attribute to buying an electric toothbrush for my spouse a couple of years ago (Figure 6-2). Harmless, but also a bit annoying.

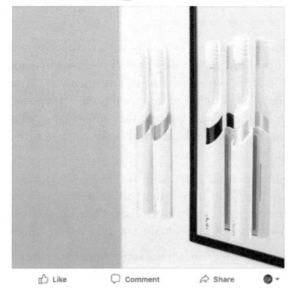

quip
March 24, 2017 · 🌐

Friday night in with the family 🦷

👍 Like   💬 Comment   ↪ Share   ⬤ ▾

It's one thing to make dental hygiene a part of our future, quite another to let it define me (source: Quip)

At scale, it looks a little different. It might mean that as a woman I see ads for jobs that pay less because salaries for women have been lower. Predictive policing software ends up perpetuating disparities in communities of color by drawing on datasets from the last decade, for example. Because machines learn on our recent past data, time shifts just a little backward. It's difficult to really move forward if we're being pulled toward the past. There's little room for us to grow or change or overcome expectations.

Even though technology is practically synonymous with the future, it has trouble taking us there. Design method, startup mindset, and even the underpinnings of tech itself conspire to make future thinking more difficult. Recently, a new field of affective forecasting has begun to look at how we make choices by looking at how we predict they will make us feel in the future. Here's where we can begin to build a new approach to future forecasting.

A Future Fueled by Emotion

In the tech world, we pay a lot of attention to the present. How well do we deliver right now? What delights when people directly engage with the app? How can we get people to stay longer?

Boosting happiness in the moment goes only so far. Surprise and delight might soothe hurt feelings, but they haven't created emotional durability. We can enjoy that confetti moment, and then have it be ruined by a lousy ending. People delete more apps than they keep, they switch between 10 tabs as they plan a trip and then forget about all of those websites after they're done, they have a positive interaction with a chatbot, never to try another conversation.

And, of course, we adapt to what once made us happy. We discover a new app, and we are happy for only a short while before we want something else. These aspirations apply to our industry leaders, too, of course. We have a million users; let's celebrate. OK, now let's get more.

If we want to be happy in the moment, there's something to be said for savoring it, trying to expand those good things (as we did in Chapter 5). But, mostly, we won't be satisfied with living in the moment. According to Daniel Kahneman, in *Thinking, Fast and Slow* (Farrar, Strauss and Giroux, 2011), our experiencing self is only one part of the picture. Happiness is just as much remembering as it is experiencing.

ROSY RETROSPECTION

When we look to the past, we often see it with rose-colored glasses. Simplifying and exaggerating memories might just be how we are able to remember in the long term. Rosy retrospection can be a good thing. It's a kind of coping mechanism to remind us about the good things in our lives and about ourselves. A host of studies have shown that nostalgia can improve mood, counteract loneliness, and provide meaning.

It creeps up on us, too. As we age, we experience a *reminiscence bump* in which the events that happened to us from ages 10 to 30 seem best of all. Our most vivid memories are emotional events, and this period of our lives is particularly rich with them. Emerging identity, biological and neurological growth, and a concentration of important life events like college, first jobs, or marriage make memories from this period especially significant. I wonder if this isn't why we are seeing a resurgence of nostalgia for the early days of the internet (Figure 6-3), including everything from quirky Web 1.0 conferences to a host of excellent memoirs[2] to the new brutalist website design trend.

FIGURE 6-3
An internet reminiscence bump; remember the 90s? (source: FogCam)

Now it might be that this only recently discovered reminiscence bump becomes a thing of the past anyway. It might flatten out with fewer people reaching emotional milestones in one concentrated period. People are going to school, starting new careers, getting married, having children, and buying homes all over their personal timelines. Milestones are shifting, just as many people are intentionally deciding not to do any of those things at all.

---

2 Virginia Heffernan, *Magic and Loss: The Internet as Art.* Simon & Schuster, 2016 and Ellen Ullman, *Life in Code: A Personal History of Technology*, Farrar, Straus, and Giroux, Macmillan, 2017.

When the past—or what we remember of it—seems so lovely, it becomes more difficult to imagine that the future will be better. The belief that society is headed toward a decline is an emotional self-soothing strategy in a way; it helps us to feel better about the present.

FUZZY FORESIGHT

Old-school psychology is obsessed with the past. Sigmund Freud hoped that people could cope well enough with the past to live lives of "ordinary unhappiness." Some days that's enough, but am I wrong to hope for more? Modern pop psychology tells us to stay in the present. Cognitive behavioral psychology aims to reprogram our present behavior. Mindfulness is the latest present-focused obsession. Definitely emotional skills to master, but how do we imagine what's next?

Two new waves in psychology, both related to positive psychology and the study of positive emotion, are concerned with time-hopping to the future. That's where we'll take heart.

Prospective psychology studies the human ability to represent possible futures as it shapes thoughts, emotions, and behaviors. And prospection—planning, predicting, developing hypothetical scenarios, daydreaming, evaluating possibilities—itself is fundamentally human. We've already noted that emotions are not only a combination of evolutionary instincts or culturally informed concepts, but also a way to guide future behavior. Prospective psychology starts to study just how this might happen.

Rather than processing our past pixel-perfect, we continually retouch our memories. We are drawn to focus on the unexpected. We metabolize the past by remixing it to fit novel situations. These memories, in various combinations, propel us to imagine future possibilities as well.[3]

Prospection isn't just fundamental to our thinking; it seems to contribute positively to our emotional well-being and mental health, too. One study asked nearly 500 adults to record their immediate thoughts and moods at random points in the day. You'd think these people would have spent a lot of time ruminating, but they actually thought about the

---

3   Martin E.P. Seligman, Peter Railton, Roy F. Baumeister, and Chandra Sripada, "Navigating into the Future or Driven by the Past," *Perspectives on Psychological Sciences*, 2013.

future three times more often than the past.[4] And they reported higher levels of happiness and lower levels of stress when they were thinking about the future.

The power of prospection is thought to be unique to humans, although I wouldn't be surprised if that was disproved in the future. Neuroscientist Jaak Panskepp (*Affective Neuroscience: The Foundations of Human and Animal Emotions* [Oxford University Press, 2004]) found that all mammals have a seeking system. Dopamine, a neurotransmitter linked to reward and pleasure, is released when we try new activities and seek out new information. So, the act of seeking itself is ultimately rewarding. Casting about for the future might just be fundamental for all mammals.

Prospective psychology says that the future guides everything we do, and that it can make us feel hopeful (or not) about the future. *Affective forecasting* tells us that we use feelings as a way to predict the future for ourselves every day. Based on the work of Dan Gilbert (who coined the term) and Timothy Wilson, affective forecasting looks at the tiny shifts toward the future we make every day.

Big decisions, everyday behaviors, relationship choices, and all kinds of other important aspects of our lives are guided by how we think we will feel. We constantly make guesses about how imagined future events will influence our emotional well-being. When we make choices about where to live, who to marry, and even what to buy, we choose based on how we think that choice will make us feel. As it turns out, we're terrible at it.

There are reasons, of course. For one, we conflate the details. We think a dentist appointment will be awful, and then it's not so bad. The problem is that as soon as our minds get to work imagining the future, we leave out important details, like the nice person at the front desk in the dentist's office or the whimsical mural on the ceiling. This *focusing effect* happens when we place too much importance on one aspect of an event, making our future predictions go awry.

---

4   Roy F. Baumeister and Kathleen D. Vohs, "The Science of Prospection," *Review of General Psychology*, March 2016.

Sometimes, we fail to appreciate the intensity or duration of a future emotion, thinking that a vacation will bring us more pleasure than it actually does or that the anger of a messy breakup will endure. For our purposes, it might be when we think we will not feel as upset by a thoughtless comment as we end up feeling. When we misjudge the emotional impact of a future event, this is called *impact bias*.

We underestimate how much we will adapt. Called *immune neglect*, we have a difficult time imagining how we will cope with things we perceive to be negative. You might, for example, overestimate the emotional consequences of an operation or the aftermath of identity theft. Discussions around work and automation amplify immune neglect, when we imagine a world in which humans will be extraneous.

We underestimate how much we will change. When I think about the future, I also don't consider the fact that I'm going to be a different person in the future—someone who might want a minivan instead of a convertible. Even though we recognize our own personal growth, we can find it difficult to imagine that we will continue to grow significantly in the future. This is called the *end-of-history illusion*, in which we imagine the person we are now is the final version, the culmination of our personal growth.[5] Seems like algorithmic decision making is founded on the end of history illusion as well.

We underestimate how much we will rationalize. After we do actually make a decision, we often end up wondering how we could ever have dreamed of choosing the other choice. When you've made an irrevocable decision, you rationalize it. When something's gone and gone forever, the mind gets to work figuring out why what it got is really better than what it lost. This one seems to lack a catchy cognitive bias label, so let's invent one: *affective rationalization*.

So, we are not just terrible at predicting what will make us happy in the future, we are terrible at it in all kinds of ways. We are a bit better at forecasting what will make us miserable than what will make us happy, but that might be because we have a negativity bias (Figure 6-4). Could this be why we see more dystopian futures in media and

---

5   Jordi Quoidbach, Daniel T. Gilbert, and Timothy D. Wilson, "The End of History Illusion," *Science*, January 4, 2013.

movies? Possibly. If it's easier to predict the negatives in our personal lives, it seems like shaping doom and gloom futures might come more readily, too.

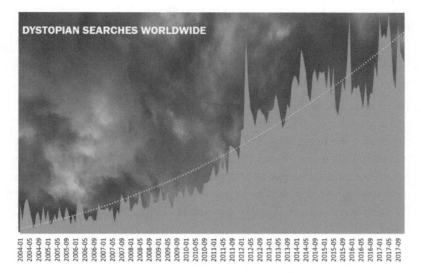

FIGURE 6-4
Are we wired for dystopian imagination? (source: GoogleTrends)

Technology is designed by flawed humans who often fail to recognize, understand, label, express, and regulate emotions. Now we find out that these same well-intentioned, emotionally-not-quite-that-intelligent (well, of course *you* are, but I'm talking about everyone else...) humans are lousy at predicting how future life will make them feel. Yet paradoxically, they are guided toward the future by feelings. In a way, what could be more human?

Knowing all this, how can designers, developers, and the entire cast of characters involved in the design of our internet things make wise choices about the future? Maybe it's by just being rational. Forget about emotion. Oh, too bad that's not really possible. Maybe we should let the machines design themselves? Oh, except they are trained by flawed predictors (aka humans) on flawed data about the same humans. No go. A more realistic choice, then, is to get a little better at imagining the future by getting better at tuning in to emotion. Let's see if we can design interventions to improve our emotional forecasting skills. First step, get personal.

Start with Future-You

Imagining future-you is not so easy. Maybe you think about dinner this weekend or maybe you set a goal to purchase a bike next summer. Imagining the far future is even more challenging. Try to vividly imagine yourself in a world 20 years from now, and it's easy to fall into platitudes about jet packs and flying cars. For our personal lives, we might imagine (on a good day) working less, traveling more, really enjoying our lives. Beyond that, it's fuzzy.

Our future selves are literally strangers to us; at least, that's what neuroscience tells us. The further out in time you imagine your own life, the more your brain begins acting as if you were thinking about someone else. This glitch makes it more difficult for us to take actions that benefit our future selves as individuals and in society. The more you treat your future self like a stranger, the less self-control you exhibit and the less likely you are to make pro-social choices. You'll procrastinate more, you'll put less money away for retirement, you'll skip the gym. As UCLA researcher Hal Hirschfield put it, "Why would you save money for your future self when, to your brain, it feels like you're just handing away your money to a complete stranger?"[6] When you can't imagine yourself in the future, your decision-making suffers.

When your future self is a stranger, it affects society, too. Legislators who undo regulations to mitigate long-term climate changes in exchange for short-term gains, and policy makers who say workplace automation can't be fathomed because it is years away, fall into this same trap. A large part of the population will be alive in 30 years to feel the impact of climate change and see the changes that AI will have on the workforce. But we have trouble imagining just what that future will look like and how we might influence it.

Clearly, we need to get better at feeling the future. Yet, putting ourselves in the future doesn't come easily. So, if we want an emotionally intelligent future with technology, it makes sense to practice *first-person futures*.

---

6   Hal E. Hershfield, Taya R. Cohen, and Leigh Thompson, "Short Horizons and Tempting Situations: Lack of Continuity to Our Future Selves Leads to Unethical Decision Making and Behavior," *Organization Behavior and Human Decision Processes*, March 2012.

PERSONALIZE THE FUTURE

A typical future forecast might be, "By 2050, sea levels might rise by as much as 9 feet and 750 million people will be displaced." You're apt to feel unmoved by a statement like that. A speculative design piece might respond with a video about an amphibious living pod. Thought-provoking, uncomfortable, but a tad too fictional to be deeply felt. Or maybe too fully realized like good sci-fi. That doesn't always leave us a lot of room to imagine ourselves in that future.

Now let's translate this to a design thinking–style future workshop and it looks like "How might we offset a rise in sea levels in 2050 NYC?" Rather than a predetermined outcome with a fully realized response, it's a problem to be solved. Certainly, we will take individuals' lives into account, but that takes a backseat to the product or service we are tasked with creating. Perhaps knowing that people will need to move, we will work with the city to create more multifamily housing space. That's a good start.

What if we enriched the challenge by making it personal? Now, a persona might get us there, especially if we've layered in emotion. Simply inserting a human being helps us to imagine the future more vividly. But if it's someone else, especially a theoretical someone else, it still keeps emotion at arm's length.

Instead, we might frame it like so, "I'll be 72 years old in 2050. The two airports I currently use will be under water. Flying will be less reliable, so I might live closer to my extended family." Future-you is bound to stir up more feeling. And to adopt affective forecasting as our model, we need to actually feel the future.

Personalizing the future builds empathy toward our future selves. More than that, it is a meaningful way to envision the future. Given that we make predictions for our future selves based on how we believe we'll feel, shouldn't we begin by asking questions about future-you?

PRACTICE COUNTERFACTUAL THINKING

In a recent study, the *Institute for the Future* found that the majority of Americans rarely or never think about the something that might happen 30 years from today.[7] When futures loom a little closer, people are more apt to think about those possibilities. If you've had a brush with mortality, you might devote a few more brain cycles to the future. When you have a child, you are more apt to engage in future thinking, too—as soon as you get past the sleep deprivation. Some people just seem to be more likely to engage in future thinking as part of their work, and I'd venture to say that people working in technology might be among those happy few.

Either way, this leaves us with a kind of future gap. Thinking about the 5-year, 10-year, and 30-year future is essential to being an engaged citizen and creative doer, but we need some strategies. Counterfactual thinking is one way to develop those skills.

Counterfactual thinking is the way psychologists describe how we create alternatives to our own stories. Although it can be a coping mechanism for trauma, it can be a strategy for positive growth, too. Thinking about how things could have been and how things could have happened is a method we can use to develop our futuring skillset.

In her 2016 Aspen Ideas talk, Jane McGonigal talks about predicting the past and remembering the future.[8] Yes, the point is to mess with your head a little. By predicting the past, she means when you think about an event in your life and then imagine that you took a different path. For instance, maybe you chose to attend a different college or took a different job. That would be the starting point for a new path that reaches toward an alternate future.

Remembering the future is a technique to create something like a memory. You craft these future memories by using an XYZ formula, where X is an activity or event in your life, Y is a person, and Z is a place. The more detailed and personally meaningful, the easier it is to retrieve the "memory." It's a pseudo-memory of a pseudo-future.

---

7   The Institute for the Future, "The American Future Gap," April 2017.

8   Jane McGonigal, "The Future of Imagination," Aspen Ideas Institute, 2016.

As I've been running futures-thinking workshops with schools, community organizations, and companies, introducing counterfactual thinking works well as a warm-up. If we put these exercises together—predicting the past and remembering the future—it looks something like this.

First, invoke autobiographical memory. Use as much vivid detail as you can recall. You can also invent details as long as they're personal ones. Let's take, for example, a trolling incident on a social network. Think of what the troll said or did. How did you respond? How did you feel? What was the reaction of the community? Where were you when it happened? What else was going on around you? What, if anything, in the design itself was relevant to the experience?

Now reimagine the encounter from your own point of view. Ask "what if" to take it in a different direction. Here's a obvious question: "What if you were speaking face-to-face?" But you might also ask, "What if I had done something else?" or, "What if someone else had responded like so?" Include as much personal detail as you can; invoking your talents and insights helps you to imagine how the situation might shift. Imagine how you want to feel.

Next, reimagine it from your antagonist's point of view. Rather than portraying that persona negatively, try to engage empathetically. Look for ways to connect without sacrificing your own values, imagining that person's everyday life, their upbringing. Next, imagine that person doing or saying something that's positive. What facilitated that turn? Could the design support that? Frame "what if" questions around imagined possibilities.

In a way, we've just re-created Dylan Marron's podcast *Conversations with People Who Hate Me*. We've rehumanized one another, counteracting the disassociative anonymity of online interactions. We've inverted the script by reconfiguring antagonists into partners. More than a positive behavioral or emotional intervention, it also gives us a path toward designing the future. Translate those what-ifs into design challenges, and the exercise generates alternatives. But let's go further.

Take your relationship forward five years. What does it look like? What supported mutual understanding? How did the design help that relationship to flourish? How did it foster understanding in a larger community?

Finally, look at what might have happened if you went back in time and followed this new path. Create an emotional timeline, but this time start five years in the future and then work your way backward. Fill in a milestone—maybe it's the admiration you felt when an influencer like Roxane Gay first used and shared the new video conversation option to engage with someone who had been trolling her. Introduce a mundane ritual, like when you began dialing up your EQ setting every time you looked at posts. Add a memory; maybe it's that warm confidence you felt when you and your community coach met in-person after so many conversations on the platform. Let's call this *emotional backcasting*.

Counterfactual thinking can help us look back on our own lives and explore a path not taken. It can also help us plant new "memories" that provide motivation toward positive goals. Another way to bend time is to reconsider the objects in our lives.

SORT THROUGH YOUR STUFF

Recently, I visited East Harlem's *Treasures in the Trash Museum*. Nelson Molina, over a period of 30 years, developed an extensive collection of discarded things while working for the New York City Department of Sanitation. He began by saving items from his route to decorate lockers at the depot. Coworkers added to the collection. When the trucks were moved out of the garage to another location, the collection of rejected things took over the space. Today, there are more than 50,000 objects in the museum, grouped by color, size, or style. As you walk through the aisles of crystal and typewriters and photographs, you might wonder at how all these objects ended up in the trash. You might wonder at the story associated with each of those objects, and how they went from wanted to unwanted, from part of a life well lived to a life abandoned.

These are the stories we need to understand to move into the future. As designers and developers, increasingly making both physical and digital objects, we have to confront the idea that we've introduced objects into people's lives that end up in the same place—the trash. So, to better imagine future objects, start at the end, with cast-offs, and move backward. This is the future we once wanted; now it's a past we disavow.

How do we decide which things keep their value and which become trash? A few exercises can work through it:

We might be past the "spark joy" craze of Marie Kondo's *The Life-Changing Magic of Tidying Up* (Ten Speed Press, 2014), but the impulse toward clearing out the old and starting fresh remains relevant. More important, this method has something to tell us about our emotional life with objects. The theory here is that we hold onto things, digital or physical, due to fear of the future and nostalgia for the past. Things trigger our affective forecasting spidey-senses.

The idea of a KonMari sort is to hold up each item you own and contemplate whether it delights. It might sound a bit gimmicky, but the idea behind it is useful. Take a minute to contemplate your emotional connection to the object. If there's none, off it goes. If there's something there, think again.

Discerning whether objects spark joy in the moment can fail to appreciate the layers of meaning objects accrue, or how our emotional relationship with objects waxes and wanes, or the complexity of emotion. But it does encourage us to shift perspective, slow down, and contemplate that relationship. Whether digital or physical objects, this technique works just as well in an interview as a workshop by encouraging people to take emotional stock.

You can start your own emotional inventory with a list of three technologies (or any objects) that spark joy. If you are looking to innovate in pet care, limit it to that space. If you already have a pet-care product, make an emotional inventory of features instead. It doesn't need to be "spark joy," strictly speaking. It could be "things you feel strongly about" or "tech that you associate with [emotion]." The point is to get right to essentials.

Emotional laddering

Asking people for an emotional reaction is a shortcut that transports us to deeper questions right away. But we can go further with it, given that people often describe emotion in broad strokes especially when they are talking to people they don't know very well. Just as we might use laddering (similar to the *five whys*) to explore the true goal behind the action, we can use that initial "spark joy" prompt to gain insight into the emotional underpinnings moving from attributes to consequences to values. The conversation might look like this:

Q: What about your dog tracker makes you feel happy?

A: The video feature lets me see my dog during the day while I'm at work.

Q: What is important to you about that?

A: It makes me feel like I'm there when I can't be.

Q: And why is that important?

A: My dog has anxiety, so I worry about him after I've been gone for a few hours. That usually kicks in mid-morning. I'll admit that I'm a bit worried about my favorite chair, too.

Q: So how do you handle that?

A: I've been working with a trainer on it.

Q: When was the last time you saw your dog getting anxious?

A: Just yesterday, as I was commuting home.

Q: How did you know?

A: I always check in on the way; it's just something I do. But I find myself just checking it a lot throughout the day.

Q: So, what did you do?

A: Well, not much. I felt like there wasn't anything I could do, but it did make me feel in more of a rush to get home. I decided to skip picking up dinner.

Q: What did you do on the rest of the commute?

A: I was glued to the screen, feeling worse by the moment.

Not every interview will reveal dog feelings, but you see how you can use this technique to get specific on a range of feelings in unexpected trajectories. What started with a big category and ended in a mix of feelings including anxiety, worry, comfort, relief. This technique showed us some of the actions that those feelings spawned, from rushing to reaching out for support to not having a way to take action at all. If these aspects of the experience aren't addressed, the relationship will suffer in the long term.

This technique revealed aspects of the experience that need design support, perhaps timed check-ins. If we are paying close attention, it shows us where we should help people disengage, so that our dog's human doesn't feel tethered to the device. Feeling overwhelmed, addicted, and increasingly anxious is a certain path to drive people away. And it uncovered new areas of opportunity, like sharing video clips with the trainer or on-demand coaching or even an emotionally attuned chatbot.

Now back to the future. We're time bending, after all. Let's try using this technique to move backward and forward in time.

Q: When was a time you felt happy with this tracker in the mix?

A: I remember this one time. I was in a meeting that was running long and I was able to check in on my phone, under the table of course. It felt like a little secret between me and my doggo. Well, and my colleague, who noticed it and, you know, my Instagram followers.

We could ask the participant to sketch what the next secret moment might look like or ask about other secret moment in any context for an analogy to draw from. Going forward, we could look at ways to embed more of these secret (or not-so-secret) moments into the experience. Maybe a cheeky nod that we are in on the secret, maybe a secret stream of other secret moments.

Q: Imagine a year from now and you no longer have this tracker.

A: Nope, not going to happen.

Q: Why is that?

A: Now that I have this view on my dog's world I feel like I have a closer connection.

Q: To your dog?

A: It's weird, but I think it might have changed my attitude toward work. I think I have more compassion for colleagues who are late or leave early or aren't always available.

Q: What if it kept going that way?

A: Maybe we need to bring more of our world with us to work? Or maybe we already do, but we just don't know it.

One emotion has expanded into a rich collection of feelings, each opening up a new possibility to sustain a fulfilling long-term relationship with the customer. It's also uncovered a world of other possibilities. Compassion for coworkers, shared secrets to bond with one another, and the feeling of calm and comfort that probably inspired the initial design. Finding the emotional resonance of the past helps us to project it into the future.

Trash track

Photographer Gregg Segal's series "7 Days of Garbage" show friends, neighbors, and strangers lying in a week's worth of trash. Every time I see it, I'm horrified imagining myself and all the trash my family produces in a week. That's the desired effect. We can take it a step further as a design exercise, though. Take a week and try it yourself, physical and digital. You'll likely identify a few different types of cast-offs.

First, you'll uncover freebies, giveaways, bargains, packaging. Lots of things you never asked for, from junk mail to junk email. Even the items that you feel you must keep just in case, often files and forms. This is the first layer. Let's hope that your product isn't in this category. The emotional weight of this type of trash is low, but as it accumulates, it can become a burden. This is why, for some people, seeing a high number in that red notification bubble is anxiety producing and why inbox zero is a lauded achievement. A few junk items are low-level irritants; at scale it's debilitating.

However, you need to go further if you are looking for emotional relationships. As you sort through the rest, you'll find three kinds of trash: trash that reveals your identity, trash that is connected to other people, and trash that represents how you view the world. If it's intentionally dumped, it's your past. And it implicitly frames your new hopes for the future.

Starting with identity cast-offs, trash that reveals who you were and who you want to be, you'll first find the *aspirational*—things that signify who you wanted to be. Maybe you purchased a fancy set of barware because you want to be the person who brings together friends for intimate dinner parties. When you give it away, are you being honest with yourself, setting new goals, or disappointed that you haven't achieved what you aspired to? In *Happy Money: The New Science of Smarter Spending* (Simon & Schuster,

2013), Elizabeth Dunn and Michael Norton found that experiences give us more long-term happiness than things. When it comes to things, objects that help us do activities we love, like tennis rackets or musical instruments, make us happy. We'll cast these aside as we change what we want to do. The multiple social media profiles that teens adopt and discard would be a virtual example.

Transitional trash is a time-hop we can make with trash. Psychologist Donald Winnicott introduced the concept of a transitional object, something that stands in for a person or even a feeling. A blanket or toy fills in for the parent relationship, but at a certain point most kids no longer need it. Adults attach to transitional objects, too, for emotional well-being to self-soothe. Is it cast off because the relationship has changed? Or the context has shifted? Or it's become associated with something else over time? Or it's no longer needed?

Then, there are the items that transport you back in time, *nostalgic trash*. It could represent a person you love, from a joyful moment to a regretful one. It could symbolize an entire period of your life. It could stand in for a place. Whatever the case, this is an item that you cherish for its power to transport you to a better time. When you give it up, it could mean you're ready to move on. Or you've changed what you value. Or your memories have shifted.

Obviously, there are certain to be other types of objects that you'll find in the trash (or that you want to save forever). Little treats in the form of small purchases can also create an intense but fleeting form of happiness. In a fit of pique or inspiration, you might get rid of things and then come to regret that, too. Our relationship with objects, physical or virtual, is subject to intentional changes as well as whims. It's very human to feel torn between wanting to change everything and become a new person and feeling extremely nostalgic for everything that's ever happened.

In truth, many objects are designed to become trash. Electronics, or items with embedded electronics (like cars or toasters), are unfixable. Fast fashion, whether clothing or home items, ties obsolescence to style. Even virtual objects, apps, and websites are obsolete as soon as they launch. Industry-wide, the decision as to whether to create objects for emotional sustainability merits urgent discussion. Until then, we can start to sort out the emotional relationship by contemplating how yesterday's treasures become tomorrow's trash.

Time capsule

After examining what we've trashed, it's time to think about what we'd save. If you ask, most people would probably say they'd save their most valuable possessions, both economically valuable objects and personally valuable ones. These grand milestone markers and treasured purchases might make us happy in the future, but perhaps not as much as we'd like to think. Revisiting ordinary, everyday experiences can bring us a lot more pleasure than we realize.

Researchers at Harvard Business School recently studied what happens when people rediscover ordinary experiences from the past, when they asked students to create time capsules.[9] Participants were asked to include the following items:

- A description of the last social event they attended
- A description of a recent conversation
- A description of how they met their roommate
- A list of three songs they recently listened to
- An inside joke
- A recent photo
- A recent status they had posted on their Facebook profile
- An excerpt from a final paper for class
- A question from a recent final exam

For each item, participants reported how they expected to feel upon viewing it three months later. They then completed the same set of ratings when they actually viewed the time capsule three months later. Most vastly underestimated how strongly they would feel about viewing those items again. Of course, you might know

---

9   Ting Zhang, "Rediscovering Our Mundane Moments Brings Us Pleasure," *Association for Psychological Science*, September 2, 2014.

this already just by scrolling through your old photos or revisiting a Facebook memory. Even the most mundane detail, what you were wearing or a favorite catchphrase, can captivate.

So, rather than assessing emotional value by what we are willing to move past, let's launch our cherished possessions and mundane moments into the future. Choose several objects for your personal time capsule. Or write a letter to your future self (Figure 6-5). Your time capsule might also include objects with an emotional value, as you found when you tracked your trash (or what you couldn't let go). Think about how you would choose the items. Predict how you will feel about them next year, or five years from now. Consider whether the meaning they have now will likely change over time. Then, tuck it away for a while. Let me know what happens.

The idea behind all these activities is to pay attention to the emotional relationships we have with our objects and how it lets us time hop, moving from past to present to future, and back again. The more skilled we become at emotional time travel, the better we will be at predicting how products and services will make us feel, individually and collectively, a few years out. The next step is to create future objects to fathom our future feelings.

FIGURE 6-5
Your future self will appreciate the most mundane details (source: Futureme)

Create Future Things

Speculative design, with its focus on designing objects that prompt conversations, can help us explore how we might feel about the future. Anthony Dunne and Fiona Raby call these *props*. "Speculative design props function as physical synecdoches, parts representing wholes designed to prompt speculation in the viewer about the world these objects belong to."[10] In other words, for people to see themselves in the future, the abstract must be made tangible.

Design studio and research lab Superflux, led by Anab Jain, explores the uncertainties of everyday life and emerging technology in just this way. A good example is *Uninvited Guests*, which shows frictions between a man and smart objects in his home (Figure 6-6). The brightly colored objects in the film are placeholders to show the tension between human and machine. The film pictures a near future in which devices offer elder support, as an extension of family or caretakers. The short film lets us feel the individual conflict. Here, design can nudge us toward predicting how we might feel.

FIGURE 6-6

Yes, we have feelings about this future (source: Superflux)

Speculative design gives us a framework to place new technological developments within imaginary but believable everyday situations. When future objects walk among us, we can better debate the

---

10 Anthony Dunne and Fiona Raby, *Speculative Everything: Design, Fiction, and Social Dreaming*, MIT Press, 2013.

implications of different technological futures before they happen. Speculative design is purpose-built for uncomfortable conversations. But it can prompt more than critical reflection. It can awaken our senses. It can help us to imagine how the future feels.

So how do we take speculative design out of the academy or the art house to evoke future feelings? Let's take everything we've learned from affective forecasting and apply it here. Time hop from past to future and back again. Practice storytelling in vivid detail. Above all, make it personal. Next, let's broaden the scope to look at future traces in the world around us.

SCAN FOR SENTIMENT SIGNALS

Science fiction writer Octavia Butler drew inspiration from what she saw on the streets. She'd walk around the poorest areas of Harlem and take note of every problem she saw. Then, she'd try to address them in her fiction and examine the implications. Speculative designers do the same, scanning the world for leading-edge examples of a local innovation or a new practice that could be translated into future products that provoke an emotional reaction.

Maybe you've wondered where to look for signals of the future. Future forecasters say they are crunching the numbers, but it still seems rather mysterious. In the marketing world, trendspotting is a closely guarded secret. Speculative designers tell us to look around for trends, without much mention of how they sort through the noise. The real secret is that there's no magic to it. It's a combination of spotters, or people all over the world who observe in-person the new and unusual, and scanners, who are sifting through reports of the new and unusual. Primary research and secondary research. Think of it as *crowdsourced ethnography.*

We've already started by looking for clues among our own objects. Now we look outward. Begin with a range of sources, a mix of academic and pop culture, news and fiction, personal and policy:

- *News* that reports on or analyzes relevant trends, from a variety of sources—even ones that make you uncomfortable and maybe even those you find questionable.

- *Conferences, festivals, and events* often posit potential futures. CES and SXSW might be obvious examples, but plenty of other conferences will be the first place where people try out ideas. Video, decks, posts, and social media reaction are all fair game.

- *Patents and trademarks.* If there was ever a place to analyze future intent, it's sifting through patents related to your topic.

- *Kickstarter* and other crowdfunded creative platforms.

- *Policies*, national and international, from governing organizations or advisory councils might be scant or tangential. Academic committees, think tanks, or nonprofit groups might publish position papers or recommendations that can fill in the gaps.

- *Public datasets*, whether with visualization tools built in or not, can help us get to know trends. Gapminder, Google Trends, Facebook Graph, Data.gov, and Pew Research Center, among others, are good resources to get started.

- *Fictions* intentionally or tangentially describe a future relevant to the discussion. This includes not only short stories or novels, movies, and shows, but also Tumblr blogs, Twitter microfiction, and even nonfiction pieces that include fictional scenarios. Fictions can be contemporary or historical, too.

- *Original research* includes qualitative interviews and ethnographies as well as social listening, surveys, and other quantitative research.

- *Random acts of design* collect ways in which people adapt the environment to their needs. IDEO's Jane Fulton Suri categorized these as reacting, responding, co-opting, exploiting, adapting, conforming, and signaling in her book *Thoughtless Acts* (2005).

- The DECIPHER model (from Chapter 3) is worth revisiting, too.

Signals will likely be a mashup of mundane predictions, negative trends, positive spin, wild speculation, imagined product benefits, whitepaper recommendations, and hopefully some tales of everyday living. At my firm, we organize trends by broad themes like Algorithmic Living or Mixed Reality and also include tags, quotes, and cross-references. Small moments and specific examples are nested inside larger trends.

What if we took it further, though, and tuned into the emotional resonance of these signals? Because we know feelings are the way we predict the future, it makes sense to pay attention to them. You could get an initial read on sentiment by text-based sentiment analysis where it's relevant. If you have a body of publicly available comments on a news story or are working with records in a public dataset, this can be a good way to start. But we know that any kind of automated emotion-reading is only a first pass; it lacks nuance.

The Geneva emotion wheel or an adaptation can identify the signals with the most emotional impact (Figure 6-7). It's been used to measure emotion in music, to sort out emotion in tweets about the Olympics, and as a way to train AI. For example, if we say your future signals are around health hacking, you could create an emotion graph for leading-edge trends like brain hacking pills, ketogenic diet apps, and self-administered vaccines to understand which ideas inspire strong feelings.

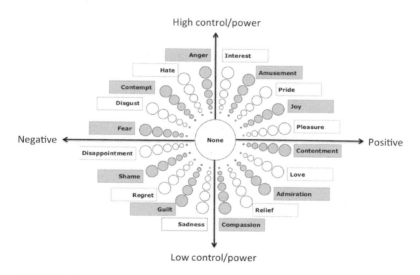

FIGURE 6-7
Sorting out signals with an emotion wheel (source: Klaus Scherer)

Now we have the emotional rough-cut. Next, we need to make the future personal and real.

STORYTELLING STRING THEORY

An empathetic leap of the imagination can be as simple as some alternative reality storytelling. Stories can convey powerful emotion, but they also help us to sort out our own feelings. Whereas designers tend to tell tales of ideal pathways, whether a hero's journey or a continuous loop, for the sake of the future let's tell stories of all manner of parallel realities so that we can sort out how we feel about each one. Here are a few ways to try:

Day in the life

> Tech writer Sara Watson plays around with a narrative that begins with her refrigerator denying her access to a favorite IPA and an autodelivery of groceries including prenatal vitamins. Her internet things somehow think she's pregnant and she's not quite sure what tipped them off.[11] The very personal story strings together a series of current, near-future, and fictional products from news stories and Kickstarter projects together into a plausible future, and one with emotional force.

Fast-forward personas

> The story of a fictional person can prompt feelings, too. Recently, UK innovation foundation Nesta shared short stories inventing "Six Jobs for 2030." Amit, the 100-year counselor, teaches and coaches people through career transitions as lifespans grow longer. Lisa works in green construction, pushing clients to take the long-term view of their green investment. More than personas that sketch demographic details, nifty graphs of purchase histories, and quick lists of typical behaviors, these well-crafted stories help translate trend signals into emotional signals.

Invent a ritual

> Rituals take a moment in time and stop it, extend it, reflect on it, fill it with new meaning. Ritual not only lets us understand emotion and build meaningful relationships, but also bends time. So, it makes sense to add ritual to our future-forecasting repertoire. You might begin by making an inventory of the rituals in your own life. Maybe you make your bed in a certain way every morning or

---

11 Sara Watson, "Data Dada and the Internet of Paternalistic Things," *Medium*, December 16, 2014.

you breathe deeply several times before heading into your home at night. Consider when these rituals come into play, mapping out a routine. Look for emotional peaks or valleys as a clue for when to intervene. What are those moments that are worth expanding?

Museum guides

In *A History of the Future in 100 Objects* (Amazon Digital Services, 2013), Adrian Hon writes from the perspective of a museum guide for the near future. Organized as a timeline of the 21st century, the book describes everything from ankle surveillance monitors (2014), to a multiple autonomous element supervisor (2039), to neuroethicist identity exams (2066). Rather than narrating histories about people, the idea here is to narrate histories of the object itself.

Social media futures

I'll confess to borrowing from a common middle school history class assignment: creating a social media profile for a historical figure. Mikhail Zygar takes this exercise to the next level, using real diaries and letters to create *Project 1917*, revisiting the Russian revolution through social media (Figure 6-8). His latest project, *Future History: 1968*, retells the story of the era in texts and Snaps of historical figures like Eartha Kitt and Neil Armstrong.

FIGURE 6-8

If we can transport the past into the present, why not the future? (source: Project 1917)

For our purposes, we won't attempt a Facebook page for Abe Lincoln or a Twitter profile for Marilyn Monroe. Instead, imagine someone famous or not-so-famous posting about the idea you are exploring, but five years into the future. You can even set up a social media account and involve the team in developing the persona and the responses from the community. If we are looking for emotional impact, social media is where emotions already run high.

Four worlds

Future forecasters often use a four-world model. In my speculative design class, we rely on an adaptation of a common model known as Four Ws: weird, worse, wonderful, whatever. PwC's Workforce of the Future Scenarios delineates four future scenarios to show paths that could diverge or coexist.[12] The Blue world is dominated by big corporations, the Red world by innovation, the Green by sustainability, and the Yellow by humans first.

The same holds true for emotional experience. Think of Patrick Jordan's model (mentioned in Chapter 2) of the four quadrants of pleasurable experience. Nicole Lazzaro's model for gaming, based on an ethnographic study of gamers, distills the best gaming experiences into four types: hard fun (challenges), easy fun (immersion), serious fun (personal growth), or people fun (social).[13] Each develops four archetypes of emotional experience. We can revisit the four emotional worlds from Chapter 3 to create future scenarios. Our four worlds, if you recall, are as follows:

- *Transformative*, experience that facilitates personal growth

- *Compassionate*, altruistic and prosocial experience

- *Perceptive*, sensory-rich experience

- *Convivial*, experience that brings people together socially.

---

12 Price Waterhouse Cooper, "Workforce of the Future: The Competing Forces Shaping 2030."

13 Nicole Lazzaro, "Why We Play Games: Four Keys to More Emotion in Player Experiences," 2004.

For each future concept, from a big idea like an emotionally intelligent city block to something narrower like personal financial health, develop stories for each of the four scenarios. Who thrives and who doesn't? What new practices flourish and which ones fade out? Consider what that world looks like at first, and then five years further.

Telling stories from the signals we collect is one step toward creating future things. Whether we imagine a personal day-in-the-life or a history textbook, a story will help us feel the future. The next step is to imagine a world with that future thing already in it.

CRAFT A CONTEXT

In 2009, Rob Walker and Joshua Glenn started an experiment called *Significant Objects*. They purchased thrift-store objects and asked contemporary creative writers to invent stories about them. Then, the objects, some purchased for only $1, were auctioned off on eBay for thousands. Context really is everything.

To understand the feelings around a future object, sometimes we don't even need an object. Unlike the typical design prototyping process, in which we rough out sketches and iterate, instead we skip to the end and create an object that points to your future object as if it already exists. Yes, it's meta.

Props leave room for the viewer to imagine. This is a bit different than current design practices. In a co-design, we might ask people to assist in creating a concept. In a usability test, we ask people to interact and sometimes critique. Here, we create a thought experiment instead. The goal is to create a way to bring the story to life.

This could be a guidebook, a catalog, user manual, newspaper, unboxing video, user review, even a patent. An FAQ could include questions that came up in writing the press release, but the idea is to put yourself in the shoes of someone using the future product or service and consider all the questions. Press releases are a rarity these days, but they have a well-defined format that can help describe what the product does and why it exists. Amazon popularized this approach, creating press releases for new features rather than presenting long slide decks to executives.

Other examples of "legit" fictions to go with the object abound. Specify your fictional object with a patent, including schematics and prior references. What if it has already gone quite wrong? Perhaps a legal petition. What if the object has become obsolete? Perhaps we create a museum plaque or exhibit. Or perhaps we stumble on it as a souvenir. Or maybe it ends up on a list of items that can be recycled. Any way that the object might be appropriated by people in a mundane context is fair game: a teaching tool, a recipe, hobby gear, a yard sale, an artwork, a screenplay, a news article, a classified ad, or an auction description.

This is a way to pay attention to nefarious uses of technology. How might the product be hijacked, misused, or trolled? Who is likely to do so? How bad are the consequences? Create a pirated version or imagine how it could be used for prison contraband or, worse yet, weaponized. For our purposes, consider how it might negatively affect mental health. Will it drive compulsive behaviors? Will it erode social norms? Will it undermine relationships?

No matter the prop, the context should feel like everyday life, but a few years or decades forward. Situating the design fiction, whether it has an object to go with it or not, in an unscripted environment is a sure way to get at the emotional impact. *Near Future Labs*, for example, created the IKEA catalog of the future to portray products from a few years forward (Figure 6-9). Obviously, we need to take care. Setting up a pop-up shop, as *Extrapolation Factory* did with *99 Cent Futures*, is less risky than trying out an artifact in a doctor's office where its placement might mislead and have real implications.

Of course, the prop itself guides how we might dramatize it. A speculative patent document might be couched in a simulated patent search. A fictional unboxing video might be best viewed on YouTube. You might have noticed that many of the speculative design projects listed here imagine an object that we have bought or a thinking about buying. That makes sense because we are making products or designing services to buy. It doesn't have to end there.

FIGURE 6-9
It feels real; now how does it make you feel? (source: Near Future Labs)

Futurists often use the STEEP (Social, Technological, Economical, Environmental, and Political) framework to explore trends or develop implications. I use a variation, influenced by global well-being indexes, like the Social Progress Index, Gallup Healthways, and the Global Happiness Index. THEMES (Technology, Health, Education, Money, Environment, Society) is a small tweak that ensures we focus on the most meaningful aspects of personal and collective experience. We can then use it to inspire new dramatizations for our imagined future objects.

Technology

> *Embed, upgrade, develop, integrate, hack.* Stage it as an accessory for another product, fictional or not. Say it is an upgrade to another product. Situate it on (faked) GitHub.

Health

Assist, care, counsel, diagnose, chart, advocate, volunteer. Show the data from the object in a medical history or chart. Role play its use in a hospital, or assisted living, or hospice. Prescribe it.

Education

Teach, study, plan, test. Use it in a syllabus. Show it being referenced in a mock lecture. Develop a study guide that includes it. Present it at a school board meeting. Create rules for its use at a school. Stage proposed legislation related to its use in schools.

Money

Sell, market, trade, review, pawn, give, price, promote. Resell it on eBay. Write a classified ad for it. Leave it at a yard sale. Set up a pop-up shop. Give it as a gift. Film a short piece describing the product as the next holiday craze.

Environment

Conserve, protect, contaminate, recycle, degrade, repurpose, dispose. Show how it degrades through three generations. Make a recycling guide. Dramatize how it is passed down through three generations. Write an investigative report on its role in damaging the environment.

Society

Regulate, legislate, celebrate, mediate, vote, debate. Stage a debate pro and con. Create a ballot to vote on regulations or restrictions. Set up an event for a user community. Plan an exhibit of it as an artifact from 20 years past.

Stories about the future that pay attention to emotion help us to imagine how we'll make a life with future technologies. Fictional products can take it even further, so let's look at some ways to make evocative objects.

MAKE A FUTURE HEIRLOOM

Every so often I receive a package that's a jumble of photos, letters, and handwritten recipes from my mom. Sometimes, I have little memory of who's in the photograph or where the recipe came from. Sometimes, there's a flicker of recognition. I'll recognize a bookcase from my aunt's house, recall a picture I saw displayed on a dresser, or catch a hint of a scent that I maybe remember. The sensory experience of these artifacts being passed around the family made me wonder about what future heirlooms might look like.

A few heirlooms are created, or marketed, with the status of heirloom in mind, like a watch or a custom-made cabinet. There might be something intrinsic to the object themselves, like the materials, the details, a handmade quality. An heirloom is often associated with luxury, like the Kronaby swartwatch (Figure 6-10), but not always.

FIGURE 6-10
A smartwatch reimagined as an heirloom (source: Kronaby)

Many heirlooms were once a common object, maybe with a low life expectancy, that somehow lasted. Perhaps because they stand in for a person. My own daughters debate who will get my shoes one day, for instance, even though none are particularly expensive or well made. Perhaps they have accrued meaning over time. Whatever the case, heirlooms reveal what (or who) we value, and some of those values have a timeless quality. Heirlooms are the antithesis of the easy, the frictionless, the ultimately interchangeable products that we buy or borrow only to shed shortly after.

What makes a future heirloom? This was the premise of a workshop I held with design students. Students began with a think-alone activity, documenting an object in their own lives that they would consider an heirloom. How would you describe the sensory experience? What emotions are associated with the object? How intense are those emotions?

Have they changed at certain times in your life? What are they like now? What does the object represent? How close is it to your identity or people you care about? What does it express about what you value? Students created stories, sketching and writing.

This prepared us to create a personal artifact that will be meaningful enough to pass on to future generations. It's a design that is emotionally durable, as designer Jonathan Chapman describes in his book *Emotionally Durable Design* (Routledge, 2005). The next phase was to build these insights to create a future heirloom. Almost all the concepts bridged the physical and virtual worlds, blending luxury and every day, nostalgia and aspiration. One student invented a crystal hologram pendant that contained family member stories, a future living locket. Another prototyped a beautifully crafted bike handlebar that remembers music and replays rides and can be displayed as an art object.

Rather than focusing on solving a problem or making life frictionless, the heirloom prompt nudges us to go deeper. It challenges us to design a meaningful, resilient, emotionally durable product or service. An emotionally intelligent future for design must consider the lifespan of our products.

DEVELOP RELATIONAL ARTIFACTS

More than 100 robot dogs were recently given a funeral in Japan. With the last AIBO repair clinic closed and Sony no longer supporting the discontinued robot dogs, owners said goodbye in a service at the Kofukuji Buddhist temple. MIT professor Sherry Turkle coined the term *relational artifacts* to describe sociable robots like Sony's AIBO robot dog. Think of it as something at once familiar (the dog) and unfamiliar (the robot-ness). In that familiar sense, the object is an extension of what came before. At the same time, they look forward. These are not just objects that we attach to, but objects to think with and to feel with. So, creating relational objects is another way to sort out future feelings.

There are two ways we can approach it. One is the way of speculative design, creating an object that shows us what the future will look like. Whether it's a furniture collection that uses miniprojectors to display our favorite music or books or photos, or clothes that nudge us toward conversation, a physical object or digital experience gives us a glimpse of that future. A thought-provoking piece can inspire conversation or leave us with a feeling, just like a painting or a poem might. It helps us to flex our empathetic imagination.

Some future objects even go further. Lauren McCarthy's Pplkpr software gives us a glimpse of a future in which technology can read our emotional response to friends and family to gauge who is good for our emotional well-being. Pplkpr is not just presented as a concept in a compelling video, but it's also available as an app to try out (Figure 6-11). So, you might learn, as I did, that your partner makes you the most angry and also the least angry, and that our communication doesn't map one to one with our feeling in the moment. Living with the technology, even for a short time, is quite different from simply being exposed to an idea.

FIGURE 6-11
It's one thing to view the future, and it's another to actually try the future out (source: Pplkpr)

These future objects bridge past, present, and future through a simulation. The more we are encouraged to live with them and reflect on them, the better we'll be able to feel the future. But there's another way to create future artifacts. What if we could create a symbolic artifact that mediates our hopes and fears about the future? Rather than creating an artifact that simulates the future, it's an artifact that is a metaphor for the future. Objects materialize our emotions, values, and beliefs, so it makes sense to model that, too. A kind of future-forward talisman.

Creative arts therapy highlights the human capacity to transform thoughts, emotions, and experiences into tangible shapes and forms. It's most often part of an integrative approach, where art techniques like painting, poetry, and music are used in combination with other methods. In therapy sessions, people are encouraged to work through complexity creatively. Post-session, the objects can serve as a reminder or a way to prompt further thought.

In Chapter 3, we experimented with making emotion data into physical objects. Designer Lillian Tong at Matter–Mind Studio has been researching how we use objects as emotional tools in the present. It's not much of a stretch to imagine creating an object that people could stand in for a possible future. For instance, what about an orb that symbolized a camera placed in a mailbox or above a door or in a kitchen to serve as a reflection point for facial recognition? Or, at one further level of abstraction, a collection of blocks that represented times of focus or relaxation that could be connected with time online?

The emotional force of the future can be explored by translating ideas into stories, or objects, or even meta-objects. Future artifacts can be more than a kind of Rorschach for the future, they can help us get better at recognizing, realizing, and regulating our emotions now and making emotionally intelligent choices about what's next.

Future Thinking as Emotional Time Bending

"Imagining the future is a kind of nostalgia." This is a line from John Green's young-adult book *Looking for Alaska* (Dutton, 2005). It's very popular on Tumblr. It's also scientifically accurate.

Humans predict the future by using their memories. Often, when you remember, you are reliving the scene. You can hear conversations, you can smell lilacs, you can taste the madeleine. You feel those emotions anew. In turn, when you imagine an experience in the future you are preliving that scene. Once you become more skilled at it, you can cultivate sensory-rich, emotionally complex futures.

The time-bending properties of emotion can help us all get a little better at imagining (and making) better futures. Emotions tug at us, pulling us toward a future we think we might want. At the same time, the future is a kind of safe space where we can temporarily transcend our current worries and project our hopes. What better way to design with emotional intelligence than to follow our feelings toward the future?

[7]

Toward an Emotionally Intelligent Future

It began innocently enough. After enough Googling for "happiness and technology"—a practice that led me to uncover everything you would ever want to know about unhappiness and technology too—I began to see ads for the Thync: a plastic potato chip that sticks to your forehead, stimulating calm or energy, that seemed a sure way to automate happiness. I had to try it. Almost everything seems like it's on demand, so why not emotional well-being?

Scientists have been working on how to stimulate the brain with electrodes for decades. Like so many of the cutting-edge technologies today, it began as assistive technology. Transcranial direct-current stimulation (tDCS) is sometimes used to treat major depressive disorder (MDD). The military has been testing it to increase focus. An implantable chip, a real-life pleasure button for humans nicknamed the Orgasmatron, made headlines a couple years back.

Although the evidence that devices like Thync actually work is unclear, that doesn't stop products from coming to market. And it certainly didn't stop me from trying it.

In the relative calm of my office, I stuck the Thync to my forehead and dialed a medium setting (Figure 7-1). After a surprised yip from me and a curious head tilt from my Boston terrier, I had to dial it down to the lowest setting. After just a few minutes—much less than suggested—I had to remove it. I might have been looking for peaceful bliss, but instead I discovered a very highly concentrated headache. An intense wave of cyberchrondria (an escalation of health concerns based on internet searching) hit. I Googled Thync and long-term effects. What I found wasn't terribly damning, but it wasn't reassuring either.

Despite the confidence that neuroscience seems to have in bokeh brain images, it seems like cracking the code of even the most basic feeling of pleasure in the brain is far from automation.

FIGURE 7-1
Can't we just zap ourselves to happiness? (source: Thync)

This means that for the time being it's up to us, as human beings co-evolving with technology and as makers of new ways of being, to take it on. The way we design our devices, websites, apps, and various internet things has a profound influence on our emotional well-being. If we want a human future for technology, we need to think seriously about our emotional life with our internet things and everything else.

By now, you know that designing emotionally intelligent tech is not just about soothing away difficult emotions with design conventions, or trying to make human emotion machine readable, or creating empathetic artificial friends, or zapping ourselves to feel more or less intensely. It's a little bit of all of these things. But it's much more than that, too. Fundamentally, it's about taking the emotional layer of our experience with technology as seriously as the functional layer. And that has implications. In this final chapter, we look at the implications for the way we live and work.

Emotional Intelligence at Scale

Technology is perplexing when it comes to our feelings. You can get to your destination in a timely fashion and still feel disappointed, or carsick. You can hold a beautifully crafted iPhone in your hand and still feel depressed. You can engage with a well-designed website and still feel angry. A delightful detail can be staring you in the face, and you will remain unmoved (Figure 7-2). Tech designers, who have tried to create a spark of joy, know only too well how futile their efforts can be.

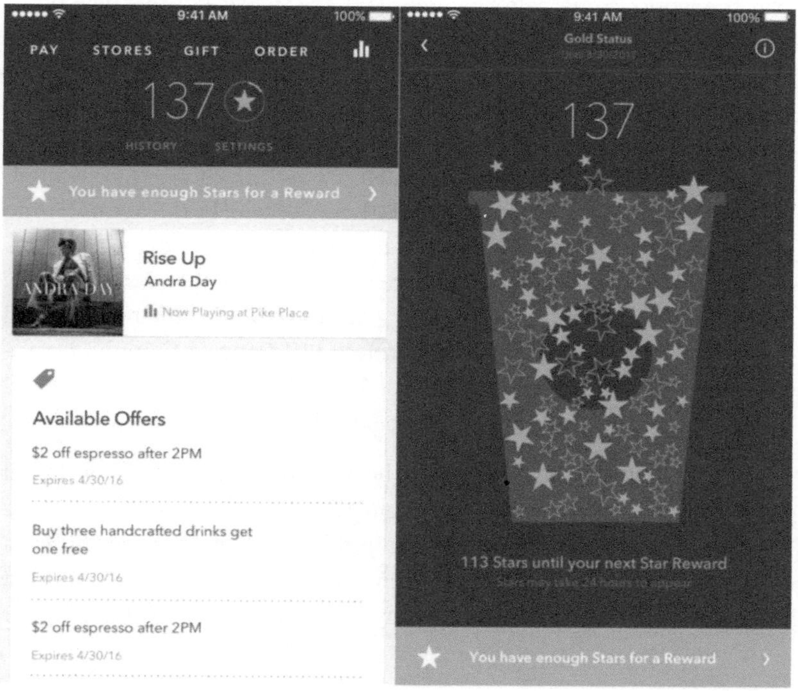

FIGURE 7-2
I could still be in a terrible mood, even after coffee and a reward (source: Starbucks)

It's more than that, though. Our emotional life is changing. Each platform demands a different expression of ourselves, from email to text messages, social media, and video chat. As the new range of technologies detects emotion and adapts to it in various ways, we will adjust accordingly. At scale, this will change what we feel, how we express it, and how we relate to one another and our machines.

THE BRAVE NEW WORLD OF EMOTIONAL LIFE

Despite the best efforts of amateur and expert alike, emotions remain elusive. Better sensed than described; better depicted through art and film than analyzed as data; better lived than simulated. We don't understand emotions unless we feel them, and then that experience becomes a blind spot. But if we look closely, we can begin to see that our emotional life is changing in a very real way.

In my own research, through a series of Future Feeling Labs held all over the world, some patterns emerge. I see the rise of five new types of feelings.

Micro—emotions atomized

Microaggressions, those brief and persistent messages that degrade individuals from marginalized groups, are not newly born of technology. But technology certainly enables them at scale. In the age of online shaming, we've all felt and maybe dealt small blows. Someone writes something unkind: bad enough. After thousands of likes and hundreds of mocking comments, you feel the giant force of the super small. Call it death by a thousand cuts or harmless torturing (a thought experiment once proposed by philosopher Derek Parfit years before social media), the micro can have an aggregate effect.

Other microemotions have yet to be identified. Think of the small compliments you might get throughout a day otherwise spent alone at home. There's the almost imperceptible thrill you get waiting for a message from a chatbot (or am I alone on this one?). Then, there's that feeling when you preface an everyday experience with TFW hoping for a little solace.

Microexpressions, thought to be a fleeting clue of inner conflict, will continue to receive more attention from the tech industry, for better and worse. Of course, humans detect microexpressions without being aware of it. Many people easily read slight changes in tone. Many more of us are starting to realize the slightest difference in tone or text can make or wreck someone else's day.

Machines will become better and better at the smaller and smaller, perhaps revealing new truths about ourselves. They will certainly unearth nuances never before detected. You will likely never see 10 million faces, from all parts of the world, all ages, and all cultures and register their every minuscule change in expression. Facial coding datasets are already more extensive. You will never hear 10 million shifts in tone, or, if you do, you will not be aware of all of them. You only need to try out voice emotion AI to see how machines will easily become more skilled at tiny changes in inflection. At the same time, how we express emotion seems like it's getting bigger.

Mega—emotional extremes

Since internet ancient times, humans have struggled to convey emotion on drab screens. In person, we can smile or twist our face in disgust, we can deliver a well-timed side-eye or quizzical gaze, we can wave away a concern or gesticulate wildly. Online, not so much. Instead, we've had a succession of stylized symbols: emoticons, emojis, animojis, gifs. The options keep coming but still somehow fail us. The conventions have changed over time, but confusion remains. Do you use :) or go with :-) old-school style? Do you choose LOL or a laughing face or the ha, ha reaction? 🤔

Conversational interfaces promise better communication but flatten out emotion, too. VR can transform the real into caricature. Whatever the new technology, the struggle is real. It's still hella difficult to express emotion with machines in the mix.

So, we do what has to be done: we select all. One exclamation point used to suffice, but now we need three!!! We add lots of emojis in our texts, or only one. We exaggerate our facial expressions, squinching for our selfies as a counterpoint to blank stares at our phones. Soon, we'll be sure to smile more often and more broadly so the machines can register it. Pair that with emotions breaking into bits and spreading through our networks, and you'll see a new age of extremes. Longing, nostalgia, and regret are compressed into enough despair to require self-care. Rage rages through our social networks. Not irritation, or skepticism, or pique—rage. It 👏 is 👏 already 👏 happening.

Macro—emotional climate

You might have a good sense of the mood in your own home or at your office or even at a concert. You might also have a good sense of the emotional relationships, whether a reaction to a shared experience or an accumulation of everyday interactions. Humans are remarkable emotional climate sensors. But now we don't need to rely only on our own read of the room.

Sentiment analysis in combination with geo-tagged social media posts, like the University of Vermont's *Hedonometer* (Figure 7-3) or Humboldt University's *Hate Map*, makes collective mood visible on a larger scale than we can imagine on our own. The latest emotion AI will go further, lending a more nuanced note to detecting and displaying emotion. The XOX wristband, worn by event-goers, registers and reveals crowd emotion at concerts and conferences, to build excitement or reinforce a communal feeling. On the flip side, it's not difficult to see how it could just as easily divide the crowd.

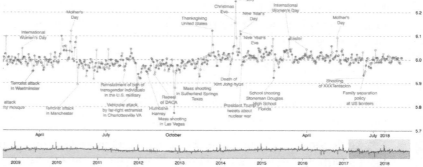

FIGURE 7-3

The emotional climate of a nation (source: Hedonometer)

With new exposure to emotion at scale, emotional contagion takes on a new shape. Emotional contagion, in which your emotions trigger another's emotion, happens on a small scale every day. We synchronize with the expressions and gestures of those around us. Neuroscientists study mirror neurons that embody this resonance. When it's a positive, it's usually called attunement. Contagion seems negative, even though that might not always be the case.

The network effect amplifies emotional contagion. Researchers at Facebook demonstrated this by skewing what roughly 700,000 people saw in their feeds.[1] By tinkering with more positive or more negative posts, they were able to show just how easily emotion traveled from person to person. People shown negative status messages made more negative posts; people shown positives posted positive. Emotional contagion isn't just face to face.

It turns out, certain feelings take precedent in this macro world of emotion. Just a few years ago, researchers thought that positive emotion, like curiosity and amazement, was the fuel behind viral content.[2] That seems to be shifting toward the extremely negative, mostly outrage. Either way, high-arousal emotions like joy and fear and anger seem to travel with more speed and force—so much so that we are often highly aware of the emotions of others, especially certain emotions, whereas we miss many others that don't travel quite so far, like sadness or loneliness or relief.

At the same time, we simply don't register other network effects. In another recent experiment, psychologists showed people sad and happy faces in fast succession. Afterward, people were asked to drink a new type of beverage. People exposed to the happy faces rated the drink higher than those people shown the sad faces. The researchers interpreted this as evidence of unconscious emotion, or feelings we have without really even being aware.[3]

Macro emotions are never fully our own. Our awareness of the degree and impact of emotional climate is already changing with the aid of technology. Growing awareness of the emotional climate will likely prompt us to reflect on how we feel about feelings, too.

Meta—emotions about emotions
In everything from art appreciation to child rearing to romantic relationships, researchers have studied the feelings we have about other people's feelings. You might tend toward dismissive, disapproving, or

---

1   Adam D. I. Kramer, Jamie E. Guillory, and Jeffrey T. Hancock, "Experimental Evidence of Massive-Scale Emotional Contagion Through Social Networks," *PNAS*, June 17, 2014.

2   Kelsey Libert and Kristin Tynski, "The Emotions That Make Marketing Campaigns Go Viral," *Harvard Business Review*, October 24, 2013.

3   Jim Davies, "You Can Have Emotions You Don't Feel," *Nautilus*, March 9, 2018.

even overly permissive in your assessment of other's feelings, but right now that judgment is usually reserved for those close to you. What happens when tech becomes involved?

As we become more aware of the tiny moments, the rising tides, and the grand movements in emotion, meta-awareness is likely to be a part of our everyday life. Take a moment to review Lev Manovich's experiment, *Selfie City* (Figure 7-4). In this collection of Instagram self-portraits from five cities across the world, you can see the range of expression across cultures. By using a slider, you can gain an understanding of how emotion takes shape, no doubt affecting your own affect.

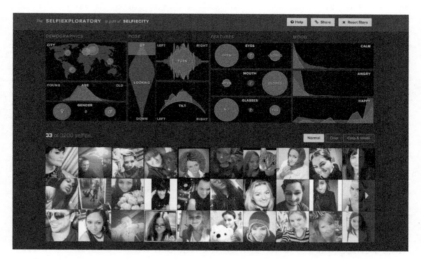

FIGURE 7-4
Feelings about feelings that shape more feelings (source: Selfie City)

A big part of our life is a tacit comment on other people's feelings. We might perform emotional work at work, out of consideration for others' feeling or to influence them. Online we perform emotion, often in an exaggerated way to make sure that emotion is felt by others. As we become aware of technology detecting our emotion, we likely start performing emotion in a certain way for the machines in our lives, too.

As we are exposed to our own emotions in new ways, whether we see it as aggregate data to detect patterns or receive nudges based on how we are feeling, we'll start to have feelings about that. Feelings that will, in turn, create new kinds of feelings.

Mixed—emotion reformulated

Awe, an emotion triggered by the vastness of the Grand Canyon or the beauty of Florence (in the days of the swoon, known as *Stendahl syndrome*), is a mix of emotions from inspiring to afraid to humble. Other emotions are culturally unique blends—for instance, *saudade*, that mix of nostalgia tinged with longing that is uniquely expressed in Portugeuse. But even those are changing. Consider *schadenfreude*, taking joy in other's misfortune, shape-shifting in the form of an internet-specific pile-on.

All of these already-quite-complicated feelings are being stretched to capacity. As online and offline seep together, we keep extending our concepts of certain feelings. Maybe it's that new addition to your annoyance repertoire that evolved from one too many humble brags, or the newfound infectious joy you experienced staying up all night to watch a raccoon make it to the top of a building with a band of fellow insomniacs. As the internet's own unique culture intersects with global pop culture and amazing human diversity, feelings flourish in new ways.

Many more mixed emotions, yet to be uncovered, are unique to the new lives we are living. That undeniable urge you have to correct strangers online or that feeling when it seems like you're the last person on earth to find out about something that happened minutes ago, are unnamed but widely felt and shared. The very spirit of the internet, after all, is in the remix—our emotional life included.

Machine—feelings by, for, and of technology

Researchers have long studied the emotional relationship between humans and machines. As noted in Chapter 4, it doesn't take much for us to attribute emotion to machines and to attach to them. Companion robots are probably not going to replace human companionship; nevertheless, they will certainly be a part of many people's lives in the near future (if not already). And they'll take all kinds of forms: childlike droids to childlike simulations (Figure 7-5), disembodied therapy bots to rubbery sex bots, friendly giants to fluttery fairies. Some will be amazing, some will be awful, many we'll love anyway.

FIGURE 7-5
Some of you will feel real love for this unreal baby (source: Soul Machines)

It can be a red herring to debate whether they will "have" emotions, because we don't really know what that means anyway. David Levy argues in *Love and Sex with Robots* (HarperCollins, 2007) that if a robot behaves as though it has feelings, it can be difficult to argue that it doesn't. With devices exposed to human emotion on a scale more extensive than many of us experience in a lifetime, bots will certainly have some kind of emotional intelligence, though. More than that, just as certain breeds of animal have coevolved with humans to understand our emotions and express emotion so that we feel that they have emotions like ours, bots will likely move toward that, too.

Annette Zimmermann, vice president of research at Gartner, said, "By 2022, your personal device will know more about your emotional state than your own family." Gasp if you must, but that might already be the case. You probably wouldn't hand over your phone even to someone close to you, much less a mere acquaintance. Whether you believe that our devices will know more about us than our family members, they will certainly begin to know not just what we do but how we feel.

For now, the worry is that technology is taking too much of a toll on emotional intelligence. People are less self-aware as emotions are exaggerated online. Empathy might seem diminished in the wake of more screen time. Impulse control becomes more difficult in an era of attention-grabbing. So far, that's more correlation than causation. And it's not the entire story. For each of these negative takes, there are also positives. As our emotions atomize or crescendo or radicalize, we'll relearn emotional intelligence, too.

Technology will reshape our consciousness in ways that won't be evident for years to come. The new tech-infused emotional intelligence will reshape not only our private lives but our public lives as well.

EMOTIONAL INTELLIGENCE AND PUBLIC POLICY

In the 21st century, emotional health is a key goal of public policy, championed by psychologists, economists, charities, and governments. Those lucky enough to enjoy emotional well-being are less likely to suffer from a range of mental and physical disorders, such as depression, addiction, anxiety, anorexia, irritable bowel syndrome, or heart disease.

Scientists, doctors, philosophers, and politicians now talk about emotions such as anger, worry, fear, and happiness as causes or symptoms. But what is the perfect recipe for emotional health? Who decides which emotions we should feel, and when?

In the past few decades, the emotion driving policy has been loosely defined as happiness. Smart Dubai, for instance, use sensors and analytics to promote happiness (Figure 7-6). By tracking what people do and how they behave in combination with online sentiment, they aim to cultivate happier citizens. The citywide Happiness Meter makes happiness transparent to policy makers, affecting spending on transportation, health, and education. Smart Dubai is an ambitious initiative, but it's not only one. From the *Bhutan Gross National Happiness Index* to *Santa Monica Well-Being* to the *World Economic Foundation* sustainable development goals, happiness is an emotion that drives policy big and small.

FIGURE 7-6
Citizen happiness already shapes public policy (source: Smart Dubai)

Whereas happiness is an explicit emotional goal, there are others that drive public policy without formal adoption. Legal institutions, charged with regulating individual emotion and responding to public sentiment, are shaped by anger and remorse. Outrage, simultaneously tracked and fueled by technology, is driving political action all over the world. Empathy, whether through real-life or VR-based refugee experience simulations, assists policy makers to assess impact as well as influence public support. For example, MIT's Deep Empathy initiative simulates how cities around the world would be transformed by conflict using deep learning. Emblematic Group walks people through devastated Syrian cities (Figure 7-7).

As cities begin to profile more data through cameras, sensors, and biometrics, the emotional experience of public life will become even more evident. The opportunity to improve the design of cities and to raise the well-being of all citizens is real. In the near future, designers will be tasked directly with using this data to create environments that support emotional well-being.

FIGURE 7-7
Virtual witnessing potentially influences policy (source: Emblematic Group)

EMOTIONAL INTELLIGENCE IN THE ORGANIZATION

Emotional intelligence, at scale, is not just changing our personal lives but is becoming foundational to organizational culture. I challenge you to go a day without coming across a headline in *Harvard Business Review*, *Forbes*, or *Inc.* about the importance of emotional intelligence in the workplace. The World Economic Forum, in its report "The Future of Jobs," ranked socio-emotional skills as increasingly critical for future careers. Business schools are adjusting their curricula to include emotional intelligence. Companies like Google offer emotional intelligence courses. Organizations like the *School of Life* or *Brain Pickings* are on a mission to bring emotional intelligence to the masses. Tools to measure EQ or track employee happiness (Figure 7-8) are near-ubiquitous.

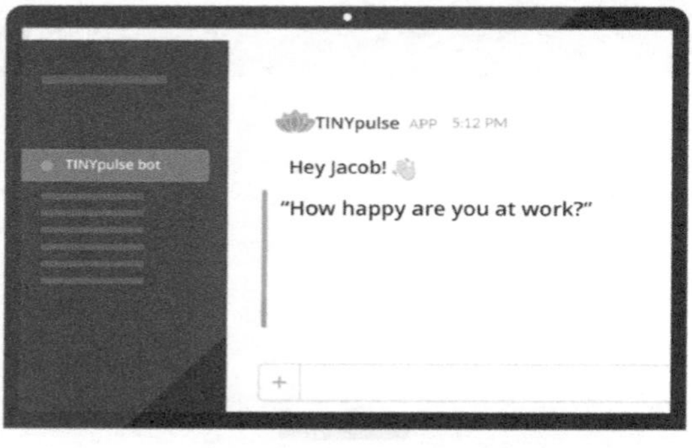

FIGURE 7-8
How do you like me now? (Source: TinyPulse)

> TINYpulse APP 5:12 PM
>
> Hey Jacob!
>
> "How happy are you at work?"

Although organizations seem to value the emotional intelligence of leaders and the emotional well-being of employees, emotional labor itself is undervalued. Customer service agents, caretakers for the young and the elderly, and social workers are not paid well relative to other professions. The concept of emotional labor isn't new. Arlie Hochschild first published *The Managed Heart: Commercialization of Human Emotion* (University of California Press) in 1983. But the mental health issues associated with emotional labor are more relevant than ever.

It looks like this is an area where emotion AI is ready to assist. AI to augment the emotional intelligence of human customer service reps is already in use. Japan is leading the charge to develop emotionally intelligent AI to care for the elderly, from robot therapy pets (Figure 7-9) to home health chatbots. Perhaps the required relentless cheer of Disney employees and Walmart greeters will be next for an emotion AI upgrade.

FIGURE 7-9
Where humans won't go, robot seals dare tread (source: PARO)

Whether it's leadership or team building or individual success, creativity or collaboration, organizations have already embraced emotional intelligence for humans. Emotional labor is beginning to get its due, with emotion AI potentially supplementing roles or even providing relief. What will it take for emotional intelligence to become a part of product design in the organization?

The market for emotion AI is estimated to grow exponentially. It's easy to see why. Companies will want to get a competitive advantage by learning more about what people feel. For tech companies relying on personal data, it's a wide-open world of customer insight. And it's easy to imagine how that could veer toward manipulation, especially given the trend toward optimizing for transactional emotion.

All of the tech giants have tried to crack the psychological code for emotion, however indirectly. So far, the tech industry optimizes around key metrics that favors some aspects of emotion. In-the-moment behaviors like time spent or scroll depth or number of clicks stand in for in-the-moment engagement or even delight. For Amazon, it might be evident in product recommendations. For Facebook, it's determining which posts show up in the feed. For Candy Crush Saga, it's knowing what to offer for free or not. Optimizing for short-term emotional gains is still the primary mode of operation for tech companies, and it often comes at the expense of emotional sustainability.

Moving forward, products and services that are more emotion-aware will provide real value. Market positioning is one factor. If given a choice (and in certain sectors that is less and less the case), frictionless can translate to blandly predictable. Think already of the experience of planning travel, where a typical journey consists of 20-odd sites that are quite disposable after booking. Think of the speed at which people try to "get through" certain experiences, often not just out of time-saving or convenience.

Easy and efficient, those pillars of user experience are still relevant, of course. You probably appreciate the ease of tracking travel expenses or making a remote deposit at your bank. But easy and efficient are often synonymous with expendable and interchangeable. An emotionally satisfying experience is one that stays with you.

People are becoming increasingly aware of how some apps make them feel distracted or even creeped out. More and more, people are beginning to wonder about the emotional toll. People are actively looking for products that support emotional well-being in all kinds of ways, from fitness to mental health to mindfulness. Emotionally intelligent products will become a key selling point.

With the advent of emotional AI, expectations will shift to demand more of technology, beyond ease and efficiency. Rana el Kaliouby, CEO of Affectiva, says that "10 years down the line, we won't remember what it was like when we couldn't just frown at our device, and our device would say, 'Oh, you didn't like that, did you?'"[4] Products that acknowledge emotion and enhance well-being without breaking trust will stand out.

Attracting talent will drive further organizational change. The talent marketplace has never been so competitive. A company offering an emotionally intelligent product or service will attract and retain talent, particularly among designers and developers who have a strong impulse to change the world for the better. And by showing that the company values its relationship with its customers, by extension, it means that it's likely to value the relationship with employees.

Whether organizations slowly adopt new measures or radically shift values or try to continue along their current path, change will happen anyway. Metrics like page views and retweets and likes will inevitably fade. Persuasive tactics that work now will be exposed and become less effective. These measures will have to be replaced by something. Future-forward companies will start to think differently about creating a relationship with customers by doing some of the following:

- Consider the emotional layer of experience, not just the functional layer.

- Measure on multiple factors, including emotion and other aspects of subjective well-being.

- Develop for long-term goals that offer emotional support, personal growth, and social connection.

---

4 Raffi Khatchadourian, "We Know How You Feel," *New York Times*, January 19, 2015.

- Frame value to a broader range of stakeholders, not only shareholders and business partners.

- Make emotional factors legible so that the relationship is meaningful and respectful.

The value of a long-term relationship aligns with growth. If we look at what people choose, when given a real choice, it's often emotional. If we look at what makes people stay, it's an emotional investment. If we look at what contributes to a good life, it's technology that supports emotional well-being.

EMOTIONAL INTELLIGENCE AND ETHICS

Designers struggle with the unintended consequences of the products they create, from spreading hate speech to exacerbating mental health problems. Beyond "do no harm" or "don't be evil," conversations about ethics in tech are often framed around personal autonomy. But I wonder if this isn't another area in which we should let emotional intelligence guide us. Where there are strong or conflicted feelings, you are sure to find the most pressing ethical conundrums.

Philosopher Martha Nussbaum, in *Upheavals of Thought: The Intelligence of Emotions* (Cambridge University Press, 2001), argues that emotions are central to any substantive theory of ethics. The most important truths about humans are not grasped by intellectually activity alone, but by emotion. Emotions expose our values. Grief, for example, presupposes the belief that whatever has been lost has tremendous value. So, if you believe someone is important in your life and that person dies, you will experience grief. This extends to bigger issues of identity, too. If someone says they are a feminist but witnesses an act of abuse without reacting, people might question the sincerity of those convictions, for example.

Anger seems like one possible emotional starting point for tech ethics. If there's any one emotion that characterizes the internet, it's anger. We've evolved from flame wars to fake news. We inexplicably feel the urge to argue with strangers on the internet. Since we disassociate a bit when we're online, we might express our rage more virulently. Moral outrage prompts comments and sharing. That rage multiplies. After we log off (or whatever, you know what I mean), we might feel a kind of anger hangover for a while or a longer-lasting rage flu. Anger shows what we value, certainly. But it takes on its own life. And it's rewarded by attention, human and machine. What if we started with anger and, instead of letting it spread or fester (or profiting from it), we looked at ways to encourage the hard work of self-examination or civic engagement? The more we understand the emotional undercurrent of experience, the more emotions can become an ethical compass, guiding us toward what we value.

Human emotion has been proposed as the antidote for a future where artificial intelligence takes over so many of the things we do now. Quite honestly, we are not all experts at emotional intelligence just because we are human, either. We have trouble recognizing our own emotions, we often don't respect the basic humanity of other people, we discount emotion or go to great lengths to avoid it. So, while I'd like to remain hopeful that the dawn of AI will lead humans to develop even greater compassion, lead us to value emotional labor highly, and teach emotional intelligence, it's not quite so simple. The idea of the human as the emotional layer of the operating system has its own limitations to overcome. But one thing is clear—we need emotionally intelligent humans to develop emotionally intelligent technology.

A New Hope for Empathetic Technology

An emotionally empty future of sleek glass houses and glossy white robot servants speaking in soothing feminine voices is not my ideal vision of the future. I bristle at seeing ambitious future museum projects divorced from everyday realities. Donut-shaped tech campuses designed for living full-time at work don't seem like an emotionally satisfying way forward. Living forever doesn't much appeal to me (from an emotional well-being perspective, it's fraught, too), and I wouldn't be likely to afford it anyway.

The future we are living toward is quite a bit messier. If you look at your day-to-day life, you'll uncover how much of the internet and all its related technologies have a hold not just on your home but also on your experience of nature, your social life, and your psyche. You'll also realize that you are still using all kinds of technologies from previous eras, no matter how thoroughly modern you try to live. We aren't going back, but we will have to live with the mess of the past too.

Maybe there is a hint at the future in the undercurrent of how people already use the internet. We design devices, apps, websites, and internet things for speed, efficiency, and productivity, yet another set of values lies just below that clean veneer. The handmade, authentic, vulnerable, amateur, stupidly funny, tragicomic, flawed—these are the values of internet culture such as it is. Those values have persisted since the dancing hamsters of Web 1.0. They persist despite the corporatization of the internet. You'll find them in how people engage with technology every day.

Lately, people have asked me how it's possible to be hopeful given the pileup of negatives—fake news, AI gone wrong, a widening technology divide, net neutrality under threat, the creepiness of emotional surveillance, and well, *gestures broadly at everything* all of it. One minute you're "techsplaining" how it will all be okay, and the next you're seriously considering opening up a bakery. And isn't it selfish to think of something as frivolous as feelings when there is so much at stake? How can you write a book about emotions when the world is spinning out of control?

Despair is not an emotion that propels us into the future. It tells us that nothing we do matters, issues are too complex, and one person can't make a difference. It ensures that those benefiting from the continuation of the problem are safe. It breeds apathy. Cynicism might look like rebellion, but it's not. It's status quo. So perhaps we should consider another emotion—hope.

Hope, in contrast to despair, can be revolutionary. Hope is optimism that is deeply thoughtful and fully engaged. Hope is lucidly mobilizing. Hope is a belief that meaningful change is possible. Hope is choosing to contribute to a positive future.

Rather than neatly tying up loose ends, together we can encourage people to tell their own stories. Rather than looking toward a utilitarian logic that rewards the most efficient, together we can redefine success. Rather than optimizing for convenience, we can make room for a messy, emotional meaning surplus. Together, we can craft bolder visions, tell better stories, and embody them persistently to support a different idea about the future.

Let's start.

[Index]

A

ability model (Salovey/Mayer), 67
ACLU Dash button, 105–106
ACT model, 101
Adams, Edie, 33–34, 101
adaptive models, 135
Addiction by Design (Schüll), 163–164
addiction, internet, 11
adrenaline, 85
advertising, emotion AI and, 44, 47–48, 49, 60
Affectiva automotive AI, 53, 250
affective computing. *See* emotion AI
Affective Computing (Picard), 43
affective empathy, 46, 76, 174
affective forecasting, 199, 203, 207
Affective Neuroscience (Panskepp), 28, 203
affective rationalization, 204
Against Empathy (Bloom), 174
Agreeableness (OCEAN model), 132
AI (artificial intelligence), 198, 221. *See also* emotion AI
AIBO robot dogs, 230
Airbnb (company), 102
Airtime app, 176
Alexander, Christopher, 192
Allport, Gordon, 177
Aloebud app, 89
Alter, Adam, 164
Alterity relations (Ihde model), 115
altruism, 181–186
Amazon (company)
    altering behaviors, 15
    crafting emotional interventions, 154–155, 163, 184
    emotion AI and, 49–50
    key emotion metrics, 249
    machine-human harmony and, 129

work productivity tools, 7
ambient awareness stage (tech relationship), 137
American Association of Pediatricians, 175
Amusing Ourselves to Death (Postman), 9
analogies, 98–100
Anderson, Stephen, 101–102
animal emotion, 27–30, 129
anonymity, sense of, 12
antithesis, 21
Apple (company)
    calm technology and, 40
    emotion AI and, 41, 47
    iOS Driver Mode, 167–168
    work productivity tools, 7
AR (augmented reality), 46, 163
Aristotle, 20
artifacts
    developing relational, 230–232
    making future heirlooms, 228–229
artificial intelligence (AI), 198, 221. *See also* emotion AI
The Art of Screen Time (Kamenetz), 153
art therapy, 88, 232
Aspire (STAGE model), 157
Atlas of Emotion, 69, 100–101
attachment
    as Fisher stage of love, 136
    as tech relationship stage, 139
attention
    augmented reality and, 46
    calm technology and, 39–40
    DECIPHER model, 104–108
    diverting, 9–11
    emotion and, 30, 38
    self-awareness and, 160–161
    self-managing, 164–169

[*About the Author*]

Pamela Pavliscak studies the future of feelings. Obsessed by our conflicted emotional relationship with technology, her work is part deep dive research, part data science, part design. As a researcher, she creates experiments that challenge us to see technology—and ourselves—in new ways. Whether documenting new internet emotions or asking people to confront their digital alter egos, Pamela's research is aimed at understanding how technology can help us be human.

Pamela's work with organizations like Google, IKEA, The New York Public Library, and Virgin draws designers, decision-makers, and community members into creative collaboration. She's also co-founder of SoundingBox, a new online research platform. Her insights have appeared in The New York Times, the LA Times, NPR, Slate, CBC, and Quartz. She's spoken at SXSW, TEDx, TNW, and Web Summit among many others. Currently, Pamela is on faculty at Pratt Institute where she teaches the next generation of tech designers.

Learn from experts.
Find the answers you need.

Sign up for a **10-day free trial** to get **unlimited access** to all of the content on Safari, including Learning Paths, interactive tutorials, and curated playlists that draw from thousands of ebooks and training videos on a wide range of topics, including data, design, DevOps, management, business—and much more.

Start your free trial at:
oreilly.com/safari

(No credit card required.)